CW00712659

F. R. Leavis

The following titles are available in the Modern Cultural Theorists series:

Hélène Cixous by Verena Andermatt Conley
Jacques Lacan by Madan Sarup
F.R. Leavis by Anne Samson

Modern **C**ultural
—**T**heorists—

F. R. Leavis

Anne Samson

 HARVESTER
WHEATSHEAF
New York   London   Toronto   Sydney   Tokyo   Singapore

First published 1992 by
Harvester Wheatsheaf,
66 Wood Lane End, Hemel Hempstead,
Hertfordshire, HP2 4RG
A division of
Simon & Schuster International Group

© 1992 Anne Samson

All rights reserved. No part of this publication may be
reproduced, stored in a retrieval system, or transmitted, in any
form, or by any means, electronic, mechanical, photocopying,
recording or otherwise, without prior permission, in writing,
from the publisher.

Typeset in 10 on 12 point Ehrhardt
by Inforum Typesetting, Portsmouth

Printed and bound in Great Britain by
Biddles Ltd, Guildford and King's Lynn

British Library Cataloguing in Publication Data

A catalogue record for this book is available from the British
Library

ISBN 07108 13430 (hbk)
ISBN 07108 13449 (pbk)

1   2   3   4   5   96   95   94   93   92

Contents

For Bernard

Preface

It is enjoined on authors in this series to outline their critical stance, and their attitude to their subject. But that is the task of my book, for I undertook to write it in order to re-examine my response to F. R. Leavis. My attempt at definition must accordingly confine itself to the conclusion of this book. Leavis was a potent influence in my student days when I was taught at Swansea by Ian Robinson, who later supervised my research. If Leavis was one influence, then Wittgenstein was another, and my interest now lies not so much in literary criticism as in that area where it intersects with philosophy and cultural history. Accordingly the focus on critical theory over the last decades seems to me to have been stimulating and fruitful, although it may raise questions about the value of English Studies as they are presently constituted.

I am grateful to Ian Robinson for his generosity and commitment as a teacher, and count myself fortunate to have studied under him and the late David Sims.

My greatest debt, however, is in the present, and to my husband who has listened, criticised, given good advice and helped in every conceivable way.

F. R. Leavis 1895–1978
Chronology

1914–18	First World War Stretcher-bearer with the Friends' Ambulance Unit.
1919	Undergraduate at Emmanuel College, Cambridge, reading History.
1920–1	Reading Part 2 English.
1924	Ph. D. 'The Relationship of Journalism to Literature: Studies in the Rise and Earlier Development of the Press in England'.
1927–32	University Probationary Lectureship in English, Cambridge.
1929	Married Queenie Dorothy Roth.
1929	Wall Street Crash
1930	*Mass Civilization and Minority Culture*
1930	*D. H. Lawrence*
1932	Director of Studies in English at Downing College, Cambridge.
1932	*New Bearings in English Poetry*
1932	*How to Teach Reading: A Primer for Ezra Pound*
1932	*Scrutiny* launched.
1933	*For Continuity*
1933	*Culture and Environment*

1933	*Towards Standards of Criticism* (edited)
1934	*Determinations: Critical Essays* (edited)
1935	College Lecturer at Downing.
1936	Assistant Lecturer in the University and Fellow of Downing.
1936–9	Spanish Civil War
1936	*Revaluation*
1939–45	Second World War
1943	*Education and the University*
1944	The Butler Education Act
1948	*The Great Tradition*
1950	*Mill on Bentham and Coleridge* (edited)
1952	*The Common Pursuit*
1953	Last issue of *Scrutiny*
1954	Member of English Faculty Board in Cambridge.
1955	*D. H. Lawrence: Novelist*
1959	University Reader at Cambridge.
1962	Retired from teaching at Cambridge. Appointed Honorary Fellow of Downing.
1962	*Two Cultures? The Significance of C. P. Snow*
1963	The Robbins Report on Higher Education
1964	Resigned from Honorary Fellowship at Downing.
1965–7	Visiting Professor at York.
1966	Lecturing in USA.
1967	The Clark Lectures at Cambridge. Honorary Visiting Professor at York.
1967	*'Anna Karenina' and Other Essays*
1968	*A Selection from Scrutiny* (edited)
1969	Visiting Professor at University of Wales.
1969	*Lectures in America*
1969	*English Literature in Our Time and the University: The Clark Lectures, 1967*
1970	Churchill Visiting Professor at Bristol.
1970	*Dickens the Novelist*
1972	*Nor Shall My Sword*
1973	Britain enters EEC.
1975	*The Living Principle*
1976	*Thought, Words and Creativity*
1978	Companion of Honour.

Abbreviated Titles

MCMC	*Mass Civilization and Minority Culture*
DHL	*D. H. Lawrence*
NBEP	*New Bearings in English Poetry*
HTR	*How to Teach Reading*
FC	*For Continuity*
S	*Scrutiny*
CE	*Culture and Environment*
D	*Determinations*
R	*Revaluation*
EU	*Education and the University*
GT	*The Great Tradition*
MBC	*Mill on Bentham and Coleridge*
CP	*The Common Pursuit*
DHLN	*D. H. Lawrence: Novelist*
AK	*'Anna Karenina' and Other Essays*
SS	*Selection from 'Scrutiny'*
LA	*Lectures in America*
ELOTU	*English Literature in our Time and the University*
DN	*Dickens the Novelist*
NSMS	*Nor Shall My Sword*
LC	*Letters in Criticism*
LP	*The Living Principle*
TWC	*Thought, Words and Creativity*
CAP	*The Critic as Anti-Philosopher*
VC	*'Valuation in Criticism' and Other Essays*

Introduction: Historical and critical context

F. R. Leavis was nineteen when the First World War broke out. He was the son of a piano dealer in Cambridge, where he was to live all his life. His family was cultured, he had attended the Perse School, famous for its successful teaching, and had won a scholarship to Emmanuel College to read History. The war, 'the great hiatus' as Leavis later called it, thrust him out of this sheltered life and onto the battlefields of France as a stretcher-bearer (he had conscientious objections to fighting). One can only guess at the impact of such a continual exposure to the pain, mutilation and death of those he tended. Leavis returned, plagued by insomnia, and reputedly suffered all his life from the effects of gassing (though in some anecdotes he seems to have denied this) – his small appetite, and the open-necked shirts which he always wore were interpreted as a response to respiratory troubles. At the same time, his pride in running and cycling is equally attested. The familiar photographs – balding, domed head, chin jutting out, the flowing shirt beneath – recall with uncanny closeness the famous painting of Wordsworth by Haydon, a painting that emphasises the poet's status as seer and literary figure, a status to which Leavis, too, came to have some claim.

After the war, in 1919, he entered Cambridge University to read History, but moved to the new and still fluid subject of English at the beginning of his second year. He submitted his Ph.D. in 1924, and after a period of free-lance lecturing was made a Probationary

Lecturer in the newly formed English Faculty in 1927. He married
Q. D. Roth in 1929, and so began a working partnership that was to
last throughout his life. In 1931 Leavis's Probationary Lectureship
came to an end, and although he was given a College Lectureship by
Downing in 1935, it was not until 1936 that he obtained a University
Assistant Lectureship. This impediment in his career was to rankle
with him all his life.

Despite opportunities elsewhere, and the hostility of the
Cambridge academic establishment, which seriously hindered his
advancement – he was made a University Reader only in 1959, a few
years before his retirement – Leavis remained in Cambridge for the
rest of his life. His most sustained absences from the town were
probably those in 1965–7 when at the age of 70 he was appointed
Visiting Professor at the University of York and spent part of the
week there for two out of three terms. In 1966 he also lectured in
America, a country which, since the 1930s, had represented for him
the worst attributes of modern civilisation.

Leavis published his first book, *Mass Civlilization and Minority
Culture*, in 1930, his last, *Thought, Words and Creativity: Art and
Thought in Lawrence*, in 1976, two years before his death in 1978.
Since then two collections of his essays have appeared. Throughout
an academic career of over forty years he attracted respect, venera-
tion, suspicion, contempt, even hatred – but rarely indifference. Despite his rather retired life and the neglect of Cambridge his
reputation extended beyond the academic world. He was frequently
a subject for discussion in the 'quality' newspapers and journals he
so much despised. Such was his influence in the 1950s and 1960s
that an article in *The Observer* of 11 March 1962, 'The Hidden Network of the Leavisites', claimed that his 'disciples' were 'spread all
over the world'. In keeping with its title the piece has a somewhat
melodramatic tone, hinting at conspiracy in its description of
Leavis's supporters as 'little cells of Leavisites' and in the claim that
they occupied 'strategic positions in provincial universities'.

Two articles appearing in the same newspaper on 23 April 1978,
shortly after Leavis's death, encapsulate the variety of response he
aroused. In the longer, more prominent – and predominantly hostile
– piece, 'The Battles of Dr Leavis', Russell Davies, after dwelling on
what he defines as Leavis's intolerance and irascibility, limits his
value to his influence on those students 'strong enough to resist intellectual intimidation and flexible enough to pursue [him] through

the minute analysis of texts'. In contrast to Davies's condescension, John Carey (a rather more distinguished figure than Davies) described Leavis as 'not just a great literary critic and pedagogue', but 'a spiritual leader [who] aroused, accordingly, irreconcilable animosities'. He concluded, 'We are unlikely to see a critic of his stature again, if only because we have lost his confidence in the capacity of literature to influence "the powers that rule the world"'. A similar tone of admiration can be heard in another eminent critic. Writing in *The Guardian* of 24 January 1981, Raymond Williams stressed Leavis's intellectual contribution to English. The context of Williams's comment was an acrimonious dispute which had broken out in the Cambridge English Faculty between traditionalists and those who attempted to incorporate critical theory, particularly post-structuralism, into the subject. Williams, who supported the innovators, likened their impact to that made in the 1920s and 1930s by Leavis and his circle, whom he described as 'the distinctive shapers of what became internationally known as Cambridge English'. In Williams's view Leavis's contribution to the subject had been to combine 'close literary analysis and fierce moral and cultural criticism'. 'Cambridge English had been shaped by that kind of urgency, in deep social and cultural crisis', he added.

Svengali-figure, rancorous bully, spiritual leader, intellectual innovator and social critic: whatever their different evaluations of him, the writers of these newspaper articles testify to Leavis's power to influence and persuade – or to provoke.

Williams's assessment of Leavis as one of the main shapers of Cambridge English and his stress on Leavis's combination of moral and cultural criticism with literary analysis is important. Leavis, like many of his associates, was middle class, with a developed social conscience, and hostile to the then dominant public school ethos with its exclusivity and dilettantism. As Terry Eagleton pointed out in an obituary in *The Tablet* of 13 May 1978: 'One of his achievements was to detect, and defy, the clear class-connotations' in the study of English when he entered it. Literature mattered to Leavis because he believed it to be the means, above all others, of combating the ills of a mechanised, constantly changing world and of restoring the heritage of those dispossessed by the machine. Like his mentor, I. A. Richards, he rejected aesthetic theories, and saw the function of literature as moral and educational, though not in any doctrinal sense. But if literature had the power to change the world then the role of the critic was correspondingly important. Indeed, Richards's description of his influential *Principles of Literary Criticism* (Kegan Paul, Trench, Trubner, London, 1924) as 'a loom on which it is proposed to re-weave some ravelled parts of our civilisation' (p. 1) might equally be applied to everything Leavis wrote. Literature, and the study of literature, could never be confined to some aesthetic and emotional enclave; literature mattered in the world at large, and both producing it and understanding it rightly demanded the implication of the whole person. It was, perhaps, this urgent belief that made Leavis important and attractive to so many people. Certainly, teaching English in a northern polytechnic in the 1970s, I found Leavis's fervour more sustaining, and his approach more to the point than the carefully hedged world of the New Criticism or the aridities of empirical scholarship. His diagnosis of educational ills, too, seemed sadly accurate at that time. If I have moved away from his beliefs, it may be, paradoxically, in no small part because of what I have learned from him.

Redefining the function of literature in the early days of Cambridge English entailed a corresponding change in the kind of literature to be valued. Rejecting still dominant nineteenth-century notions of the poetic, Leavis commented with characteristic astringency in *New Bearings in English Poetry*:

> Poetry, it was assumed, must be the direct expression of simple emotions . . . the tender, the exalted, the poignant, and . . . the sympathetic . . . . Wit, play of intellect, stress of cerebral muscle had no place: they could only hinder the reader's being 'moved' – the correct poetical response. (p. 16)

Although there have been some changes of emphasis in recent years such a judgement still rests securely within our critical idiom. Its revolutionary quality when it first appeared in 1932 can be gauged by setting it alongside an excerpt from Harold Nicolson's *Tennyson*, published only a few years earlier. After defining lyrical poetry as 'the poetry of personal experience and emotion', Nicolson continues:

> . . . the songs . . . are among the best in the English language, and in them we find . . . the absolute vatic ecstasy; the 'purest' poetry, perhaps, which he ever composed . . . his poetic energy was concentrated wholly on the magic of words . . . they vibrate, these songs of Tennyson, with something vague and poignant . . . (p. 293)

As much as anything, it is Leavis's crisp tone, and not merely his rejection of the assumptions that Nicolson held unquestioningly, which marks him as one of the initiators of modern English studies. Despite his wartime experiences and his concern with wide social and educational issues, it was from a peculiarly enclosed world that Leavis looked out onto the subsequent events of the century: the Wall Street Crash, the Depression, the Second World War, the founding of the Welfare State, the expansion of Higher Education in the 1960s, and Britain's entry into the EEC. Partly because of this enclosure, perhaps, there is a consistency of response to events, a theoretical purity which refuses to be deflected from what Leavis considered to be the real ills of his society. The events, and the solutions they called forth, were in his eyes mere subsidiary manifestations of those real ills themselves. His concern was with the fostering of 'finer values' rather than with improving the material conditions of existence of the least prosperous in society. Somewhat ascetic himself, he displayed at times a rather chilling ignorance of the disabling effects of working-class poverty, to the extent that he seemed unconscious that it might preclude the acquisition of a decent education or even under some circumstances erode the capacity for subtleties of feeling. His claustration in Cambridge is perhaps emblematic of his lack of engagement with the complexities of major events in the latter half of the century. Although he had much to say about them, it was as they represented dangerous tendencies within our society that they caught his attention. This lack of real engagement, showing itself in a refusal to accept any change, suggests that these events are not the best or most illuminating context in which to place his work. A writer's context, after all, is not just what happens in his lifetime; it is what he uses in his life to shape his ideas, and what he is used and moulded by in turn. The context for Leavis's work is strongly intellectual. His set of mind, his body of beliefs were shaped not so much by contemporary events as by writers, both past and present, who provided him with the means of interpreting those events. Defining his context as primarily intellectual, I shall take four influences as seminal to Leavis's work.

First of all, there is the extension of the Condition of England debate into the twentieth century. In his strictures on mechanisation and urbanisation Leavis placed himself in a line which included Carlyle, Dickens, Arnold, Ruskin and, in the twentieth century, the social history of the Hammonds and the writings of George Sturt.[1] The debate is one that many writers engaged in on occasion, and all those I have mentioned believed that the Industrial Revolution and the coming of the machine had altered for the worse, not merely people's material conditions, but their very consciousness. Dispossessed of their rural past and sucked into the manufacturing cities, people lost their traditional ways of life, lost a culture that was truly popular, an art of living. Others, including H. G. Wells, saw the coming of the machine as a liberation; and Engels, for example, believed that the material privation in the industrial cities led ultimately to a greater solidarity and raised consciousness among the workers.[2] This debate about the value of industrialisation connects with the almost ageless country/city opposition that runs through literature, and which has been explored so subtly by Raymond Williams.[3]

Another major influence upon Leavis was literary modernism. He attacked the fashionable literary world of the 1930s and, although he later came to dislike the work of James Joyce, was one of the first people in this country to discuss *Ulysses* in classes. He was also one of the strongest supporters at that time of T. S. Eliot and D. H. Lawrence, writers whom he continued to admire throughout his life although, as we shall see, he came to revise his estimate of their relative merits. *New Bearings in English Poetry*, his first book devoted entirely to literary criticism, is both an examination of twentieth-century poetry and a working out of Eliot's ideas of tradition and culture, ideas which, rather like Wordsworth's Preface to the *Lyrical Ballads*, provided a theoretical underpinning for poetic practice. It is important, too, that Leavis entered English when he did, for the subject had gained separate, free-standing status within the Cambridge curriculum only in 1917. Leavis thus became closely implicated in the pioneering new subject. Elsewhere English literature had been taught in extension colleges, and in courses designed in the nineteenth century for the working and lower middle classes and was generally regarded as a low status subject, suitable only for weaker students. The English School at Oxford was not founded until 1893, and contained a strong component of Anglo-Saxon to make it academically respectable. At Cambridge, when English eventually gained acceptance, the emphasis within the new subject was more akin to cultural studies and its links were with history rather than philology. The comparatively fluid state of the subject and its previously low status find their reflection in Leavis's attempts to define it, to make of it what he believed it ought to be, and in his obsession with standards.

The final phenomenon I want to suggest as a context for Leavis's thought bears a different, more shadowy relation to his work than the others I have mentioned. It is also one likely to be rejected by many, both by those who remember Leavis's hostility towards philosophy and those who lay stress on his Englishness, as he himself did (he described himself on one occasion as 'the scion of a line of Little Englanders)'.[4] However, despite both the Englishness and anti-philosophical bias, it is possible to trace some influence from late nineteenth and early twentieth-century philosophy on his thought, most particularly in its concern to find a way of describing human behaviour which was not borrowed from the natural sciences, to find a way, that, is, of taking into proper account the fact of human consciousness. Michael Bell has recently drawn attention to the closeness of Leavis's thought to that of Heidegger, and it seems likely that the parallels are ultimately the result of similar influences, mediated in Leavis's case by Coleridge and the Romantics, and then through the modernists with their vital interest in Continental thought and literature.[5] One writer emanating from the Continental configuration, and encountered directly by Leavis, was the historian Spengler whose briefly popular work, *The Decline of the West*, was translated and published in England in the 1920s (George Allen and Unwin, London, 1961). Despite such parallels and resemblances Leavis was steadfast in his contention that the methods and assumptions of philosophy had no relevance to English studies until, in his later books, he acknowledged with excitement the influence of the philosophers of science, Michael Polanyi and Marjorie Grene. Foundational to their thinking are the facts of language, of human consciousness, and of human existence within time – all central preoccupations in Leavis's work. This acknowledged influence seems to testify to earlier unconscious and therefore unacknowledged borrowings from, and modifications of, a philosophical tradition.

The Condition of England debate, Cambridge English, literary modernism, and Continental philosophy, variously mediated, these four influences on Leavis's thought were not completely disparate, but, as I have suggested in the case of modernism and Continental philosophy, interconnected in various ways. Most importantly, the contexts in which Leavis found his meanings combined to speak in almost one voice of the horror and uncontrollability of the modern world. This intellectual despair, matched by raw event, seemed to find its ground in the mud of Flanders and the convulsions of a capitalism that relentlessly produced goods that there was not enough money to buy. In Britain literature seemed to offer some hope in this gloom. Seen as the repository of national history, as the memory of a better past, it had been hailed in the previous century as a civilising force on the brutalised workers. Now it was to be the means by which a sense of nationhood could be restored and an instrument for social stability. To Leavis it offered the possibility of recreating a properly human culture out of the devastation of the modern world.

Leavis's consistency of approach, his refusal (or incapacity) to be swayed by raw event, shows itself in his methods of production and reproduction of work. Because he did not consider his work to be vitiated by changing circumstances he was ready to quote himself and to publish and republish particular essays often after very long intervals, and without modification. In fact, nearly all his books are made up of essays produced for *Scrutiny* or other periodicals, or of lectures given on different occasions. Given this tendency to regard his work as, at least within his lifetime, timeless, Leavis is not a writer who fits easily into a schema of development.

However, Leavis's thinking *did* change over his long career: he abandoned, for instance, Eliot's theory of impersonality, and came to value Lawrence's writing more than that of Eliot. In his later books his ideas about the place of language within culture changed under the influence of Grene and Polanyi. Such change and development needs to be registered alongside consistency and commitment to a world view. Usefully, Leavis's work divides itself more or less neatly into two chronological periods, for, apart from his Richmond Lecture, 'Two Cultures', published in 1962, there is a hiatus between *D. H. Lawrence: Novelist* (1955) and *English Literature in Our Time and the University* (1969). Within the first period Leavis's work from 1930 to 1943 is a mixture of cultural, educational and literary criticism, often within the same pieces. From 1943 to 1955 his publications are primarily literary critical. The work from 1962 onward changes in tone, and once more engages with cultural and educational topics, and facets of the 1930–43 period are developed and elaborated. Accordingly, I have treated his cultural and educational criticism as falling into two or more separate and distinguishable periods, but have adopted a roughly chronological approach to his literary criticism.

CHAPTER ONE

Leavis and the Growth of English Studies

I suggested in my introduction that in understanding Leavis it was important to situate him in the context of the new subject of English at Cambridge in the early part of this century.[1] English is now a large, if perhaps declining, empire assailed by financial pressures from without and the rather tired feuding of different factions within. Student numbers are high, teaching methods fairly standardised, and changes in the curriculum of an individual degree call for long discussion and formal, institutional agreement. Teachers of the subject are expected to have not only a good first degree but research qualifications in the area they propose to teach. In the 1920s things were very different, for then English, particularly at Cambridge, was a newly independent subject in the process of establishing itself as a respectable discipline, and seeking with all the fervour of an emergent state to define and justify its constitution. The antecedents to this independence were such that both the object of study and its methods were matters of dispute within the academic world. Perhaps unusually for an academic subject, beliefs about the value and purpose of the study of literature were widespread outside the academy, and long-held: it was seen as being of great social and psychological value by many, though others, anticipating the perhaps dominant attitude today, saw it as a soft option designed to accommodate the weaker students.

9

D. J. Palmer has given an invaluable account of the history of
the subject in which he brings out its predominantly humble origins, first as a substitute for Classics in colleges for dissenters barred
from Oxford and Cambridge, and then in evening classes for
working men and women. It was taught in Mechanics' Institutes,
and later in the nineteenth century in redbrick universities. Palmer
describes, too, the early hostility towards, and contempt for, the
subject at Oxford and Cambridge. Widely regarded as unrespect-
ably easy, English literature at Oxford hardly existed as a subject
until Sir Walter Raleigh was made Professor of English Literature
in 1904, although the English school was established in 1893. At
Cambridge its introduction was later, for although it was possible
to study English Literature as part of the Medieval and Modern
Languages degree it was not until the foundation of the English
Tripos in 1917 that the subject was allowed a separate existence,
though even then it was assumed that undergraduates would study
another subject for Part 1 of the two-part Tripos. Further changes
in 1926 allowed for English to be studied throughout the degree.

Although at Cambridge before 1917 English was grouped with
other languages, as at Oxford study of literature entailed study of
Anglo-Saxon and medieval texts. In that year, however, the break
with Anglo-Saxon was made, and Literature, Life and Thought
from Chaucer to the Present Day became the syllabus, though
students were expected to make a study of the literature of other
languages. In 1926 two new papers, The English Moralists, and
Practical Criticism were added. Whereas at Oxford the emphasis
was linguistic and historical, Cambridge English studies were
wide-ranging, comparative, theoretical and analytic.

The establishment of English was controversial in both universities, the disputes and political in-fighting bitter, so that there was
stress from within and outside the subject. The sense many early
teachers had of being embattled, of breaking new ground, of being
in the vanguard of progress needs to be kept in mind when one
thinks of the beginning of Leavis's career, for he was one of the
most fervent innovators. That period has been glamorised by a
fund of legends, and accounts of those studying there at the time
describe its intellectual excitement with nostalgia.

The new Tripos demanded new teachers and the task of recruit-
ing was left largely to Mansfield Forbes, whose brain-child the
new course was. Looking back from the 1960s Leavis described

Forbes as 'Young, convinced, contagiously charged with energy and irrepressible'.[2] Like Forbes, who was a historian, founding members of Cambridge English came from other disciplines. E. M. Tillyard was a classicist and I. A. Richards, recruited almost casually by Forbes, had graduated in Mental and Moral Sciences. Trained in Philosophy, and studying to become a psychoanalyst at the time Forbes enlisted him, it was I. A. Richards who initially gave Cambridge English its characteristic cast; a rationale (his *Principles of Literary Criticism*, first published in 1924, grew out of his lecture courses) and a new technique, practical criticism.[3]

At first the new subject had few teachers. Even in 1927, the year in which the English Faculty was founded, there were only twelve permanent lecturers. These were augmented by the appointment of Leavis and five others as Probationary Faculty Lecturers. Initially both content and methods of teaching were fluid and lecturers chose their own topics for lecture courses and were paid according to student numbers; I. A. Richards recalls how, given a chance to lecture as a free-lance by Forbes, he was able to 'collect fifteen shillings a head from anyone who came six times to the course'. He gave two lecture courses in that year, one on The Principles of Literary Criticism – 'for distinction', and one on The Contemporary Novel – 'for lucre'.[4]

The newness and intimacy of the English Faculty was not the only source of its intellectual vigour in those early days; many students, of whom Leavis was one, were bourgeois rather than upper class and, like him, newly returned from the war, older, more independent, with a weight of experience the conventional students were unable to match. The wartime experiences of many had been cataclysmic, and had roused in them a spirit of serious-ness and idealism; a need to find point and value in human life and to work actively for a better society. This search, combined with long-held notions about the value of English Studies, invested many of the students of the new subject with an almost religious belief in its value as a civilising, humanising force outside the confines of the academy.

There had been, throughout the nineteenth century, a belief that the external, mechanical age of the industrial revolution and Utilitarianism, identified as early as 1829 by Carlyle in (*Essays*, Dent, London and New York, 1915, p.223) 'Signs of the Times', might be mitigated by the study of literature. Palmer quotes the

Reverend H. J. Rose, a leading figure in the founding of King's College, London, as declaring in a sermon delivered in 1826 that literature teaches 'the wisdom of men better and wiser than ourselves' and prepares for the 'examination of those moral and intellectual truths which are not only the worthiest exercise of our reason, but most concern our future destiny'.[5] In a more romantic and less moralistic vein Dickens's *Hard Times*, dedicated to Carlyle and published in 1854, makes a wider plea for the world of the imagination. For Dickens fantasy is a human need, a value to combat the deathliness of Utilitarian society.

Perhaps the highest and most rationally argued estimate of the value of literature is Matthew Arnold's in 'The Study of Poetry', first published in 1880 (*Essays in Criticism*, 2nd Series, Macmillan, London, 1895). In his eyes it is to be an effective barrier against impending social dissolution:

> The future of poetry is immense, because in poetry . . . our race, as time goes on, will find an ever surer and surer stay. There is not a creed which is not shaken, not an accredited dogma which is not shown to be questionable, not a received tradition which does not threaten to dissolve. Our religion has materialised itself in the fact . . . and now the fact is failing it. But for poetry the idea is everything . . .   (*Essays in Criticism*, p. 1)

For Arnold, poetry, a substitute for religion, was a force for cohesion. Like him, many of his contemporaries and successors in the world of education recognised the power of literature to persuade and indoctrinate.

But if nineteenth-century writers, no less than those of the twentieth century, recognised a political dimension as well as a moral in the teaching of literature, their conservative stance exposes with some clarity the extent to which in the earlier period this country was indeed two nations, not only of rich and poor, but of educated and uneducated, where the rich and educated adopted a tutelary, somewhat fearful attitude towards 'the poor'. Speaking in the House of Commons after the passing of the 1867 Reform Bill which radically extended the right to vote, Robert Lowe, Viscount Sherbrooke, commented, 'I believe it will be absolutely necessary that you should prevail on our future masters to learn their letters' (Oxford Dictionary of Quotations, 2nd edn, 1975,

p. 4991). Education was perceived as a need on both sides of the fence, for it offered the hope of some advancement to the working classes, an escape from poverty of the more absolute kind. Such advancement, however, was often accompanied by the acceptance of values propounded in the literature students were taught.

The early twentieth century brought an increased awareness of the danger of social upheaval and the need for reform. The Labour Party expanded, and between 1910 and 1914 trade union membership increased dramatically. There was also a series of riots and strikes in response to the material deprivation of the working class. The unaccustomed proximity into which men of different classes were thrown during the First World War revealed seemingly unbridgeable social fissures. To many of the upper and middle classes the deprived, physically stunted and often uneducated conscripts from the towns seemed to belong to a different species, and the Russian Revolution of 1917 enforced the danger of such radical class divisions. Against this context of unrest the Newbolt Report, *The Teaching of English in England*, published in 1921, and written in the years after the First World War, brought out the patriotic bias of English Studies and was decided in defining liberal education as an instrument of social cohesion. 'Culture unites classes', it declared roundly, echoing Matthew Arnold. Morality and patriotism are nicely blended in the report, for by the study of literature (and science) 'the child's natural love of goodness will be strongly encouraged . . .'. The study of *English* literature is peculiarly appropriate since influences from other countries 'have been subdued to form a stream native to our own soil'; the literature is 'the native experience of men of our own race and culture'. Also emphasised is the importance of the English language as a force for cohesion, for 'English is not merely the medium of our thought, it is the very stuff and process of it'.[6] It is important to notice the kind of patriotism that imbues the report, which is not concerned with the nation as a political unit, as a collection of different interest groups interacting at a particular time, but as a physical entity, a collection of people persisting through history. The metaphor of literature as a stream moves into the metonymy of 'our own soil', emphasising literal physical location as an important component in the imagination. Even language in this way of describing it is invested with materiality. I stress this, for this kind of patriotism, which is very much a part of Leavis's mental set, is characteristic of the early years of the century. Edward Thomas's poem 'Lob', for example, evokes Englishness as rural, implicated in the landscape, and reaching back to time immemorial. His Lob-figure who has named the features of the countryside undergoes transformation through successive generations:

> He is English as this gate, these flowers, this mire.
> And when at eight years old Lob-lie-by-the-fire
> Came in my books, this was the man I saw.
> He has been in England as long as dove and daw,
> Calling the wild cherry tree the merry tree,
> The rose campion Bridget-in-her-bravery;
> And in a tender mood he, as I guess,
> Christened one flower Love-in-idleness . . .   (ll.56–63)

The idealism of the Newbolt Report was matched by the seriousness and urgency I. A. Richards showed in constructing a rationale for literary criticism. *Principles of Literary Criticism* was seminal both for Leavis – though it was not long before he attacked Richards for his utilitarianism – and for English studies in general. It was an important book because it attempted to theorise the subject, not on aesthetic grounds (Richards gave aesthetic theories very short shrift) but in terms of the psychological and ultimately moral value of literature. Despite Richards's greater debt to Coleridge, pointed out by Michael Bell, Arnold's ghost is yet a potent presence to be felt in Richards's high claims for his enterprise.[7] Like Arnold, he is concerned with the state of contemporary culture, but the difference between Arnold and later writers is that even as the former bewailed a decline in cultural standards he could yet rely on shared assumptions in his readers. Richards felt the need to argue his position. The language in which he invokes the master in the conclusion to *Science and Poetry* is an index of his perception of an increased threat:

> It is very probable that the Hindenburg line to which the defence of our traditions retired as a result of the onslaughts of the last century will be blown up in the near future. If this should happen a mental chaos such as man has never experienced may be expected. We shall then be thrown back, as Matthew Arnold foresaw, upon poetry. It is capable of saving us; it is a perfectly possible means of overcoming chaos. But whether man . . . can loosen in time the

entanglement with belief which now takes from poetry half its power . . . is another question . . .[8]

It is not just the language, of course, that measures the distance between the two writers. It is precisely the felt absence of any common belief within his society which necessitated Richards's attempt to produce in *Principles of Literary Criticism* a compelling definition of value independent of any cultural constraints, and therefore avoiding the stiffness of 'obsolescent codes'. However, there is something analogous here to Arnold's seeing the 'free play of the mind' as a defining mark of culture. An agnostic and a relativist, Richards defined his 'proper task' as 'the attempt to outline a morality which will change its values as circumstances alter' and which 'will explain . . . the place and value of the arts in human affairs'.[9]

The sanction Richards found for his scheme lay in his model of the human psyche as a bundle of a myriad conscious and unconscious, sometimes warring, appetancies. The good could be defined as the satisfaction of any appetancy, provided such satisfaction did not thwart a more important appetancy. True morality, then, lay in the satisfaction and harmonisation of as many appetancies as possible. The ideal was a complex, delicately ordered, constantly developing human psyche.

Richards extends the tolerance of his relativism not only to different societies but to individuals for, since values are dependent upon conditions of life, different conditions will produce different systematisations of values appropriate to the occasions of specific lives. Clearly, however, some conditions are privative, forbidding the fulfilment of appetancies, and it is here that criticism and the arts enter his scheme. In a passage seminal to Leavis's criticism Richards describes their respective tasks. The medico-militaristic language of the opening anticipates some characteristic Leavisian vocabulary.

> . . . it is not true that criticism is a luxury trade. The rear-guard of society cannot be extricated until the vanguard has gone further . . . The critic . . . is as much concerned with the health of the mind as any doctor with the health of the body. To set up as a critic is to set up as a judge of values . . . For the arts are inevitably and quite apart from any intentions of the artist an appraisal of

existence. Matthew Arnold when he said that poetry is a criticism of life was saying something so obvious that it is constantly overlooked. The artist is concerned with the record and perpetuation of the experiences which seem to him most worth having . . . he is also the man who is most likely to have experiences of value to record. He is the point at which the growth of the mind shows itself. His experiences, those at least which give value to his work, represent conciliations of impulses which in most minds are still confused, intertrammelled and conflicting.[10]

It is consonant with Richards's refusal of any separate aesthetic category that the artist should be defined in terms of the quality of his response to life. Artist is artist by virtue of the fact that the work (though not necessarily the life) harmonises and fulfils the psyche's appetancies and records the complexities of this experience. Critics are important to society because of their diagnostic powers; they are able to judge the worth of the recorded experience. Thus artist and critic are in the vanguard of progress. The means by which art changes the conditions of existence for 'the rear-guard' is not doctrine or statement, for that would be to reintroduce the forbidden idea of belief. It is rather that by opening himself or herself to the new psychic organisation the reader is able to re-enact the processes by which the artist's impulses are conciliated. It is this re-experiencing of the artist's experience which changes the conditions of the reader's life, and this change can in turn lead to a change in values.

Such a summary outline of Richards's theories in *Principles of Literary Criticism* is necessarily reductive. However, even when Richards's careful qualifications of his position are taken into account difficulties remain. Pamela McCallum has argued that a fundamental contradiction within the English liberal tradition to which Richards, Eliot *and* Leavis belong (despite Leavis's attempts to reject it) shows itself in their work. She points to a conflict between an empiricism that portrayed the individual as moulded and restrained by environment and an idealism which saw 'human capacities as structurally identical transcendental essences awaiting actualisation'. She argues that all three writers abandon 'insistence on the distortions in consciousness by the whole socio-historical context'.[11] Writing specifically of Richards she pinpoints his 'refusal to temporalise rationality'. While he recognises that beliefs may change from society to society, Richards still sees the operations of the human psyche as uniform from one society to another, and is therefore unable to take into account the culturally induced distortions in perception that led him to embark on his project.

Leavis, eventually alienated by Richards's subsequent scientific stance, accused him of succumbing to the technologico-Benthamite ethos which he (Leavis) regarded as inimical to a proper human culture. 'Benthamite' was a term of extreme disapprobation in Leavis's vocabulary, for Jeremy Bentham, the late eighteenth-century philosopher and exponent of Utilitarianism, was a symbol to him of all that was wrong in nineteenth and twentieth-century thought. Bentham's assertions that self-interest was the motivating force of all human nature, that pain and pleasure were quantifiable, and that 'It is the greatest happiness of the greatest number that is the measure of right and wrong' seemed to him to have eroded moral values and helped create a diminished world. It is certainly true that Richards's notion of the psyche as a bundle of warring appetancies makes of the individual a microcosm of Benthamite society. As well as enforcing McCallum's criticism, this seems to me to have some bearing on Leavis's avoidance of philosophical modes of explanation for – whatever his individual cast of mind – Richards was engaged in justifying the study of literature in psycho-philosophical language and working from assumptions he deemed to be acceptable to scientists and philosophers as well as to students of literature. This being the case, it is hard to see how he could have avoided a utilitarian bias. Leavis's refusal of the methods of philosophy, to which I shall return, can thus be seen in one aspect as an attempt to avoid the utilitarian contamination, as well as to find – as he claimed – a language sufficiently precise for his purposes.

If Richards's psychological theory of value found no lasting place in English studies and was eventually repudiated overtly by Leavis (although it seems to have exerted a strong influence on all his criticism), the two men shared a high valuation of literature, and a sense of cultural decline. It would be wrong, however, to see Richards and Leavis as isolated disseminators of cultural gloom, for a sense of crisis predominated during the inter-war years of this century. There was unease throughout the western world, from both the right wing and the left as the abomination of war was succeeded by the lurching of a capitalist system between recession and recovery. While Marxism seemed to many the only viable way forward, others saw only catastrophe. W. B. Yeats in 'The Second Coming' and 'A Prayer for my Daughter', published in 1921, envisages a time of anarchy and 'roof-levelling wind', and Eliot's *The Waste Land,* appearing a year later, can be read (*was* read by Leavis) as a description of the collapse of our world. Spengler's *The Decline of the West,* one of the most systematic predictions of ruin of the period, was widely read and influential in England in the 1920s, and I shall discuss its impact on Leavis in a later chapter.

The cultural pessimism of Richards and Leavis, then, was no eccentric phenomenon, but a widely shared attitude. What was all Richards's own, and probably his greatest contribution to English studies, was practical criticism, 'criticism in practice' or 'judgement and analysis' as Leavis preferred to call it. Close reading is so much an indispensable technique in English studies now that it is hard to imagine the constitution of the subject without it. Its importance was recognised at the time, and its introduction as part of Richards's interest in the formal features of literature was claimed by Leavis to give Richards a special place in the history of criticism:

> The histories of literary criticism contain a great many names, but how many critics are there who have made any difference to one – improved one's apparatus, one's equipment, one's efficiency as a reader? At least two of them are of our time: Mr Eliot and Mr Richards . . . Mr Richards has improved the instruments of analysis . . . Mr Eliot has not only refined the conception and the methods of criticism; he has put into currency decisive re-organising and re-orientating ideas and valuations.[12]

According to Joan Bennett's account Richards's practical criticism classes were 'hilarious, salutary and revealing'.[13] Their heterogeneous composition suggests some of the excitement of Cambridge English in those days, for the classes were attended not only by undergraduates from all years, but by graduates like Leavis, some of whom were engaged in teaching, and sometimes by Forbes himself. Classes consisted of Richards's discussions of the participants' written responses to poems distributed the

previous week. Poems tended to be obscure and were not identified or dated. In *Practical Criticism*, the book that derived from the
classes, Richards emphasises the newness of his enterprise as he
discusses his purposes, defining them as the introduction of 'a new
kind of documentation to those who are interested in the contemporary state of culture', then the provision of 'a new technique for
those who wish to discover for themselves what they think and feel
about poetry', and finally to contribute towards teaching 'discrimination and the power to understand what we hear and read'.[14]

Although, as he acknowledged in both *English Literature in our
Time and the University* and *The Living Principle*, Leavis's name
became inextricably associated with practical criticism, he was at
pains to distance himself from Richard's title and, indeed, was cool
about Richards's capacity for close reading. In *The Living Principle*, dating his objections to Richards's title as beginning some
quarter of a century earlier, he justifies his own nomenclature thus:
'I didn't, that is, like the implication – it had come to inhere in the
formula – that "Practical Criticism" was a specialized kind of
gymnastic skill to be cultivated and practiced as something apart'.[15] In fact, even in *Education and the University*, much of which
was written in the 1930s, Leavis is at pains to stress that his notion
of practical criticism is not that of some kind of drill, or the
unthinking application of quasi-technical terms. His discussion of
'realization', to him an 'indispensable' term, emphasises the subtlety and flexibility needed in its use.[16]

Leavis's concern here is important, for it has bearings on his
own practice in so far as his ends are closely allied to Richards's
dual purpose to teach discrimination *and* to enable readers to come
to a personal response to poetry. These two ends, at least in some
acceptations, are mutually contradictory, for the former implies
standards by means of which we are able to judge – hence the
tendency for the practice of criticism to move towards a kind of
drill and its language to become technical – while the latter seems
to imply that we need to shake off conventional trammels in order
to discover what we really feel. Language and practice may thus
function as a kind of manual for confession. The capacity for self-
contradiction emerges with some absurdity in Denys Thompson's
Reading and Discrimination (Chatto & Windus, London, 1934).
Leavis's collaborator in *Culture and Environment*, a co-editor of
Scrutiny and a leading Leavisite in the educational world,

Thompson envisaged the collection of excerpts of which the book is composed as having use both inside and outside schools. He defined its purpose as 'to provide material for the training of discrimination in reading, and for the formation of judgements at first hand', citing Richards and Leavis as influences.[17] However, in Thompson's mind a first-hand judgement has to be right or it is nothing, so passages inviting comment are followed by a couple of pages of guidance, perforated to allow of neat removal, and bearing the instruction, 'This sheet should be detached before the book is used in school'. Among the 'right' comments students have to guess at, but teachers are helped out with, are these on poems by Quiller-Couch (A) and George Herbert (B): 'The feeling of A tends to be unctuous; B has exquisite "tact", and the humility is genuine' (*Reading and Discrimination*, p. 157). Thompson's judgement throughout is stern and uncompromising: 'A is hysterical, the ejaculation is overworked; B is magnificent in rhythm and palpable expression' (*Reading and Discrimination*, p. 157). Depressingly, the passages are chosen to enforce tenets of Leavisian orthodoxy; for example, seventeenth century good, nineteenth century (except for Hopkins) bad, and there seems little trace of individuality in a book ostensibly designed to foster that quality.

The potential self-contradiction I have identified is not one that Leavis was unaware of. The impulsion to resolve it is a major motivation in his writing, leading eventually to his notion of language as the medium in which extra-personal standards and personal judgements may be reconciled. More worrying is the issue of freedom within the curriculum that Thompson's book raises, for, like some of Leavis's suggestions in *Education and the University* which I shall discuss in Chapter 3, the terms and scope of the enterprise and its manner of conduct combine to make the desired conclusions inevitable, despite the feint that the student is to be active in judgement.

Leavis claims that he was identified with practical criticism in later days by an adversary who saw it as an outworn mode of study associated with literary modernism.[18] Although one might agree with him that the days of practical criticism are not yet over, such a view of it is important in reminding us that its genesis in Cambridge coincided with a lively and institutionally sanctioned (not to say required) interest in modernist literature. It is no accident that at Oxford where the syllabus extended only to 1830 until recent years, practical criticism was never an examination subject.

The interest in modernism that was almost a defining feature of Cambridge English in its early years is attested to in Leavis's praise of T. S. Eliot as being, with Richards, a critic of outstanding worth. Eliot is a pervasive influence on Leavis's criticism, particularly his earlier work, and *New Bearings in English Poetry* and *Revaluation* are essentially a reshaping of the canon according to Eliotic criteria. Two of Leavis's earliest pieces of writing are on Eliot and D. H. Lawrence, writers to whom he returned obsessively throughout his life. Although he reversed his relative valuation of them he never altered his view that they were the most important of modernist writers. Yeats, Pound and Joyce also received his attention.

The title of Leavis's first piece on Eliot, 'T. S. Eliot: A Reply to the Condescending', is significant, for the merits of most modernist writers were a matter of controversy.[19] Most controversial of all was James Joyce's *Ulysses*, at this time banned in England for obscenity. Leavis's (entirely law-abiding) attempt to import a copy earned the attention of the police and the university authorities. His teaching of Joycean extracts, as he recalled, was not well received.[20]

To recognise that modernism was controversial in the early decades of this century is important. My stress up till now has been on the excitement and newness of Cambridge English, and it is certainly the case that the outcome has vindicated the innovatory. However, Cambridge was an ancient university with a strongly conservative bias, and not surprisingly, the combination of new ideas with a more than usually heterogeneous and independent student body after the First World War helped to create a combative and factional atmosphere. Francis Mulhern, in an excellent account of *Scrutiny*, the magazine with which the names of the Leavises are so closely associated, traces well the different forces at work at the time.[21] However, if one were to leave aside any but intellectual causes of tension, modernism would have to be seen as the sword in the midst of English studies. There is more than one reason for this state of affairs. Modernism did not comprise the whole of modern poetry at the time, and more conventional practitioners sometimes had a place in the academy – as Thompson's use of a poem by Sir Arthur Quiller-Couch, the

Edward VII Professor of English Literature, reminds us. As Leavis never tired of pointing out, those whose taste was formed by the study of classics found modernism offensive and held up the successors of the Georgian poets for admiration.

There is a tendency to assume that difficulty is always attendant on the new, but when considering their reception, it is as well to remember that modernist works were frequently designedly difficult, and frequently designed to shock. C. K. Stead (using a variant of M. H. Abrams's schema in *The Mirror and the Lamp* of the relations between Universe, Work, Artist and Audience) has argued that modernist poets saw their nineteenth-century predecessors as being in collusion with their readers to avoid contact with reality; to write anything that mattered, then, entailed a distancing of Artist from Audience:

> The poet in each case has had to begin by finding a style – his own way of knowing and describing 'Reality' – and he has had to achieve this alone, since the common reader's idea of what a style should be simply would not serve. But once a style was achieved, an audience could be encouraged to understand it, though never to demand modification.[22]

If the modernists' alienation from their audience produced on the one hand an attitude of uneasy contempt within the wider literary establishment, epitomised for Leavis by the growing use of the word 'highbrow', it associated on the other with the conviction, held by both Richards and Leavis, that culture was a minority pursuit, and with an almost obsessive concern for 'standards'. This concern on the part of critics is congruent with the far-reaching significance many modernist writers attributed to their work. '. . . speech impelled us/To purify the dialect of the tribe . . .' wrote T. S. Eliot in *Little Gidding*, and Joyce's Stephen Dedalus proclaims at the end of *A Portrait of the Artist as a Young Man*, 'I go . . . to forge in the smithy of my soul the uncreated conscience of my race'. Modernist writing, then, was contentious in every possible way. New, difficult, iconoclastic, contemptuous of established pieties and susceptibilities, often convinced of its mission to reshape a misshapen world, it induced in its supporters a corresponding stance, and an urgency capable of disrupting the conventional niceties of university life.

In 1927, the year in which Leavis was appointed Probationary Lecturer, he also started to contribute to the *Cambridge Review*. It is interesting to look at his early pieces in that periodical. On the whole they show a generosity of sympathy and tone. Edmund Blunden, T. F. Powys, William Empson and Richard Eberhart are singled out for praise and, although Leavis is scathingly funny about Richard Aldington and roundly dismissive of the Sitwells, he usually writes with great urbanity, and delivers radical criticisms with tact and courtesy. Even more interesting than the reviews themselves, however, is the company they keep. A trenchant piece on Sacheverell Sitwell, 'More Gothick North', sorts oddly with the flowery tone of the next piece, a review of a life of Alice Meynell.[23] It is easy to understand why he aroused unease within the English Faculty, particularly since the Leavisian wit was sometimes deployed against his colleagues in lectures. Leavis's marriage to Q. D. Roth in 1929 consolidated his adversarial relationship with the Cambridge English establishment. Less witty and more offensive than Leavis, she shared his beliefs to the full, and contributed her own brand of acerbity to the partnership.

The hiatus in Leavis's career between 1931, when his Probationary Lectureship came to an end, and his appointment by the university in 1936 as an Assistant Lecturer rankled with him all his life. For Leavis Cambridge English existed in its purity until the foundation of the English Faculty in 1927 gave power to 'the natural ward-bosses, who were well-prepared to take their opportunities, took them, and had a rapid triumph that was almost complete'.[24] While Leavis's later treatment at Cambridge was quite scandalous in the light of his achievements and influence, and suggests a malice at odds with any serious intellectual interest (he was not made a member of Faculty Board until 1954, and given a Readership only in 1959, three years before his retirement), it is not so clear that he was as badly treated in the 1930s as he believed himself to have been. There was a shortage of permanent posts, and Leavis was not the only Probationary Lecturer later to have a distinguished career who was forced to wait his turn. He was young, earnest, iconoclastic, but there was probably nothing in his achievement up to that point to make his appointment *intellectually* compelling. He had not, for instance, the brilliance of William Empson, a younger contemporary who after taking a First in Mathematics in his Part 1 examinations trans-

ferred to English and gained a starred First. Some of the undergraduate work Empson produced for I. A. Richards formed the
basis of his still-famous book, *Seven Types of Ambiguity*, published
in 1930 before Leavis had written anything substantial.

However, Leavis's perception of events had some justification.
There had been strong opposition both to the creation of the
Tripos in 1917, and to the reforms of 1926, and the founding of
the English Faculty in 1927 gave institutional status to some of its
most forceful opponents while denying such status to many of the
enthusiastic free-lance lecturers recruited by Forbes and Richards,
both of whom were less active in the subject than in earlier years.
F. L. Lucas, trained in Classics, was particularly hostile, and attacked the new English viciously and comprehensively in *University Studies*. Summarising the attack, Mulhern quotes specific
criticisms of Q. D. Leavis's doctoral dissertation, which Lucas
held up as an example of what research work should *not* be: 'angry
arrogance', 'Pharisaism, asceticism and fanatical intolerance' are
some of the phrases he used. Lucas's vitriolic language, published
in what Mulhern describes as a 'quasi-official conspectus', testifies
to the bitterness of the struggle, but the struggle at this point does
not seem to have been that of the time-serving and ambitious
against the self-evidently right, as Leavis so frequently claimed.
Time has been on the side of Leavis and 'the critical school of Mr
T. S. Eliot' which Lucas so much hated; and Lucas himself has
been consigned to the obscurity of the occasional footnote; but he,
no less than Leavis, was filled with *intellectual* hatred and naturally
fought against the appointment of one who had a view of English
studies which he believed to be pernicious. His attack has both
intelligence and panache, and he is concerned to distinguish between I. A. Richards, whom he treats with politeness, and Q. D.
Leavis, whom he likens to 'Saturn masticating stones'.[25]

Hostility to the new English was not universal, so after his
Probationary Lectureship had come to an end Leavis was able to
survive precariously on the money from supervisions he gave at
Christ's and at Girton, Q. D. Leavis's old college, until in the next
academic year he was made Director of Studies in English at
Downing College.

Although Leavis had been passed over by the English Faculty in
1931, he was even then not without influence. The idealistic temper of the Tripos's founder members was not betrayed by any

idleness on his part, and students seem to have been drawn to him both for the excitement of what he had to teach, and because of his concern for their intellectual well-being. His urgency made him for many, but by no means for all, a charismatic figure among undergraduates and research students. Evidence for Leavis's impact as a teacher in these years comes from, among other things, the foundation of the Minority Press by Gordon Fraser, an undergraduate at St John's College. In 1930 Fraser published two pieces by Leavis as Minority pamphlets: *Mass Civilization and Minority Culture* and *D. H. Lawrence*. Q. D. Leavis was also influential, and her thesis, published in book form as *Fiction and the Reading Public* became a central text in the Leavisite attack on the lowering of cultural standards.[26] Leavis and his wife, then, guarded the flame of the Ricardian torch, and it is not without justification that in later years he referred to their circle as representing 'the essential Cambridge'. It is a real achievement that they kept alive the enthusiasm and integrity of the previous pioneering decade.

Circles need somewhere to meet, and it was at Friday tea-parties in the Leavises' home that much of the opposition to the institutional conception of English shaped itself. These tea-parties, Leavis claimed later, made possible the launching of the magazine *Scrutiny* in 1932, the year in which his first full-length book, *New Bearings in English Poetry*, was published. The magazine was launched, not by Leavis, but by an American, Donald Culver, and L. C. Knights, later to be Edward VII Professor of English. They edited the first two issues and were then joined on the editorial board by Leavis and Denys Thompson, a former student of Leavis's, and soon to co-operate with him in the production of *Culture and Environment* in 1933. In that year, too, Culver was replaced by D. W. Harding, later to become Professor of Psychology at the University of London. The editorial board remained the same until 1939 when Denys Thompson, a school-teacher, left to edit a new magazine, *English in Schools*, and Wilfrid Mellers, a regular contributor of music criticism, joined. The magazine survived, surprisingly in view of all its difficulties and the disruption of the Second World War, until 1953. That it did so was very much due to the tenacity and dedication of the Leavises who alone of the editors remained in Cambridge throughout *Scrutiny*'s life. In his preface to *A Selection from Scrutiny*, published in 1968, Leavis declared, 'My wife and I bore the major burden of *Scrutiny*:

for two decades we did the donkey work and had the responsibility'.[27] In fact, *Scrutiny*'s closure came, not through any decline in popularity – its circulation of 1, 500 in 1953 was half as much again as in 1947 – but through the difficulty of maintaining a circle of regular contributors of the right calibre. Added to this was the Leavises' exhaustion. Q. D. Leavis had been diagnosed as having cancer in 1948, and the strain of coping with this as well as with what Leavis in a letter to Storm Jameson described as his 'ostracism' at Cambridge proved too much.[28]

A glance at the contents pages of *A Selection from Scrutiny* suggests that the periodical was not merely organised by the Leavises, but largely written by them too. However, the circle of contributors, particularly in the early days, was wide and their positions varied.

Clear, however, from the Manifesto written for the first issue by L. C. Knights was the debt the magazine owed to Richards's conception of English studies, and behind Richards stood Matthew Arnold. For the editors it was 'axiomatic that concern for standards of living implies concern for standards in the arts' (S, vol. I, p. 2). The appropriation of the phrase 'standard of living' to a cultural use in 1932, when economic issues were inescapable, marks the large claim the periodical was making for high culture (later Richards's description of the arts as 'the storehouse of recorded values' is quoted), and its own, correspondingly large, ambition to intervene in the life of the nation. The method of intervention is self-consciously Arnoldian in its rejection of political alignment: what is necessary is 'a play of the free intelligence upon the underlying issues'. Accordingly articles were promised, not merely on the arts, but on topics and books of general social interest, with a particular emphasis on education. The word 'standards' recurs almost to the point of monotony throughout the Manifesto and the standards of criticism found in literary journalism are particularly deplored. The chosen title, *Scrutiny*, which referred back to a series of articles, 'Scrutinies', in the by then defunct *Calendar of Modern Letters*, was an earnest of its editors' more serious intentions.

On the whole, the promises of the Manifesto were performed, and with notable success, though different political and social circumstances produced different emphases at different times. Mulhern distinguishes three phases, 1932–9, 1939–45, and 1945–

53. He suggests that in much of the criticism of the first phase the idea of an ideal, vanished past became an enabling myth for planning a better future; it was 'a myth that functioned principally as a critical device in a discourse on the actual state and possible futures of modern society'.[29] Although quite a large number of contributors had left-wing inclinations, *Scrutiny* continued to refuse political alignment. For Leavis, Marxist communism, seen by many at this time as the proper solution to otherwise intractable social problems, was itself a part of those problems rather than an answer to them, and therefore to be resisted along with other manifestations of a utilitarian world.

The promised attention to education took two forms. There was much reviewing of text-books and of material for classroom use by school teachers; there was also a series of attacks on different aspects of the educational system. In 1933 a meeting of teachers was organised at the Leavises' house, and attempts were made to set up a movement with 'cells' in different geographical locations.[30] The idea of 'cells' seems to be indicative not only of the time, but of Leavis's personal sense of being engaged in a resistance movement of almost military dimensions.

Criticism of the arts included articles on the cinema and on music. Both cinema and jazz were unfavourably received on the whole, both being regarded as symptomatic of the contemporary decline in taste.

In the war years *Scrutiny*'s sensitivity to propaganda and the cruder manifestations of nationalism entailed a certain detachment from the war, demonstrated in its extensive coverage of German literature. The detachment was not of disaffection, however. Unlike the 'great hiatus' of the First World War, this war – if only to non-combatants – offered an opportunity: 'By some of the group at least, the war was consciously treated as an historical adjournment, a time for reflection, consolidation and, most important, preparation'.[31] Mulhern describes Leavis's movement, consummated in the series of articles later to become *Education and the University*, from guerrilla-like opposition into a belief that his ideas for educational reform might find institutional acceptance in the climate of optimism generated by plans for post-war reconstruction. However, this optimism was soon to be dashed by the Butler Education Act of 1944 which attracted to it the familiar charge from Scrutineers that it was a part of the process of the levelling down of standards.

During these years there was a shift from poetry to novel as the object of critical attention. Again, this could be related to a change of consciousness induced by the war, to the recognition in the face of a qualitatively different opposition of an actual, enabling community, still existing despite its tensions and conflicts. Arguably this shift of attention to the novel had serious consequences for Leavis's criticism, since it opened the way to a collapse of the distinction – always precarious in his work – between literature and life.

This elision of the distinction between life and politics on the one hand and literature on the other accompanied a bifurcation, noted by Mulhern, in the post-war years of literary and cultural criticism along their separate paths. The literary criticism, liberal and modern in its outlook, and sure in the conviction that the text had laid down a politicrl, or at least a moral, agenda seemed to withdraw from 'the large contemporary issues that had once been objects of direct and sustained concern' (Mulhern, p. 268). At the same time, there was an increase in social and cultural criticism notable for its conservatism and preoccupation with past splendours. Mulhern sees this preoccupation with the past as having an entirely different function from the myth of the organic community. Rather than being an instrument for the definition of fruitful change, the new concern with the past and attendant obsession with the loss of order in the present became a 'search for images, both critical and consolatory, of the unity of politics and "culture"'. Thus, in Mulhern's analysis, literary and cultural criticism, superficially so opposed, met in a rejection of social democracy.[32]

The history of *Scrutiny* could be, and is, read in other ways, but Mulhern's account seems fundamentally convincing. There is certainly a marked change in tone between Leavis's early criticism and that stemming from the last period of *Scrutiny*. With my liberal humanist leanings, I would lay more stress on Leavis's individual concerns than on the material circumstances in which he found himself, for although other contributors shared his preoccupations, most were people he had chosen. However, although the change in tone can be attributed to an increasingly conservative and dictatorial choice and censorship of the periodical's contributors, *Scrutiny* was taken too seriously at the time of its demise to allow one to explain its conservatism as Leavis's purely idiosyncratic response to post-war Britain. Lawrence Lerner writes of the magazine in terms that suggest its centrality, as well as its inevitable capacity to arouse controversy. Just a little over a year after the magazine's closure he speaks of the 'shock' to both 'friends and enemies'. Distancing himself from Leavis's complaints about his treatment by Cambridge, which he describes as 'the wail of nobody-loves-us', he asserts that 'The centre of the picture should be, not that Leavis is bad-tempered, but that he is a genius'.[33] Lerner also takes it for granted that publication in *Scrutiny* was prestigious. Interestingly, he confines his attention to the literary criticism of the magazine. *Scrutiny*'s political stance, then, and its compartmentalisation of literary and cultural criticism may have been one of the signs of the times, for a dispirited apolitical conservatism seems to have been characteristic of the 1950s.

A recurring motif in Leavis's comments on *Scrutiny* is the continuing sacrifice he and his wife made to keep it going. This sacrifice is indisputable. However, compensations can be discerned or guessed at. For a couple as combative as the Leavises' it could only be a comfort to belong to a circle of right-minded friends and acquaintances. Leavis's altruism and his urgent sense of mission could find some satisfaction in the belief that by means of *Scrutiny* he was intervening directly in the fight to save culture; the written word could bring about such practical consequences as the meeting of teachers at the Leavises' house in 1933 and the organisations that seem to have followed from that meeting.

More practically, although the non-writing tasks associated with *Scrutiny* may have been a time-consuming burden, reviewing introduced him to a wide range of writers: poets, novelists, social commentators and reformers, so that although he used some as exemplary figures – either angels or beasts – the variety of reference helped to avoid the repetitive note of his later writing. Most of Leavis's major books were made up from articles published in *Scrutiny*, and for one who reputedly found writing slow and difficult the discipline imposed by facing a relentless series of deadlines may have been more useful than otherwise. Also, a more precise sense of his audience than could have been generated by the conventional methods of producing books may well have been useful to one who prized the spoken word so thoroughly. Then, too, that *Scrutiny* was a platform additional to, and not a substitute for, his books must also have been important for, impelled by his sense of mission, Leavis was a great recycler of his works. *For Continuity*

(1933) contained not only book reviews and pieces from the early issues of the magazine, but also two Minority pamphlets, *D. H. Lawrence* and *Mass Civilization and Minority Culture*. *Revaluation* (1936), *The Great Tradition* (1948), *The Common Pursuit* (1952) and most of *D. H. Lawrence: Novelist* (1955), all literary critical works, had their genesis in *Scrutiny*, as had *Education and the University* (1943). With customary thrift Leavis added to this collection of essays on education an appendix containing a recent *Scrutiny* review, 'T. S. Eliot's Later Poetry', and a pamphlet, *How to Teach Reading: A Primer for Ezra Pound*, first published by the Minority Press in 1932. To the second edition of *Education and the University*, when Leavis's disillusion with post-war educational reforms was complete, and his stance toward society was once more adversarial, he added 'Mass Civilization and Minority Culture' as his definitive statement on the ills of modern life.

This willingness to republish, even after the lapse of a considerable period of time, receives its most notable expession, perhaps, in the early chapters of one of Leavis's last books, *The Living Principle* (1975); these were originally essays first published in *Scrutiny* in 1945 and 1953. Changes are minimal. Such long-term adherence to one's critical views is unusual and connected, I think, with Leavis's search for an absolute order, his rejection of the relativism of our century. Unlike T. S. Eliot (and this is part of his later animus against the poet) Leavis, the free-thinker with Protestant forbears, was unable to locate this order within the structures of any institutional belief, for such an order would be imposed from without, unvalidated by the light of inner experience. However, although Leavis rejected such a belief as Eliot's as in some sense unearned, he had a sense of the religious, more and more frequently appealed to as time went on. Leavis's notion of the religious involved wonder, an openness to the not-I, and above all, creativity. These attributes all associate with commonly held notions of art; for Leavis, however, taken together, they were nothing less than life, the kind of life possessed to the full, as Leavis saw it, by the great creative artist, but also capable of being attained by the intelligent (in the special Leavisian sense of the word), mature individual. Life, then, properly achieved life – and Leavis always uses the word normatively – takes on in his work the aspect of an art-form, and is thus capable of possessing the necessary order of art.

Yeats, in holding that 'There is a myth for every man's life, did he but know it', kept art and life distinct, even as he pressed the claims of art to interpret life, but in some ways Leavis confused and conflated the two realms, particularly in his later work. Curiously for a critic with such a fascination with the novel, that great book of bourgeois individualism, Leavis seems to have interpreted his life in mythic rather than novelistic terms, so whereas in his literary criticism he would praise the heuristic processes of a novel, and the capacities of its characters to change and grow, in life he valued the mythic qualities of constancy and endurance and tended to see events and circumstances, not as occasions which might significantly modify his perceptions but as either aids or obstacles (and usually the latter) to his quest. Thus, what he had written was, as a part of himself as unchanging entity, itself unchanging, and what he had once condemned usually remained condemned. The conservatism of the post-war years is marked and unyielding. It is important to take this mythologising bent into account when one considers both Leavis's complaints about his treatment by the literary establishment and his notoriously vicious attacks on those he opposed; it is similarly important not to succumb completely to the mythologising, and to recognise an all too human mixedness of response and complexity of motive. Thus, the list of Leavis's frustrations so frequently enumerated is not, on his reading (though we may read a little differently), designed to arouse our pity but to demonstrate the parlous state of English studies. His case is exemplary rather than individual. His opponents are similarly mythologised and reduced to bloodless, two-dimensional figures, important only as examples of wrong-headedness.

This cast of mind partially accounts for Leavis's attack on C. P. Snow in his Richmond Lecture, *Two Cultures? The Significance of C. P. Snow*, given at Downing College in 1962, and printed in the *Spectator* almost immediately afterwards.[34] A response to C. P. Snow's Rede Lecture of 1959, *The Two Cultures and the Scientific Revolution*,[35] it roused a storm of protest and controversy extending across the Atlantic. The interest Leavis's lecture and the subsequent correspondence aroused is suggested by the production in the United States two years later of an educational textbook, *Cultures in Conflict: Perspectives*, containing extracts from both lectures and from a variety of writings on science and literature, including excerpts from H. G. Wells, D. H. Lawrence, E. M. Forster and Erich Fromm.[36]

The furore caused by Leavis's lecture stemmed not so much from his opposition to Snow, but from what was taken as a crudely personal attack. Leavis declared of Snow, 'he is intellectually as undistinguished as it is possible to be' (NSMS, p. 42), accused him of 'blindness, unconsciousness and automatism' (NSMS, p. 43), and poured scorn on his novels, suggesting maliciously 'that they are composed for him by an electronic brain called Charlie' (NSMS, p. 45). It was only after this attack that he engaged in detailed criticism of Snow's actual argument that modern conditions have created two cultures, the scientific and the literary, and that each culture should know more of the other than is the case. Snow's argument was loaded against the literary in a variety of ways – he characterised the literary culture as 'luddite' and suggested that scientists were likely to know more about literature than the students of literature did about science – and he argued the need for a broader, less specialised education at school level, all obvious causes for Leavis's dissent. Leavis's line of argument was that the intellectual content of Snow's lecture was so thin that at the time of its publication he had not felt it worth arguing against; it was only its acceptance at large and dissemination in schools that led to his attack:

> Snow is a portent. He is a portent in that, being in himself negligible, he has become for a vast public on both sides of the Atlantic a master-mind and a sage. His significance is that he has been accepted – or perhaps the point is better made by saying 'created': he has been created as authoritative intellect by the cultural conditions manifested in his acceptance.   (NSMS, p. 42)

The mythologising bent – which is also a dehumanising one – is strong here, and allows Leavis to claim that his criticism is not personal, for he is, after all, criticising a portent who has been 'created' by those most likely to object to his criticisms, and who are his real object of scorn. Snow thus suffers demolition upon demolition, for the comments on his novels establish that he has no claim to be the proper object of attack. There seems to be more at work than Leavis's mythologisingbent, however, for it was precisely through the violence of his attack that Leavis was able to get publicity for his cogent intellectual arguments against Snow's lumbering analysis of our culture. Leavis, that great attacker of modern journalism, was prepared to exploit *its* simplifying, mythologising tendencies in order to get a hearing.

As well as being the year of the C. P. Snow controversy, 1962 marked Leavis's retirement as University Reader and as Fellow of Downing, although he continued to hold an Honorary Fellowship there for two years longer. After this he embarked on a variety of lecturing assignments both in England and in the United States, and held in this country a number of visiting professorships. Freedom from teaching, changes of audience, and perhaps the sense of being properly recognised led to a new spate of books, which in their mixture of cultural and literary concerns recalled the productions of the 1930s. As in his early prolific days these books are made up of lectures and essays rather than produced as complete works *ab initio*. These last works are notable for a kind of religious fervour and a great sense of urgency. If culture was in crisis in the 1930s, by the 1970s Leavis saw little to hope for. However, the fight for civilisation could never be abandoned. Leavis died in 1978, two years after producing *Thought, Words and Creativity*, his third work on Lawrence, that novelist who had become for him the supreme prophet of our era.

CHAPTER TWO | Leavis's World Picture

Introduction

However unwillingly, Cambridge provided Leavis with an occupation and professional status. It also provided the conditions within which it was possible to create, in *Scrutiny*, a forum which extended beyond the lecture hall. It gave him much more, for in the 1920s and 1930s it provided a milieu in which a multiplicity of cultural and social theories circulated, mingling with and modifying one another. The very nature of literary studies as they had been theorised by I. A. Richards demanded involvement in social and cultural questions, for if the *raison d'être* of literature and its study was not aesthetic, but psychological and moral, and if the critic were assigned a therapeutic role in his society, then that role implied investigation and diagnosis.

Although in his introduction to *Determinations*, a collection of critical essays culled from *Scrutiny* and published in 1934, Leavis endorsed T. S. Eliot's dictum that poetry is to be considered primarily as poetry and not as something else, he also held that literary studies necessarily led outside themselves. Following Richards he consistently denied that there were any purely literary values, holding it as self-evident that 'judgements of literary value involve extra-literary choices and decisions' (FC, p. 183). In

Leavis's acceptation 'criticism, when it performs its function, not merely expresses and defines 'the contemporary sensibility'; it helps to form it' (FC, p. 183), and does so by making known to those capable of judging it the literature which is 'the consciousness of the age' (FC, p. 183), the work of those genuinely creative artists who represent in Richards's phrase, 'the point at which the growth of the mind shows itself'.[1]

Licensed by such Ricardian doctrine, Leavis occupied himself almost as much with social and cultural as with literary criticism, or perhaps it would express his position better to say that he made no hard and fast distinction between the literary and the social. So, while his first two full-length books, *New Bearings in English Poetry* and *For Continuity*, could reasonably be claimed to have distinguishable concerns, the former literary critical, the latter cultural, it would have to be with the proviso that *New Bearings* articulates and depends upon a clear idea of the place and function of literature within a society, and that many of the essays of *For Continuity* perform at least some of their cultural criticism by means of literary criticism. *Culture and Environment*, a textbook for schools and colleges produced in collaboration with Denys Thompson, uses the methods of practical criticism as a means of alerting its users to the dangers of advertising and other cultural phenomena.

From the beginning of his career Leavis presented his criticism as opportunistic, reactive, a collection of immediate responses to particular, specific situations. 'For Matthew Arnold it was in some ways less difficult'; this, the opening of his pamphlet *Mass Civilization and Minority Culture*, is typical of the Leavisian rhetoric whereby an argument is presented as stemming from a particular moment or event rather than as representing an already worked-out position. Typical, too, is his claim in the prefatory essay of *For Continuity*, 'Marxism and Cultural Continuity', that the collection was written in 'the reverse of an academic and purely theoretical spirit' (FC, pp. 1–2). 'Theory' and 'philosophy' are almost always terms of contempt in Leavis's vocabulary, signifying an arid intellectualism and reductive, over-simplifying thought processes. The implicit claim is that each situation requires for its understanding a fresh engagement of the whole being.

Whatever the rhetoric, Leavis – although the fact is somewhat obscured by his method of presentation – is one of the grand system builders, and the texts I have already mentioned, together with *Revaluation* and *Education and the University* emerge from and articulate a remarkably totalising and seemingly coherent world picture forged from a number of different intellectual sources. They also represent social interventions of different kinds, for Leavis and his fellow Scrutineers saw their enterprises as practical, as directed toward the creation of an influential and self-aware reading public able to apply its intelligence to extra-literary as well as to literary matters.

Social and Cultural Criticism 1930–43

Urgency is the dominant note sounded in Leavis's early criticism, and in the 1930s he was not alone. Few at the time would have disagreed with his assertion, 'It is a commonplace today that culture is at a crisis'.[2] However, the causes, nature and duration of this state of affairs were perhaps less easily agreed upon. Indeed, it might be fair to say that the sense of crisis sprang from significantly different origins within different groups, and that in some sense at least those of different persuasions addressed themselves to, or defined for themselves, different concerns, different crises persisting over different periods of time. Allan Megill emphasises the length of time over which a sense of crisis persisted within European philosophy, attributing it to the collapse of historicism, and the failure of faith in progress that occurred in the late nineteenth century.[3] His analysis differs from a view held more commonly in the 1920s and 1930s, and not uncommon today, which linked the felt sense of dislocation with the disappearance of authoritative standards in the early part of this century.

By contrast with those stressing the primacy of intellectual causes, the perception of crisis among those of the left was conditioned by political and social factors; by the poverty and dislocation of the 1930s, and by the threat of Fascism. The stress in James Klugman's reminiscences of the period is upon the intractability of raw events, rather than upon Marxist theory.[4]

Despite the left-wing sympathies of some Scrutineers – among them one of the founder members, L. C. Knights – and the attempts of some communists to enlist Leavis and *Scrutiny* as allies, there was a gulf fixed between the two groups. For communists, improvement in the material conditions of life was a primary concern, for Leavis what, for want of a better word, might be called the spiritual was central. Put like this, and given Leavis's assertion that he believed 'some form of economic communism to be inevitable and desirable' in the circumstances following the Wall Street Crash and Depression, it might seem that there was not so much a conflict between the two sides as a difference in emphasis.[5] However, Leavis shows himself to be essentially conservative in his attitude to change, and to have a quite different conception of the ills of society from that of the communists. In their eyes radical change was necessary in order to bring about economic and social justice, whereas Leavis and most of the Scrutineers believed that change was an enemy in itself. The changes already brought about by industrialisation had destroyed customary patterns and limited the influence of that small minority upon whom, in Leavis's view, 'depend the implicit standards that order the finer living of an age'.[6] Whereas it seemed to the communists that their ends could be attained only by revolution, Leavis saw revolution as yet another stage in the process of destruction and, setting a word against a word, he countered their call to arms with an insistence on the need 'for continuity', a phrase which, as we have seen, he used as the title of his second book. Why Leavis regarded continuity as essential emerges in his strictures against Trotsky's *Literature and Revolution* when he speaks of 'the delicate organic growth that "human culture" is', and in his description as 'rootless' of such a culture as he alleges is envisaged by Trotsky.[7] Leavis's metaphors here are botanical, and function as something more than metaphors throughout his writing, validating his proposition, imbuing it with the self-evidence of tautology, that without continuity there can be no growth. However, the past is important not only as the necessary condition of growth, but as that which will guide our sense of what is worth having. For Leavis it is normative, just as the future is for Trotsky; for the one the present state of affairs represents a falling off from, to, the other a preliminary to the ideal state.

It is in *Culture and Environment*, perhaps, that Leavis most explicitly evokes the past he considers us to have lost, and it is important to notice his insistence that it cannot be revived:

What we have lost is the organic society with the living culture it embodied . . . an art of life, a way of living, ordered and patterned, involving social arts, codes of intercourse and a responsive adjustment, growing out of immemorial experience, to the natural environment and the rhythm of the year . . . It is not merely that life . . . has become urban and industrial. When life was rooted in the soil town life was not what it is now.   (CE, pp. 1–2)

The continuities which characterise the prelapsarian society evoked by Leavis are manifold: most obviously there is continuity over time, allowing the growth of 'social arts' and 'codes of intercourse' – and words like 'immemorial' and 'time-honoured' are honorifics in the Leavisian vocabulary. There is also continuity between the human and the natural worlds; 'a life rooted in the soil' and a 'responsive adjustment to the rhythm of the year'. Continuity, too, between the rural and the urban is suggested, though not explicitly stated. Later in the book the relation between work and leisure in the organic society is contrasted with that existing in our own time:

. . . it was in their work for the most part that the folk lived . . . The modern labourer, the modern clerk, the modern factory-hand live only for their leisure, and the result is that they are unable to live in their leisure when they get it . . . Men are now incapacitated by their work, which makes leisure necessary as it was not before, from using their labour for *humane* recreation . . .   (CE, pp. 68–9)

The continuity posited here is between all aspects of life, so that life is not assumed to be identical with leisure and antithetical to work, as in the machine age. Work is fulfilling, a principle of order and a source of enjoyment for the common people. Using George Sturt's *The Wheelwright's Shop* as evidence, Leavis expands on what he takes to be the workmen's relation to their work, and the concomitant relations with their employer:[8]

. . . they were never merely 'hands' but always 'the men' . . . The workmen were men and not 'labour', not merely a factor necessary to production as 'power' and 'capital' are, and on the same level. Besides their hands their brains, imagination, conscience, sense of beauty and fitness – their personalities – were engaged and satis-

fied. Just as their master was not concerned merely for his profits,
so they were not concerned merely for their wages.   (CE, p. 75)

The work employed the whole man, and 'master' and workmen
were mutually dependent rather than necessarily, structurally, opposed to one another. Leavis correspondingly asserts a relation of
interdependence between what I shall call for the moment polite
and popular culture (later in the chapter we shall see why these are
not the terms he himself uses) which he saw as sharing a common
tradition and language. He contrasts this state of affairs not only
with the demonstrable split between 'highbrow' and popular culture in modern times (and for Leavis the very word 'highbrow'
measures what has been lost), but with the 'rootless' leisure society
which he believed to be the inevitable outcome of the communist
utopian ideal. This strong sense of the importance of physical
place in conjunction with Leavis's stress on the cohesion and
mutual supportiveness of different social groups suggests a
nationalistic perspective of the kind I have already noticed in
discussing the Newbolt Report, defined in such expressions as
'rooted in the soil' and 'the folk'. This latter is probably impossible
to use now without overtones of condescension attaching to the
implicit glamorising approval.

Implicit in the passages I have quoted is a correspondence between individual and society. In an organic society, it is suggested,
individuals will be whole, with all their faculties brought into
harmonious play with one another. By contrast, the literature of
the modern world, starting from after the Civil War, exhibits a
dissociation of sensibility as intelligence and feeling become increasingly compartmentalised.

This brief delineation of Leavis's ideal of the organic society has
also necessarily suggested the shortcomings he found in the modern world. The swift and disorientating changes characteristic of
the machine age, soul-destroying jobs unfitting workers for the
creative use of leisure and encouraging a passive materialism, an
urban, denatured environment obliterating national differences –
the megapolitan culture. Leavis regularly evoked these deficiencies
in his unholy trinity of 'mass-production, standardisation,
levelling-down', processes which he believed invaded all aspects of
life, and most importantly, the intellectual-spiritual. In his view
the effects of the machine could be felt in every corner of the world

of ideas and literature. Advertising, the popular press (Northcliffe, the press baron, held a prominent place in Leavis's demonology), book societies, in their need for mass sales had pandered to the public, and in 'giving the public what it wants' had debased taste and coarsened sensibilities. Such phenomena as mediocre literature, films and (perhaps surprisingly) the BBC induced passivity and stock responses in their consumers; at the same time such consumers were encouraged to dismiss serious works as 'highbrow'. Correspondingly, serious writers now wrote for a tiny minority, producing works of such difficulty as to repel most readers, and neither works nor their minority readership wielded any longer the influence they had had in the past. The process of levelling down had nothing to counter it.

Within this world of constantly declining standards and incessant change it was only tradition, specifically literary tradition, that in Leavis's scheme of things offered the possibility of performing David's function against the modern Goliath the machine had created. To Leavis literary education was vital to the preservation of what was left of our culture. His argument can be summarised as follows: literary tradition, the literature of the past, is what we have left of the organic community. This literature is not so much *evidence* of a past culture as a part of that culture itself, embodying its values and a whole way of life. It speaks to us of a time before the split between 'highbrow' and mass communications, of a time when 'the cultivation of the art of speech was as essential . . . as song, dance and handicrafts' (CE, p. 2). Importantly, Leavis does not see himself as engaged in any kind of antiquarian reconstruction, but in establishing continuities, for the literature of the past has its life 'in the present or nowhere'. In fact, literature is literature precisely to the degree to which it is alive for us. Healing the breach between past and present, such a literature is a necessary condition for that growth which is all but precluded by the deracinating changes of the machine, and that which keeps some part of the old tradition alive in us.

That Leavis is able to make such high claims for literature and literary studies depends of course upon Richards's theories which confer a high status on the great writer, and in 'Mass Civilization and Minority Culture' Leavis quotes Richards approvingly:

For the arts are inevitably and quite apart from any intentions of the artist an appraisal of existence. Matthew Arnold when he said that poetry was a criticism of life was saying something so obvious that it is constantly overlooked. The artist is concerned with the record and perpetuation of the experiences which seem to him most worth having . . . he is also the man who is most likely to have experiences of value to record. He is the point at which the growth of the mind shows itself.[9]

On this interpretation the writer, above anyone else, is uniquely qualified to judge his or her world, and to reveal that world to itself, changing it into something different through the new consciousness s/he has created.

The largeness of Leavis's claims for the writer also constitutes the justification of his claims for literary criticism, for if the writer represents the growing point of a culture, it is the small group of readers, 'the very small minority', who are able not only to recognise the value of past literature but who can detect the growth of the mind in the present, in their own age, who are the preservers and transmitters of culture:

Upon this minority depends our power of profiting by the finest human experience of the past; they keep alive the subtlest and most perishable parts of tradition. Upon them depend the implicit standards that order the finer living of an age, the sense that this is worth more than that, this rather than that is the direction in which to go, that the centre is here rather than there. In their keeping, to use a metaphor that is metonymy also and will bear a good deal of pondering, is the language, the changing idiom, upon which fine living depends, and without which distinction of spirit is thwarted and incoherent. By 'culture' I mean the use of such a language.[10]

Crucial here is the identification of culture with language – though, it is important to notice, Leavis does not see the boundaries of the two as being coterminous. Crucial also is the association of 'culture' with 'fine living' and 'finer living' (the comparative is important). 'Culture' in Leavis's use here refers not to that network of practices and beliefs that go to make up a society, but to what he sees as most valuable within that society. Used of the modern world the term is always value-laden; used of the past 'culture' is given more of an extended, anthropological sense, but in those instances the past, the organic society itself, is a value so that 'the living culture it embodied' remains valorised. 'Culture', that is, is almost always a value, hardly ever a neutral term, though its relation with society is not necessarily the same from one period to another.

Leavis's sense of the ills of his society fell within a tradition of social criticism persisting throughout the nineteenth and into the twentieth century; it was also defined, although far more tenuously, by facets of the European philosophical tradition as they were mediated in attenuated form through modernism and oversimplified in Spengler's *The Decline of the West*. Important influences, too, were accounts of the American experience of the machine age, whether favourable or monitory. Although these different sources may all be pressed to tell stories of decline their varying constructions of past and present leave traces in the picture Leavis draws from them, inconsistencies and aporia which bring into question the historicity of his myth.

That Leavis could speak of the organic society as 'a phrase now familiar', together with his emphasis on the devastation caused by the machine, allies him with a strain of concern stretching back in this country into the nineteenth century, showing itself in one aspect in the cultural criticism of such writers as Thomas Carlyle and Matthew Arnold. As early as 1829 in 'Signs of the Times' Carlyle, criticising his society and predicting worse to come, defines the 'mechanical age' in which he lives: 'Not the external and physical alone is now managed by machinery, but the internal and spiritual also. Here too nothing follows its spontaneous course, nothing is left to be accomplished by old natural methods.'[11] He reiterates and expands on his definition a few paragraphs later:

> . . . the same habit regulates not our modes of action alone, but our modes of thought and feeling. Men are grown mechanical in head and in heart, as well as in hand. They have lost faith in individual endeavour, and in natural force, of any kind.

Written a hundred years before, Carlyle's analysis of his society is strikingly similar to Leavis's of his. There is the same opposition of the mechanical to the natural and spontaneous. Anticipating Leavis, Carlyle refuses his contemporaries' diagnoses of crisis and locates the malaise in the changes of consciousness wrought by the impact of the machine on every department of life, and deplores the inadequacy of empiricist and utilitarian philosophy, founded as it is on the methods of the natural sciences, to speak of the human, to give a proper account of human individuality. Leavis's fulminations against such phenomena as the Book Club, the BBC, and the Arts Council echo Carlyle's blistering description of the plight of culture in his time:

> In defect of Raphaels, and Angelos, and Mozarts, we have Royal Academies of Painting, Sculpture, Music; whereby the languishing spirit of Art may be strengthened, as by the more generous diet of a Public Kitchen. Literature, too, has its Paternoster-Row mechanism, its Trade-dinners, its Editorial conclaves, and huge subterranean, puffing bellows; so that books are not only printed, but in a great measure, written and sold, by machinery. ('Signs of the Times', p. 228)

Both writers stress the materialism of their societies, and in almost identical terms. Like Leavis, Carlyle deplores a concentration on the physicalities of existence: 'It is no longer the moral, religious, spiritual condition of the people that is our concern, but their physical, practical, economical condition, as regulated by public laws'. ('Signs of the Times', pp. 232–3). Given such identity of concern, it seems rather surprising that in *Mill on Bentham and Coleridge* Leavis should deplore the time students had to spend on Carlyle (MBC, pp.13–14).

Although the content of Leavis's diagnosis of society's ills follows Carlyle's so closely, Matthew Arnold is the Victorian sage with whom Leavis most self-consciously and overtly aligns himself in *For Continuity*, and with whom he enters into dialogue in later essays. From the Arnold of *Culture and Anarchy* (1869) he adopted a rhetorical stance of detachment from his society, a persona whose scathing wit became the expression of moral urgency. Where Carlyle's use of first person plural pronouns signals, at least at times, his acceptance of implication in what he deplores ('the deep almost exclusive faith we have in mechanism', 'our modes of thought and feeling') on the whole Arnold and Leavis embrace in their use of 'we' only that small band of the enlightened: 'Here we have the plight of culture in general'

(FC, p. 31). It becomes in their hands a means by which the great mass of the unworthy are excluded.

Leavis also uses Arnold as a measure of the decline in intellectual standards between his time and Leavis's own ('For Matthew Arnold it was in some ways less difficult') and his, Leavis's, correspondingly more difficult task. In 'Mass Civilization and Minority Culture', the essay which opens with the above statement, Arnold is brought forward both as a reference point and an authority; his definition of culture, together with that of I. A. Richards, seemingly accepted as self-evident to the few capable of thought: 'When . . . having started by saying that culture has always been in minority keeping, I am asked what I mean by 'culture', I might (and do) refer the reader to *Culture and Anarchy*; but I know that something more is required' (FC, p. 13). Although Leavis's notion of culture and what it comprises is by no means identical with Arnold's, what they crucially share is an idea of it as something we assimilate and which alters us; it is an active pursuit involving nothing less than every facet of our lives; it is freeing and enlightening, and it has a public importance: it is 'the great help out of our present difficulties' (*Culture and Anarchy*, Cambridge University Press, 1932, p. 6). Interestingly, for both writers it is predominantly verbal.

Nineteenth-century concern for the state of society found expression not only in social and cultural criticism, but also in creative literature, most notably in the novel. The Condition of England debate was widespread and wide-ranging. While such writers as Disraeli and Mrs Gaskell explored in their fiction the material conditions of working-class life, Dickens in *Hard Times* (dedicated to Carlyle) focused on the spiritual constrictions produced by Utilitarianism and rampant capitalism. Within these novels and others with similar themes, life in the town is presented as both sullied and sullying, as brutalising and ultimately destructive. By contrast the countryside tends to appear as a place of recreation providing the chance to cast off the restraints of the urban which is also the alien.

Attacks on the machine age came from all quarters and continued into the twentieth century. Ruskin contrasted the 'degradation of the operative into a machine' with the working conditions leading to the building of the great cathedrals; and William Morris's textiles, furniture and books were a product of his hatred of the mass-produced shoddy goods that flooded the nineteenth-century markets.[12] Economic and social historians, too, exhibited a tendency to read the present in terms of decline. One of the important issues was the decay of the peasantry. The work of the Hammonds who were prolific and gifted historians is important here. Although the Hammonds' findings have been substantially modified by later research *The Village Labourer* (1911) and *The Town Labourer* (1917) ran into numerous editions and attained classic status.[13] Central to Leavis's account of the organic community is the work of George Sturt (who wrote under the name of George Bourne); he used both *Change in the Village* (1912) and *The Wheelwright's Shop* (1923), which I have already mentioned. Although Sturt wrote from his own experience of village life and of the erosion of traditional skills, it is important to recognise that his perspective is still to some extent that of the outsider, a former schoolteacher who, under the influence of Ruskin, 'felt that man's only decent occupation was in handicraft' (*The Wheelwright's Shop*, p. 12), and so returned to the family business. While it may be true, as Geoffrey Grigson, his editor, suggested, that this distance is essential to his work, his picture of his village and his trade is coloured by the craft movement and the work of the Hammonds (*Change in The Village*, p. x).

The writers and works I have mentioned all speak of dispossession and loss, of an impoverishment of life. For some the decline is predominantly in material standards of living, for others such as Sturt it is located in the loss of customary skills, a loss which is finally the loss of a whole way of life. Yet throughout the nineteenth century the dominant belief was in progress rather than decline, and in the benefits of the new industrialisation. Despite the increased pessimism of the twentieth century, the idea of progress still had its exponents; notable among them is one of Leavis's *bêtes noires*, H. G. Wells, who in *The Work, Wealth and Happiness of Mankind* presents an essentially optimistic view of life with the machine. In Wells's novel *Tono-Bungay* (1908) the implication is that adherence to the machine and the intricacies of capitalist society entails the privileging of town over country, and the narrator–protagonist mounts a defiant attack on the rural myth, overturning its most cherished tenets. His position is not dissimilar to that of Engels in the opening chapter of *The Condition of the Working Class in England*:

In the English countryside there are no books at all, no songs, no drama, no valiant sin even; all these things have never come or they were taken away and hidden generations ago, and the imagination aborts and bestialises. That, I think, is where the real difference against the English rural man lies. It is because I know this that I do not share in the common repinings because our countryside is depopulated, because our population is passing through the furnace of the towns. They starve, they suffer no doubt, but they come out of it hardened, they come out of it with souls . . .[14]

If the machine is a focus for polarity this is, at least in part, because it takes its place within an opposition of country to city transcending the coming of industrialism by centuries. As Raymond Williams has shown, the opposition is pervasive and stretches back to classical times, undergoing transformation after transformation with the impact of different historical circumstances.[15] To recognise this is not, however, to dismiss its proponents as backward-looking sentimentalists. The changes wrought by industrialisation were swift and all-encompassing, and the disruption it entailed must have seemed to be unalleviated by any real improvements in living standards. At the beginning of the century Charles Booth and Seebohm Rowntree conducted surveys of London and York respectively which revealed that in London 30.7 per cent of the population was living in poverty, and 27.84 per cent in York.[16] Included in the bibliography of *Culture and Environment* is *Middletown*, a study of the impact of industrialisation on a mid-Western town in the United States. The work emerges the more powerfully as an indictment of what it describes because of its attempt to be non-judgemental, and because of the detail amassed in order to avoid 'smooth generalisations'.[17] Perhaps the most poignant feature of the society described by the Lynds (but not singled out by Leavis) is the destruction of a sense of future for male workers, who could look forward to being sacked in their early forties since speed and stamina, and not experience, were the valued qualifications in the new industries.

Also included in Leavis's and Thompson's bibliography is E. M. Forster's 'The Machine Stops', first published in book form in 1928, a story which adds another dimension to the urban/machine complex in its creation of a machine world designed to extrude the physical and to isolate each individual in her or his own capsule;

within this world human contact is to be avoided, and living confined to the realm of concepts and ideas, all completely dependent upon the (only seemingly) perpetual machine. A pattern looking back to Carlyle and Dickens is thus articulated with perhaps too obvious neatness, and the rural/physical/craft-based/feeling/ intuitive human is placed in opposition to the urban/cerebral/ machine-using/emotionless/isolated intellect. This discrediting of the intellect in so far as it operates in isolation from feeling and sensation is one of Leavis's constant preoccupations; his mistrust of philosophy is vociferous as he attempts to shape within his criticism a discourse he conceives to be more adequate to the expression of human truth.

Leavis in rejecting philosophy equated it with the dominant empiricist–positivist tradition in England which tended to use models derived from the natural sciences to categorise human life, and to define metaphysical questions as illegitimate. However, as H. Stuart Hughes has shown, philosophers on the Continent had addressed the problem of finding a distinctive way of speaking of the human[18], and in England the writings of T. E. Hulme, published posthumously in 1924, introduced the work of Bergson to the intelligensia and attacked the privileging of intellect over intuition.[19] According to Bergson, as he is mediated by Hulme, 'the ordinary use of the logical intellect' 'distorts instead of revealing', and both intellect and intuition are necessary to 'obtain a complete picture of reality'. Intellect alone, although it is capable of dealing with matter, reduces 'vital phenomena' to 'very complex mechanical phenomena' (Hulme, p. 174). The distortions of the unchecked intellect thus figure an entirely determined, mechanistic universe for us. The reason for this is that the logical intellect operates from within the process it seeks to define; it has been abstracted, created by the model it investigates and so it transforms the phenomena it observes into what is compatible with it: '. . . this surprising unanimity in the results of the different sciences is not due to the nature of the phenomena they investigate, but rather to the nature of the instrument we use in explanation. We find atoms everywhere' (Hulme, p. 177). Against this atomism, which he believes to be caused by always thinking in terms of extension in space – that is, analytically – Hulme sets a more holistic means of knowing, a kind of immediate, intuitive grasp of certain situations or states of affairs which he describes as 'intensive manifolds' (by contrast analytic thinking sees in terms of 'extensive manifolds'). Implicit in his ideas is a belief in some sort of correspondence between the means of knowing and the object of knowledge. Intuition gives us a different picture from that provided by the intellect. At the same time Hulme asserts the reality of that which will be lost without the operation of intuition. Intuition, that is, does not create its object; rather, it recovers or discovers it. Although Hulme died in the First World War, before his work could be refined and extended, he was influential among modernist writers. Frank Kermode has pointed out that, despite the way in which T. S. Eliot's name has come to be linked indissolubly with the notion of the dissociation of sensibility, 'Hulme was one of the first of the English to discover, what was later to become a dominating concept in modern criticism, some kind of disastrous psychical shift, some original moral catastrophe, in human history about the time of the Renaissance'.[20] He notices that Pound, too, shared the belief. If we look at Eliot's formulation the link with Hulme's idea of intensive and extensive manifolds is clear: since the seventeenth century there has been a split between intellect and emotion which has prevented an intuitive grasp of the whole event:

> The difference is not a simple difference of degree between poets. It is something which had happened to the mind of England between the time of Donne or Lord Herbert of Cherbury and the time of Tennyson and Browning; it is the difference between the intellectual poet and the reflective poet. Tennyson and Browning are poets, and they think; but they do not feel their thought as immediately as the odour of a rose. A thought to Donne was an experience; it modified his sensibility. When a poet's mind is perfectly equipped for its work, it is constantly amalgamating disparate experience; the ordinary man's experience is chaotic, irregular, fragmentary. The latter falls in love, or reads Spinoza, and these two experiences have nothing to do with each other, or with the noise of the typewriter or the smell of cooking; in the mind of the poet these experiences are always forming new wholes.[21]

Yeats, another great modernist poet, produced his own formulation: 'In literature . . . we have lost in personality, in our delight in the whole man – blood, imagination, intellect, running together' ('Discoveries', *Essays and Introductions*, London, 1961, p. 266).

Like Eliot, Yeats connects this fragmentation with the seventeenth century and, like Hulme, with mechanistic ways of seeing: 'The mischief began at the end of the seventeenth century when man became passive before a mechanised nature' (*The Oxford Book of Modern Verse*, Oxford, 1936, p. xxiii). Although Hulme is not an acknowledged influence on Leavis's thought (and on occasion referred to dismissively), Eliot's 'theory' (the poet's own word) of the dissociation of sensibility is crucial to Leavis's construction of literary history, and to his cultural criticism.[22] The theory is also closely tied to his rejection of empiricist philosophy; indeed one might say it entails that rejection. Thus, doubly mediated, through Hulme via Eliot we can see the shadowy outlines of European philosophy in Leavis's thinking. It may be because of filiations such as these that the parallels between Leavis and Heidegger which Michael Bell points out are so striking.[23]

Leavis's most direct contact with European philosophy, however – albeit in somewhat debased form – was probably through Spengler's *The Decline of the West*.[24] Although Leavis repudiated the determinism of Spengler's vast and rather turgid system-building which encompassed the whole of human history and pontificated on the characteristics of successive cultures, there are some striking resemblances between the thinking of the two men. Leavis adopted the Spenglerian opposition of Culture to Civilisation ('*Culture and Civilization* – the living body of a soul and the mummy of it' (*The Decline of the West*, p. 186)) and the Spenglerian term, 'megapolis' to refer to the modern city, which both writers saw as being divorced from any idea of nationhood. Such adoption was possible because both, sharing a common revulsion against twentieth-century society, attached similar associations to the two terms. In the familiar opposition, culture was organic/natural/rural/rooted/traditional/intuitive and its members shared a feeling of community and a capacity for wonder. By contrast civilisation was mechanical/megapolitan/urban/rootless/ rationalist-intellectual/utilitarian/irreligious, its inhabitants an atomistic mob. Such polarisation has been evident in many of the thinkers I have referred to in this chapter, but Spengler in his urgent theorisation perhaps expresses it most explicitly. One of the most insistent likenesses between Leavis and Spengler is the importance they both attach to the physical roots of nationalism. Both emphasise the importance of place and landscape rather than a political system in its constitution, and in his early essay on D. H. Lawrence, Leavis quotes at length Spengler's description of the withering of Being into intellect when it is 'separated from the power of the land'.[25] Like Leavis, Spengler gives his metaphor an almost literal force: 'A race has roots. Race and landscape belong together. Where a plant takes root, there it dies also' (*The Decline of the West*, p. 251). Unlike Leavis, however, Spengler seems to distinguish between a race and a people; a distinction which leads to a crucial difference between the writers, for where both would define an authentic society as having a sense of community, of shared life, Leavis would locate this sense of sharedness in the possession of a common language entailing shared values, while Spengler, citing America and Rome as examples, declares that 'Neither unity of speech nor physical descent is decisive. That which distinguishes a people from a population . . . is always the inwardly lived experience of the "we"' (*The Decline of the West*, p. 260). Spengler's notion of the origin of group consciousness makes of it something reactive, brought into being by factors external to itself, for 'The great events of history . . . *created the peoples*' (*The Decline of the West*, p. 260). Both writers assert that rootedness is a necessary condition for a living, vital society – what Spengler calls 'a high Culture' and Leavis an 'organic community'. Spengler's 'Whatever disconnects itself from the land becomes rigid and hard' (*The Decline of the West*, p. 311) strikes a note which echoes in Leavis's writing. In another essay in *For Continuity*, 'Joyce and "The Revolution of the Word" ', Leavis comments on the metaphor explicitly, claiming the popular basis of culture to be agricultural, and supporting a linguistic theory that linked features of language with ' "kinaesthetic" images' deriving from physical labour (FC, p. 216). Such a stress on the physicality of language, as it were, connects interestingly with Leavis's valuing of tactile imagery, and also with his insistence that poetry needs to be read aloud to be properly understood.

Against his picture of our past Spengler sets the horrors of the modern world city, the megapolis, inhabited by a mob rather than a community, and in which the individual is homeless:

> The world-city means cosmopolitanism in place of 'home' . . . To the world-city belongs not a folk but a mob. Its uncomprehending hostility to all the traditions representative of the Culture . . . the

keen and cold intelligence that confounds the wisdom of the peasant . . . all these things betoken the definite closing-down of the Culture . . . (*The Decline of the West*, p. 49)

In such a city, Spengler argues, democracy and plutocracy are the same thing, for the expenditure of money on a vast scale is necessary for 'the preparation of public opinion' (*The Decline of the West*, p. 350) – and here we might remember Leavis's fulminations against the purveyors of popular and middlebrow culture and his instinctively anti-democratic stance. In Spengler's megapolis, the world of the twentieth century, 'the mechanistic conception of the world stands at its zenith' (*The Decline of the West*, p. 330), and marks the death of culture for 'Culture is ever synonymous with religious creativeness' (*The Decline of the West*, p. 330). Instead we have 'The whole world a dynamic system, exact, mathematically disposed, capable down to its first causes of being experimentally probed and numerically fixed so that man can dominate it' (*The Decline of the West*, p. 330). Like Hulme and Leavis, Spengler seeks to find a means of exploring the human which does not reduce it to mechanism, and like Leavis's his implicit claim for his work is that it is praxis as well as theory; that the new form reveals/ creates its content: 'The means whereby to identify dead forms is Mathematical Law. The means whereby to understand living forms is Analogy. By these means we are enabled to distinguish polarity and periodicity in the world' (*The Decline of the West*, p. 30).

Since Leavis refers to Spengler and has read him, the parallels between the two writers suggest straightforward indebtedness on Leavis's part. That Spengler did in fact influence Leavis's thinking seems indubitable, but it is perhaps more important to stress the ubiquity of the ideas he propounded than to insist on the debt. How widespread such ideas were can be seen in the resemblances between *The Decline of the West* and Yeats's *A Vision*, published in 1925, which depicts the twentieth century as the end of a cycle of civilisation. According to his biographer Joseph Hone, Yeats, reading Spengler in translation 'had found in it whole metaphors that were also in his *Vision*, and many of the same dates as well'.[26] What we seem to have are numerous lines of connection between different writers and theories; cross-fertilisations and contaminations, filiations of many different kinds which all testify to the centrality of Leavis's cultural concerns and to his status as a representative rather than idiosyncratic figure in the 1930s. His version of the myth of catastrophe emerges from a dialogue with others haunted by similar fears and holding similar values.

The doctrines of the dissociation of sensibility and the loss of the organic community are foundational to Leavis's criticism, but although the two ideas seem logically tied, focusing respectively on individual and social fragmentation, Leavis tends to make use of the former in his literary criticism, basing his construction of English literary history upon it. This is no doubt partly because literature in Leavis's acceptation exhibits most clearly in its revelation of inner, spiritual states, the psychic fragmentation of our time and the psychic wholeness of our forbears. The tendency to allow the different ideas slightly different areas of operation may also derive from their different pre-histories, for the notion of a dissociation of sensibility was from the beginning primarily a means of accounting for and/or justifying poetic practice. Frank Kermode presents it as a kind of enabling myth for symbolist poetics: 'They seek, in short, a historical period possessing the qualities they postulate for the Image: unity, indissociability; qualities which, though passionately desired, are, they say, uniquely' hard to come by in the modern world' (*Romantic Image*, p. 145). By contrast, the idea of the 'organic community', as we have seen, was not confined to the literary world for most of its history, but was used by artists, historians and cultural critics to embrace every facet of a society. Beyond this difference in application these seemingly logically tied states appear to be set at odds with one another by their dating, for the dissociation of sensibility is held to show itself at the very latest after the Civil War, while the organic community is assumed to be destroyed by the industrial revolution.

The discrepancies between the two terms are matched by the uncertainties within them. In *The Country and the City* Raymond Williams points out how each generation of rural writers is imbued with a sense of recent loss so that the search for the organic community becomes an almost infinite regress (pp. 9–10), and Frank Kermode points to a similar problem of dating the dissociation of sensibility (*Romantic Image*, p. 143); Yeats and Hulme agreed in seeing Byzantium as the moment after which all was decline; for Eliot and Leavis it was the Civil War which marked the individual's alienation from himself. The quality both ideas share is the inaccessibility of the wholeness they celebrate. In a sense, both are versions of the Edenic myth, for the Fall is located at the moment of consciousness; yet consciousness is precisely the condition of dissociation, for in Hegelian terms it is through consciousness that the individual becomes the object, the other, to him or herself. A modern version of the myth seems to be that of the French psychoanalyst, Jacques Lacan, according to which the child's perception of himself at the mirror-stage of development is accompanied by entry into the symbolic of language, an entry which is described in terms of loss, of relinquishment of the imaginary and its attendant sense of wholeness.[27]

It seems necessary to reiterate, however, that to emphasise the mythic qualities of these two ideas so crucial to Leavis's thought is not to deny them all historical truth. There *have* been changes of consciousness over time, and there *is* a difference in consciousness between pre-industrial and industrial societies. It is also true that some times and places are better or worse for some people to live in than others, and that unregulated industrialism all too frequently condemns people to degrading and stultifying living and working conditions. *Middletown* and (unwittingly) Henry Ford's *My Life and Work*, and other books Leavis made use of testify to that.[28] It is probably also true that, other things being equal, an established rural community offers more protection against hardship than a new urban settlement; there is likely to be a greater diversity of employment in the country, and at least some opportunity to live off the land or to exchange favours, but above all there is the sense of being known, of belonging to a network of kinship.

And yet the myth as it is presented to us smoothes out the irregularities of history, ignoring those who found work in the city an escape from rural poverty; ignoring also the possibility of brutalisation and oppression inherent in the country. In the end it figures as a kind of Utopian vision, providing through its particularity, through its claim to truth, a set of values promising to be realisable. As such it seems to me morally suspect. A Utopian vision looking toward the future lays no claim to the real. It is professedly ideal. But to make a Utopia of the past, to present the complexities of a historical situation so simply is to break faith with the people who lived and suffered in it, to deny them their full humanity and resourcefulness. Those living in the country are made the objects of aesthetic admiration, while the supposedly passive and denatured industrial workers become the subjects of a rather patronising pity. The brutalising (in more than one sense) tendency of myth shows itself in Sturt's description of the sawyers in *The Wheelwright's Shop*. Sturt's sawyers slouch dispiritedly through his pages, and his literary dealings with them seem to present him with as many problems as his business transactions did. His shifts in discourse have an air of social embarrassment, seeming to function as attempts to find the right company for this group whose diwith what one might call without too much unfairness a zoological, Darwinian perspective:

> As a wild animal species to its habitat, so these workmen had fitted themselves to the local conditions of life and death. Individually they had no special claim to notice; but as members of old-world communities they exemplified well how the South English tribes, traversing their fertile valleys, their shaggy hills, had matched themselves against problems without number, and had handed on, from father to son, the accumulated lore of experience. (Sturt, p. 32)

Then, after a detailed and admiring account of their skills, Sturt comes clean, relapsing into employer-talk in which exasperation, condescension and admiration mingle uneasily:

> In my experience they were drunken to a man . . . one sawyer was no good without his mate – he was as useless as one scissor would be. So, on a Monday morning, the one who reached his work first would loaf about waiting for the other, and then, sick of waiting, drift off to a public-house – his home perhaps for a few days or weeks. His mate, coming at last, would presently find that his predecessor had begun boosing; and was likely enough to end a disgusted and wasted day following suit . . . I have known sawyers unable to get together and start their week's work until Thursday morning. (Sturt, p. 39)

In the chapter on the sawyers we see one model follow another; a physical rootedness so extreme as to convert the human, by way of a regression through the animal, into a part of the landscape by means of the metonymy of 'their shaggy hills'; this is followed by the model of the craftsman, and finally the recalcitrant reality of the sawyers, after yet another attempt at dehumanisation ('he was as useless as one scissor would be') is tamed by the note of admiration that makes of them 'cards' or 'cases'. The tone is condescending throughout, but perhaps the sawyers win, peering out through the dislocations in Sturt's tone.

Memories of my own, and evidence all around speak against the myth as well. I know something of the hardships of industrialisation in the 1930s through accounts of the life of my maternal grandfather, a shipyard worker. At best he worked long, numbing cold hours in a draughty shed; at worst he and his family endured spells of real poverty when he was unemployed, but his work did not denature him so that he was too passive to enjoy his leisure. He had a zest for invention and elaboration; his garden was a work of art; he made furniture, and above all wonderfully witty and detailed toys for his children and grandchildren, pressing into service the most unlikely materials imaginable. True, my grandfather was a tradesman, and our part of the world significantly rural, but in the big cities there is physical evidence of an active use of leisure and a delight in inventiveness. Allotments with flowers and vegetables carefully tended for shows, or holding pigeon lofts built with a pleasure in the fantastic that would not have disgraced Wemmick. Such books as Richard Hoggart's *The Uses of Literacy* describe urban working-class culture from the inside, providing further modifications to the myth.[29]

As well as being distasteful, Leavis's mythologising of historical reality seems to me to give rise to inconsistencies and confusions in his thinking about culture. In the introductory essay of *For Continuity* he defines culture:

> The positive preoccupation throughout is, in various ways, with the conditions and function of the extra-individual mind – consciousness, sense of value and memory – that a living culture is; to insist that, in civilisation of which the machinery becomes more and more overwhelming, the life and authority of this mind must be worked for consciously.   (FC, p. 10)

The most noticeable thing about the definition is the way in which it places culture in the world of ideas – 'consciousness', 'memory', 'mind', 'value'. Although the ethereality of the notion seems consistent in some ways with Leavis's frequent contention that in the modern world culture is cerebral, the possession of a minority, and no longer rooted in the materiality of existence, it has to be noticed that he is speaking of *any* culture and, moreover, any culture that is *living*. In 'Under Which King, Bezonian?' his attacks on Trotsky's notion of culture are essentially strategic and polemical. Like Trotsky, he seeks to assert the material basis of culture, paving the way for his own definition of what culture successfully had been in the pre-industrial past, a definition which might provide a norm for the future, a guide by which new culture-bearing efforts were to be judged. In this new definition the suggestion is of a nexus of social practices, not merely an intellectual milieu or activity. However, the suggestion seems to remain precisely that, a suggestion and nothing more:

> . . . it is true that culture in the past has borne a close relation to the 'methods of production'. A culture expressing itself in a tradition of literature and art – such a tradition as represents the finer consciousness of the race and provides the currency of finer living – can be in a healthy state only if this tradition is in living relation with a real culture, shared by the people at large . . . And when England had a popular culture, the structure . . . of it was a stylisation . . . of economic necessities; based . . . on the 'methods of production' was an art of living, involving codes, developed in ages of continuous experience, of relations between man and man, and man and the environment in its seasonal rhythm. This culture the progress of the nineteenth century destroyed, in country and in town; it destroyed . . . the organic community. And what survives of cultural tradition in any important sense survives in spite of the rapidly changing 'means of production'.[30]

Although the tortuousness of syntax, the parentheses, qualifications, phrases placed in apposition to one another suggest a muscular attempt to wrestle with words in the interest of a precision Marxist thought is incapable of, these grammatical features seem to have an essentially rhetorical function. That is, they are concerned to evoke rather than to define explicitly, framed to give weight to such phrases as 'art of living', 'seasonal rhythms', 'finer consciousness of the race', 'ages of continuous experience'. The contortions of the second sentence convey a suggestion of precision going beyond that which can be achieved by direct statement: 'A culture expressing itself in a tradition of literature and art . . . can be in a healthy state only if this tradition is in living relation with a real culture, shared by the people at large'. Trembling behind these words, its avoidance seeming to give rise to the complication and strain in expression, we sense some such distinction as high culture/popular culture being refused by Leavis as misleading, since what he means by a 'real culture shared by the people at large' is not what contemporary culture is. Only by such indirection, it seems to be implied, is he able to rescue the phrase 'popular culture' for its use later in the passage. Importantly the indirection, with its seeming attempts at definition, brings into play a vocabulary of value which is perhaps the real point of the exercise – 'fine', 'healthy', 'real'.

Curiously, what emerges from the sentence is the implication that 'a culture expressing itself in a tradition of literature and art' will represent 'the finer consciousness of the race' whether such a tradition is in a healthy state or not, and, indeed, whether or not it is in touch 'with a real culture, shared by the people at large'. The suggested continuity/unity of culture(s) in the organic community thus seems to be eroded even as it is asserted.

I write continuity/unity because there is a peculiar evasiveness about the passage which makes it difficult to decide which might be the appropriate word; there seem to be two cultures – that of the tradition of literature and art, and the real culture for, after all, a relation is posited between them – or is the relation that between the tradition of literature and art and the real culture, of which literature and art are an expression? Probably the latter, but if so, Leavis's way of putting it seems unnecessarily tortuous. Perhaps the tortuousness is the result of a sense of strain entailed by the context of the passage, for Leavis is claiming that Marxists have not properly confronted the difficulties involved in developing in a machine-created leisure society 'a culture independent of any economic, technical or social system as none has been before'. He continues, 'Whether such a rootless culture . . . can be achieved and maintained may be doubtful'. Work, then, is presented as the principle of organisation within a society. Without it the culture will be rootless. We might now question the sense in which the 'popular culture' mentioned by Leavis is 'a stylisation of economic necessities'. What Leavis means by this emerges in *Culture and Environment*, and at greater length in Sturt's works, which he so frequently quotes as an authoritative account of a vanishing rural England, an elegiac picture of the organic community.

The ideal expounded by Sturt is of self-reliance and a large measure of self-subsistence, with men living, in part at least, from the produce they grew and the animals they tended. The work by which they earned money to buy what they could not produce themselves might be hard, but was varied and demanded at least some skill – a lot of skill in more specialised occupations – skill which was passed down from generation to generation. In this society neighbourliness and consideration were prime values, for there was little chance of help from outside in the case of need. In such a society leisure as a concept hardly existed, and not just because life was hard, but because the work was interesting, and not regarded as being in opposition to living. Out of this way of life demanding so many skills and sensitivity to the physical, natural world grew the capability to create beautiful artefacts, whose beauty lay in their very functionality. There grew also an art of speech: the stories told by the fireside and at the inn, the proverbs which evolved to describe common natural and social situations. This real culture, then, both grew out of labour, out of the means of production, and expressed it.

The picture is attractive, but to spell it out in detail rather than merely to evoke it is to raise the question of the way in which *this* culture in which leisure is both unnecessary and unobtainable finds its relation with the tradition of art and literature which represents 'the finer consciousness of the race', for *that* tradition demands of its practitioners precisely the leisure that is presented as a problem for the future; neither do its products have the functionality of those coming from the 'real culture', nor (on the whole) do its practitioners share the language of the peasant. Presumably this is why Leavis adduces Shakespeare as a kind of cultural signifier, for the plays have always been taken to appeal to all levels of society, and indeed depict all levels: Shakespeare's language is the language of both the court and the peasantry; different groups speak different languages, but the groups communicate with one another. However, once we remember that Shakespeare's language is 'artfolk', and not reportage, the continuity between literary tradition and the culture of the folk remains (at least to me) undemonstrated. It may be that Leavis's position is not unlike that of the Marxist critic, Lukács who, in *The Historical Novel* (first published in Russian in 1937), saw the classic realist novels of the nineteenth century as penetrating to the essential features of their time because their authors were implicated in their society: they had not designated themselves professional novelists and taken on the role of detached observers as later naturalist writers did.[31] If so, he makes no such attempt as that of Lukács to elucidate the relation he sees as existing between writers of the past and the popular culture.[32]

Given Leavis's comments on Swift's capacity to influence events in his time, his contention that the minority 'is being cut off as never before from the powers that rule the world', and his fulminations against those who characterise the best of culture as 'highbrow', it is perhaps not so much a set of relations between different aspects of a culture he laments, but more precisely a set of relations between different social groups. In a society where many are illiterate the power and the influence is with the literate and cultured; with a widened franchise, mass-production, and some species of literacy the balance shifts, the old hierarchy becomes eroded. It is the passing of a *political* order that Leavis mourns as much as anything. Or perhaps one ought to say a political *order*, for his sense of chaos is acute: 'Here we have the plight of culture in general. The landmarks have shifted, multiplied and crowded upon one another, the distinctions and dividing lines have blurred away, the boundaries are gone . . .' (FC, p. 39).

The context of this lament confines 'culture' to the restricted sense of 'arts and literature', and references to 'the competent reader' narrow down the use still further, betraying yet again Leavis's practical neglect of all but the verbal. The culture we have here is the property of 'the cultivated person' who demonstrates his cultivation by his capacity to discriminate among 'the smother of new books'. The chaos Leavis describes is not merely a matter of there being too much to attend to (though this is important), it is primarily caused by the decay of the critical function, the lack of influence of the cultivated. Order, cultural order, depends precisely upon a system that gives power to the cultivated. Put starkly, the cultural continuity that Leavis attributes to the organic society seems to amount to little more than the acceptance by the ruled of the importances of the rulers. Whatever the value of the popular culture, however sustaining it was for those who shared it, a relationship of deference on the one hand and domination on the other does not make for cross-fertilisation. Jonson in 'To Penshurst', a glowing hymn to the organic community before it was ever thought of, gives us a landscape in which fruits and creatures are anthropomorphised ('the blushing apricot') and the peasantry treated as one more instance of nature's bounty. They are not part of the specifically human world:

> . . . some that think they make
> The better cheeses, bring them; or else send
> By their *ripe* [my italics] daughters, whom they would commend
> This way to husbands; and whose baskets bear
> An emblem of themselves, in plum, or pear.   (lines 53–7)

Leavis's stress on the importance of language to culture also seems to be at odds with his ideas of cultural continuity. While he pays tribute to the art of speech, of story-telling that he assumes to have been a part of the organic community, this art seems to have little to do with the capacities of that small minority who in any age are the transmitters of culture, upon whom 'depend the implicit standards that order the finer living of an age, the sense that this is worth more than that, this rather than that is the direction in which to go, that the centre is here rather than there' (FC, p. 15). High culture and popular culture remain separate, for there is nothing to suggest that a workman could be one of the minority.

However, to point to the discontinuity in Leavis's thinking does not invalidate his definition of culture as a minority pursuit, and it seems to me to be precisely through his stress on language that he is able to make his claim for the centrality of literary criticism to a culture. It is, after all, by means of language that we define and refine our values and shape raw event into meaningful experience; and in literature we have this process of shaping un-rolling before our eyes. It is perhaps thus that the literary critic is 'a judge of values'. And yet, to make language so absolutely foundational is extremely dangerous unless we remember that the well-turned phrase is not always a guarantor of fine feeling, or clumsy expression a sign of crude response. Relationships between words, feeling and action are complex, and sometimes seem to be contradictory. It is necessary to resist the temptation to oversimplification. In his later criticism Leavis returned to the problems of his early writing, developing more carefully the relations he saw between language and culture, and addressing more directly the problem of justifying standards within such a diverse society as ours. It is to this that I shall now turn.

Social and Cultural Criticism 1962–76

I have taken Leavis's Richmond lecture, *Two Cultures? The Significance of C. P. Snow*, as marking the beginning of a new phase in Leavis's cultural criticism, a phase which lasted until his death in 1978. As in the earlier phase it is inappropriate to try to trace a development in his thinking. He himself clearly felt that what he had written ten years earlier was still apposite in 1972, the year in which, in *Nor Shall My Sword*, he published *Two Cultures* substantially unaltered, together with a selection of essays written over the previous nine years. He made it clear in his introduction that he regarded the assemblage as representing his current stance: 'I realized that I had hit on the way of writing the book that seemed to me so badly needed' (NSMS, p. 29). Moreover, there is a striking similarity of tone and vocabulary throughout all the work of this period. Striking, too, is the continuity of this later criticism with the earlier, although some of the targets of attack have changed, the stance is more explicitly conservative, and new influences have enabled him to produce a more elaborated and satisfactory account of the centrality of language to culture. That his tone has taken on the moral urgency of an Old Testament prophet (or Blake's Bard 'Who Present, Past, and Future sees') is a measure of the threat he perceives in 'the malady under which mankind wilts'.[33]

In his criticisms of C. P. Snow's Rede lecture Leavis insisted on Snow's representative status, insisted that it was only because Snow's notion of two cultures had gained currency even within sixth forms that he, Leavis, had felt it necessary to read, let alone attack the lecture. Snow was a portent he declared. What, then, did Snow portend, and what were the 'menacing characteristics of our civilization' that Leavis claimed to have been dealing with in his Richmond lecture? The 'characteristics' seem substantially those which he attacks in *For Continuity* and other earlier writing.

In one aspect, in his belief in the power of scientists to improve the world, Snow, 'the spiritual son of H. G. Wells' occupies the place of that writer and the Communists in Leavis's earlier criticism, although Leavis considered Trotsky to merit serious criticism in a way that Snow did not. He stands, that is, for those who, in Leavis's way of putting it, are unable to make the Ruskinian distinction between wealth and well-being, and who assume that an increase in the standard of living is not only an adequate incentive to social change, but a sufficient condition for human happiness (Leavis quotes viciously Snow's phrase, 'Jam tomorrow'). As Leavis sees it, the materialism of Snow is no more able than that of the Communists to ensure a satisfying life in a society where work is predominantly stultifying, and he adduces an unnamed French sociological authority who has explored the theme of 'the incapacity of the industrial worker, who – inevitably – looks on real living as reserved for his leisure, to use his leisure in any but essentially passive ways' (NSMS, p. 60).

In another aspect, Leavis sees Snow as representative of the metropolitan literary coterie-world, 'the *haute culture* of our time', which is antithetical to proper standards and without any understanding of what a real culture might be. His attendant castigation of the quality press, *The Times Literary Supplement*, the British Council and the BBC recalls his fulminations against the intellectual 'levelling down' he saw in the 1930s, and his assertion of the need for an intelligent, influential minority. It is the whole of the fashionable literary world that he arraigns in his attacks on Snow, who 'takes over inertly . . . the characteristic and disastrous confusion of the civilization he is offering to instruct' (NSMS, p. 53). For Leavis Snow's intellectual inertia manifests itself in his capacity for cliché, a capacity which enables him to evade the questions he ostensibly discusses.

Throughout the lecture Snow is treated as exemplifying the quantifying, atomising 'technologico-Benthamite society' that Leavis despises so much, and his denunciation of Snow's odd distinction between 'social hope' and the necessarily tragic fate of the individual presages his later articulation of the relation between individual and society, an articulation which avoids the Cartesian dichotomies of mind/body, individual/society. It is precisely the need to avoid such dichotomies which is at the heart of Leavis's attack on Snow's attempt to distinguish between a scientific and a literary culture, for Snow's position, in so far as it is capable of being taken seriously, undermines the constitutive role of language within a society. For Leavis it is precisely within language that the distinction between individual and society is dissolved.

Snow's credentials as a judge of literature are exposed as sham in Leavis's eyes by his failure to mention D. H. Lawrence among 'the writers who above all matter', and his praise of 'the brutal and boring Wyndham Lewis' (NSMS, P. 53). Leavis's treatment of Lawrence as social prophet and moral authority marks a new stage in his elision of the distinction between literature and life. It marks, too, the beginning of a conservatism that to my mind sometimes verges on the brutal and not infrequently lapses into silliness.

In Chapter 1 I suggested that the violence of Leavis's attack on Snow was to some extent strategic, a way of getting his objection to Snow and what he stood for properly noticed, and in this he succeeded. John Wain, writing in the *Hudson Review* some months later, while noticing the 'brutality' of the 'attack' also remarked on the '*naïveté* and emptiness' of the flood of letters supporting Snow, taking them 'as a barometer of the present state of intellectual England'.[34]

However, to take Leavis's indignant rhetoric as in some sense strategic does not at all imply that it was manufactured. To judge from other, later utterances it was rather that he felt his outrage to be a weapon in itself. Throughout these last works his tone is embattled as he proclaims again and again 'the sickness of civilization' (NSMS, p. 105), 'our civilization, outwardly cock-a-hoop and at heart despairing' (LP, p. 10) and the 'cultural disinheritance and the meaninglessness of the technologico-Benthamite world' (NSMS, p. 104). Again and again he insists that his readers share 'the perception that the despair, or vacuous unease, characteristic of the civilized world comes of profound human needs and capacities that the civilization denies and thwarts' (LP, p. 10).

As in his earlier criticism Leavis locates the cultural malaise he feels in the lack of continuity between past and present, seeing the lack as a 'disease that threatens to destroy humanity'. As before, America with its technological culture and its lack of rootedness is cast in the role of carrier; we infected America first through the inventions of the Industrial Revolution, and the disease which was fatal there because of the lack of a national past returns to plague us. Therefore Leavis's concern is 'for a conception of society, life and *humanitas* that does not eliminate the depth in time and the organic' (NSMS, p. 145).

In specific terms he saw this as entailing opposition to all aspects of the progressivism of the 1960s, to the 'statistico-egalitarian reductivism' of the age, 'the barbarity of reformist enlightenment'. The human exemplars of this attitude included not only C. P. Snow with his two cultures and ideas of 'social hope', but Noel Annan, Provost of King's College, Cambridge; Lord Todd, an eminent chemist and President of the British Association for the Advancement of Science; and Lord Robbins, Chairman of the Committee that produced the 1963 Report on Higher Education.[35] Snow's phrase 'social hope' and Annan's advocacy of 'pluralism and compassion' provided Leavis with the sub-title of *Nor Shall My Sword*, and the title of one of the essays in the book. In that essay Leavis dismissed Annan's 'pluralism' as 'the right to be incoherent and opportunist', and suggested of his compassion, 'the actuality is self-indulgence'. He saw the stance of Annan and Snow as inviting 'irresponsibility', and claimed that by the date of the essay, 1970:

> The suggestion that enlightened reductivism, the vacuity of life in a technological world, a consequent sense that (even though there are plenty of jobs going for technicians) this civilization has little to offer one, violence, destructiveness, condoned irresponsibility in regard to sex, drug-addiction, 'student unrest' – that all these are intimately related wouldn't now be dismissed with the easy jeer of a very short time back.   (NSMS, p. 181)

Even if one were to stifle the comment that Leavis's impassioned urgency, the violence of his attacks, might be taken as symptoms of self-indulgence in the face of his new grounds for hope, the ease with which he assimilates different phenomena and different orders of experience into one composite ill needs to be resisted, particularly when such a conflation comes from one who insists on the need for discrimination, from one to whom in other contexts generalisation is anathema. His language here, and the quality of thought it conveys, seems no less clichéd than what he has attacked, and to emerge with – dare I say it? – mechanical ease.

That Leavis's is a purely emotional response is betrayed by his hypostatisation of a variety of dissatisfactions felt by students in the late 1960s into one entity, 'student unrest', which is then damned by the company it keeps as Leavis places it in the same category as 'violence', 'destructiveness', 'irresponsibility'. Whatever one's views on the events of the 1960s, Leavis's use of the phrase 'student unrest' as a pejorative term seems to leave him open to the danger of implying that no student unrest could ever be justified, that student unrest must, by definition, be wrong. Although his fencing in of the phrase with speech marks seems to distance him from such an extreme view, his comments elsewhere suggest that it is not far from his actual position. As he describes it the dissatisfaction among students was politically motivated by 'lecturer ward-bosses and demagogues' and 'young-lecturer agents' of the far left, and attributable to the rapid expansion of the universities which had filled them with 'telly- and pin-table-addicted non-students, thus making possible the pressure for "participation" and the careers of student-union politicians'.[36] The way in which Leavis refuses to allow for the possibility of intelligent and disinterested dissatisfaction, or even conscientious muddle seems to me to vitiate his otherwise powerful criticisms of the more extreme exponents of 'participation', and – more importantly – to cast doubt on his assertion that organic change is a necessary feature of life. In so far as students are a part of the academy then it should be possible, in theory at least, for them to contribute to the growth and change which in Leavis's acceptation is life, yet it seems to be precisely because the unrest was manifested by *students* that its more moderate manifestations were deemed to be not even worth refuting. Leavis's position here is a far cry from the one he held in the years during which *Scrutiny* was established.

The stance is authoritarian and paternalistic, and consonant with Leavis's comments on the working classes and women. His attitude towards the former is absolutely consistent with his insistence in the 1930s on the inadequacy of material prosperity as a measure of well-being. The new manifestations of working-class culture – transistor radios, Bingo and increased mobility – are seen as no more satisfactory than those he deplored then, though perhaps more intrusive: 'in those once very quiet places . . . to which my wife and I used to take our children the working-class people now everywhere to be met with in profusion carry transistors round with them almost invariably'. The note struck, however, is not primarily one of contempt. He continues:

> . . . as for the actual working-class people who *can* be regarded as characteristic, it's not anything in the nature of moral indignation one feels towards *them*, but shame, concern and apprehension at the way our civilization has let them down . . . The concern, I imagine, is what all decent people capable of sympathetic perception must feel . . .[37]

However much Leavis attacks other members of the clerisy and proclaims his exclusion from it he yet feels himself to be a part of it; a part of the group in whom power is vested, for otherwise 'shame' would be a meaningless term. The distinctions between 'the actual working-class people' and 'all decent people', and '*our* civilization' which has 'let *them* down' are revealing, the more so for being unconscious; to Leavis the working class seems to belong to a significantly different species from himself. His stance here is likely to be offensive to many, but perhaps not much more so than the cloudy egalitarianism of some of his opponents, which he confronts, not with the abuse he heaped on 'student unrest', but with sharp, telling arguments based on an analysis of the way in which such words as 'élite' and 'oligarchy' may be used loosely as little more than terms of disapproval. The attack is mounted first in 1970 in 'Pluralism, Compassion and Social Hope', and returned to in the following year in 'Élites, Oligarchies, and an Educated Public' (both essays are collected in *Nor Shall My Sword*). The tone is acerbic and condescending, but what he has to say constitutes a case to be answered:

> The word 'élitism' is a product of ignorance, prejudice and unintelligence . . . appealing . . . to jealousy and kindred impulses and motives. It is stupid . . . because there must always be 'élites', and, mobilizing and directing the ignorance, prejudice and unintelligence, it aims at destroying the only adequate control for 'élites' there could be . . . the word covers a diversity of things . . . There are scientist élites, air-pilot élites, *corps d'élite*, and social élites (the best people), and the underprivileged masses know that professional footballers and BBC announcers are élites. (NSMS, p. 169)

Despite his life-long collaboration with his wife, Q. D. Leavis, and the respect with which he treated her *Fiction and the Reading Public*, Leavis clearly found it difficult to envisage students other than as men – unless, that is, they were weak and timid – and *Scrutiny* is notable for its dearth of female contributors apart from Q. D. Leavis (Muriel Bradbrook was an exception in its earliest years). However, what seems to have been an unconscious set for most of his life hardened under the influence of D. H. Lawrence into what can only be described as offensive (though not uncommon) dottiness. In *Thought, Words and Creativity* we have Leavis construing the phenomenon of working women as no more than a demonstration of 'technologico-Benthamite philistinism', as something essentially abhorrent, but within the prevailing system unavoidable:

> 'Even the absorption of women on a large scale into industry and affairs that is so grave a menace to *humanitas* will have to go on . . . otherwise the economy, the whole complex machine of civilization, would break down, with unmanageable consequences (TWC, p. 13).

At this point Leavis does not define the nature of the menace. His assumption, in fact, is that it needs no definition, but he returns to the subject later, praising Lawrence's championship of women:

> Already . . . he was defending women against the enlightened stupidity that, claiming for them equality with men, offered to reduce them, in proper accord with the Benthamite ethos, to arithmetical human units. Things have got worse . . . we have reason now to apprehend that detected failure to observe the principle of equality will, like racial discrimination, very soon be punishable by law. (TWC, p. 82)

He predicts that the principle will be 'enforced in its absurdest extremes', citing as portents of the way things were going, agitation to admit equal numbers of women into Oxford colleges, and the recent use of women announcers by the BBC. Clearly this attitude has not worn well and will seem to most people merely ludicrous. It needs to be stressed that Leavis's attachment to Lawrence generates at times a kind of dishonest muddle that takes him close to self-contradiction. We have another example of that paternalism that under the guise of concern denies the capacity for choice; denies, that is, full humanity to a particular group of people, for clearly since women want to work, want to be BBC announcers, to have similar educational opportunities to men, Lawrence's and Leavis's concern must be to save them from themselves and their misconceptions:

> . . . as Lawrence insists, it is properly not a question of equality and inequality, but of difference, and the difference is essential to human life. It is essential not only in the most obvious way, the continuance of the species depending on it. The difference in that respect carries other respects – other modes of difference – along with it. Neither man nor woman can represent a complete *humanitas*; the close association that is interinfluence and mutual supplementation (and more) is necessary.   (TWC, p. 82)

The relationship of kindly tutelage implied in the first quotation has now shifted, and we are assured that influence, 'mutual supplementation' are necessary if full *humanitas* is to be achieved. The question of where this complete humanity is to be located now arises. Is it some kind of essence generated between male and female, only a function of their togetherness, or do both parties possess it, or only one? If we accept Leavis's opposition of equality to difference it might seem that it is the woman's function to help the man attain his *humanitas*, for what the opposition amounts to, translated, is that while it belongs to mac's nature to work outside the home, to engage in whatever occupation best suits him, it is misguided for women to want to do the same. Whatever their intelligence, their age, their capacity to reproduce, the fact that women as a group bear children and men do not is enough to reduce their needs and natures to uniformity, to abolish the difference between woman and woman. Under the name of difference (difference from the male), and as a protection from being reduced to arithmetical units, somewhat over half the human population is defined by, reduced to, one aspect of being and the male/female relationship elevated into the necessary condition for the attainment of complete humanity.

Predictably, the expansion of Higher Education in the 1960s, the creation of new universities and polytechnics, the foundation of the Open University and changes in the system, actual and

proposed, drew forth Leavis's criticism, although he denied vig-
orously that he was against expansion as such. While claiming that
he was in favour of expanding Higher Education 'to the utmost' he
refused to identify it with 'the university', and believed in the need
to distinguish between different modes of learning. His concern,
characteristically, was for standards, and the central thrust of his
argument is against the comfortable assumption that anything approaching a 'comprehensive' university education was possible.
Predictably, prophecies that England would have a system similar
to that of the United States by the 1980s, and that a very high
proportion of the population would follow first degree courses
drew a less than enthusiastic response from him. This is partly
because it seemed self-evident to him that not all candidates for a
degree course were capable of following one (and now that the
egalitarianism of the 1960s has been for the most part abandoned
his view would probably be widely shared), and partly because the
kind of rapid expansion envisaged would require teaching methods
he regarded as inimical to the proper functioning of the university:

> A university that is really one . . . will make it possible for the
> student . . . to feel he belongs to a complex collaborative com-
> munity in which there are his own special human contexts to be
> found, and will make him, in his work and the informal human
> intercourse that supplements it and gives it life, more and more
> potently aware of the nature of high intellectual stand-
> ards. (NSMS, p. 207)

Leavis's stress on the word 'human', here and elsewhere, signals
his rejection of the faith of the 1960s in technology, and of the
growing interest in teaching machines and the computer, which in
this phase of his writing took on for him the aspect of the arch-
machine, the triumphant apotheosis of all he most hated. To
conceive of the university as 'plant', he argued, to demand of
university teachers that they should be more productive and teach
larger classes was to introduce the practices of the factory into the
educational system: to use technological methods to produce
technologists. It was, above all, to substitute the conception of
'restructuring' for that of organic growth, the kind of life exemplified by Oxford and Cambridge, a 'distinct and strongly positive organic life, rooted in history' (NSMS, p. 206). Essentially, he

argued for the need to distinguish between education and training (although he does not use that word), a distinction which it seems more than ever necessary to make in the universities of the 1990s. While it seems likely that standards have been rather less adversely affected than he feared would be the case, much of what he fought for has been surrendered only to be regretted; its value recognised more sharply during the ruthless ascendancy of right wing philistinism than it was during that of the left. Now, with the goddess Dulness in control the danger of universal darkness is more apparent.

Throughout his career Leavis, like Carlyle, saw the mechanical and human as opposed categories, but it is in this later phase that 'human' emerges as an insistent part of his vocabulary of value, taking its place in a complex of terms including 'life', 'creativity', 'individuality', 'responsibility'. This new complex seems to mark the influence of Marjorie Grene and Michael Polanyi (the latter to some extent mediated by Grene), the philosophers of science.[38] Their work allowed him to elaborate his arguments for the centrality of English within the university, and provided a justification based on their theory of knowledge for his definition of the subject. Grene and Polanyi were so important in Leavis's thinking because of their attack on the Cartesian-Newtonian world picture which he hated, a world picture which placed individual and society, body and mind, subject and object, fact and value, in opposition to one another. Grene saw the world thus constructed as a dead world, because of the refusal to take the fact of human consciousness into account, and in the introduction to *The Knower and the Known* she proclaimed that a philosophical revolution had been inaugurated by Polanyi. Her attacks on what she regarded as the dominant philosophical school of thought are curiously reminiscent of those described by H. Stuart Hughes as taking place in Europe between 1890 and 1930, and mark a division between European and British philosophy.[39]

The basis of the position attacked by Grene and Polanyi is Descartes's *Cogito ergo sum*, 'I think (or reflect), therefore I am'. Descartes's assumption was that, by reflection, he could know himself just as he could know any external phenomenon, that he had access to his own thought processes, and because of that, access to an external reality. Knowledge for Descartes was thus timeless, objective, universal, and achievable. By contrast, Grene stresses that one does not know oneself in the way one knows the not-self. We do not *know* ourselves, we are *inside* ourselves, and generally only aware of particular traits and characteristics in so far as these are mediated through the consciousness of others. We are inside ourselves as we are inside time. We are what our past has made us. Rather than operating as pure mind we operate as mind/ body using in a variety of modes the whole of our past experience in all its variousness, so 'The knower is not simply the Transcendental Unity of Apperception, but myself, with my endowments, limitations, hopes, disappointments. It is a full, historical, not a mere logical "I" ' (Grene, *The Knower and the Known*, p. 152). This past experience is what functions in Polanyi's terms as tacit or subsidiary knowledge which we bring to bear upon the present situation. It is not a body of doctrine so much as a way of seeing, effective in so far as it *is* tacit, for to focus on it, to bring it to consciousness, would draw attention away from the current problem, the problem with which, by means of our focal and explicit knowledge we are consciously attempting to deal. Problem solving, the acquisition of knowledge depends, therefore, upon a combination of tacit and explicit knowledge, subsidiary and focal attention.

The implications of this paradigm are, first of all, that objective knowledge in the Cartesian sense is impossible. What is known is a function of the knower. We are not, that is, passive observers of reality, but implicated in its shaping. To know is in some sense to create, and knowers are responsible for (if not entirely in charge of) their creation. Secondly, if knowing is a temporal event experienced by a knower implicated in the movement of time, and growing, changing with time, it can never be absolute; there must always be a 'protensive pull' as the knower is drawn forward into a new state of being and knowing.

If we leave the paradigm there, then we seem to have a picture of humans as quite disparate entities, each inhabiting his or her own world. However, language is central to Grene's paradigm:

. . . speech . . . is the most conspicuous human achievement: speech, that is, as a structure of symbols, which again can be developed, manipulated, interpreted, and re-interpreted in an infinity of directions . . . Human language . . . becomes itself a growing world of meanings within meanings, which we not only use for practical ends but dwell in as the very fabric of our being,

> while at the same time changing it by our participation in it,
> enacting the history of our language in our history.   (*The Knower and*
> *the Known*, p. 174)

We dwell in language, and in so much as it is 'the very fabric of our
being' it is part of our tacit knowledge. At the same time it is that
which we change. Grene sees the capacity to question as foundational; it is questioning 'that marks the emergence of the child's
humanity, the emergence of the richer intangible world in which
he will come to dwell. It is truly a layer of nothingness, a fold in
being, as Merleau-Ponty calls it, that makes us human' (*The
Knower and the Known*, p. 175). The question marks the way in
which language is that which separates us from our environment
and is, by the same token, that which enables us to notice it.
Noticing, therefore, is an activity that takes place in language,
takes place, that is, within a frame of values which we share with
others. The creation of reality is a co-operative venture, and just
because it is so, is value-dominated. A fact is a fact only by virtue
of a series of prior choices as to what is important.[40]

This is not to deny the existence of a world external to the
knower. Rather, it is that this external world *is* a world, is real, is
meaningful only in so far as we have language. Reality does not
stand outside language as language's validator; rather it comes into
being, is exposed by, finds its place within that web of values
which constitutes our language. Grene brings out an important
implication of this view, Polanyi's notion of different degrees of
reality:

> This capacity of a thing to reveal itself in unexpected ways in the
> future, I attribute to the fact that the thing observed is an aspect of
> a reality, possessing a significance that is not exhausted by our
> conception of any single aspect of it. To trust that a thing we know
> is real is, in this sense, to feel ihat it has the independence and
> power for manifesting itself in yet unthought of ways in the future.
> I shall say, accordingly, that minds and problems possess a *deeper*
> reality than cobblestones, although cobblestones are admittedly
> more real in the sense of being *more tangible*.   (*The Knower and the*
> *Known*, pp. 219–20)

The world as theorised by Grene is a world of process, of life
rooted in time; a world in which entities are allowed their different

modes of being. Because humans co-operate in making it, it is a world of potentialities rather than actualities; one in which knowledge is never finally achieved. The pull is always from the future, a future which, although it is open, is necessarily, inescapably, connected with the past, even to the extent that the past itself is changed by the future as it, in turn, becomes past.

This view of the world which I have so sketchily outlined reads as though it were a working out of the implications of Leavis's stance in his early writings. Grene's description of the relation between individual and society seems to provide a theoretical justification for Leavis's insistence on the inescapably personal character of judgement, and on its more than personal genesis. It is tempting, too, to relate Leavis's refusal to define his position explicitly to Polanyi's notion of tacit knowledge, to see it as an avoidance of making the activity of knowing the object of attention. The implication of the knower in the materiality of history has, too, its clear bearing on Leavis's notion of the organic community. However, it is above all in Grene's stress upon the constitutive role of language in society that there is a meeting of minds. It is here, however, that Grene takes him beyond his previous position, allowing him to subsume culture under language rather than language under culture, as he did in 'Mass Civilization and Minority Culture' (FC, p. 15), where language was treated as a metonymy for culture.

Leavis's belief in the constitutive role of language in shaping human reality informs all his later criticism, which can be seen as a series of attempts to reshape the language, to establish as central his new vocabulary of value terms in opposition to the prevailing computer-speak. 'Life is a necessary word', he asserted, and 'life', 'creativity', 'responsibility', 'individuality' (as opposed to 'self-hood') occur again and again, defined and exemplified with tireless insistence.

The notion that language is in itself creative seemed to encourage him, too, in his elision of the distinction between art and life. Lawrence's status as a prophet is inseparable for Leavis from his status as novelist. He is a great writer precisely because he is is endowed with more than common wisdom.[41] Similarly, the moral defects which Leavis found in T. S. Eliot were held to mar his poetry. This stress on the morality of literature stems initially from I. A. Richards's refusal of the aesthetic as a category, a refusal in which Leavis concurred. However, when life is seen as something to be consciously created, and art is valued in so far as it is moral, we have something like a return of the repressed. Pushed to its limits, the exclusion of the idea of the aesthetic as a separate category perhaps entails its colonisation of the moral – hence Leavis's mythologising of the real, and the reality with which he endows the fictional.

However, it is not in his cultural criticism that this phenomenon, nor, indeed, the influence of Grene and Polanyi, is most obvious. Their world picture informs not only Leavis's passionate account of what he sees as the nature and function of English studies within the university (which he defines as a creative centre of society) but also his discussion of literary texts, where the extension of his vocabulary to include the terms 'nisus' and '*ahnung*' suggests the need to find for criticism some equivalent for Polanyi's 'protensive pull'.

English as a University Subject

An editorial in the second issue of *Scrutiny* voiced a concern which was to be important to the periodical for much of its life, and one central to Leavis's work:

> We have always intended that a positive movement should develop – a movement to propagate and enforce a clearly realized conception of education and its function. Such a conception, of course, would involve a conception of a desirable society. (Preliminary note, S2, no. 2, September, 1933)

Leavis's interest in education expressed itself in his insistence on the importance of the university in society, and on the centrality of the English School to the university. He was also as much concerned with the specifics of constructing a desirable curriculum and with demonstrating the methods of criticism as with arguments and statements of belief. In Leavis's eyes to show the content and procedures of the subject was to show its importance, to make plain its values.

His views on English as an academic subject remained remarkably consistent in many ways throughout his life. The influential *Education and the University*, published in 1943, is largely composed of pieces written earlier for *Scrutiny*, and contains as an appendix, *How to Teach Reading*, first published as a Minority pamphlet in 1932; 'Judgement and Analysis', the middle section of one of his last books, *The Living Principle* is partly based on pieces written for *Scrutiny*, two in 1945, and one in 1953, and originally intended as parts of a practical criticism manual.[1] Although there are shifts of emphasis and his ideas are more clearly articulated, there is also a clear continuity of interest with the earlier work in Leavis's Clark lectures, published as *English Literature in Our Time and the University* in 1969.

The university is important to Leavis because of the possibility it offers of 'resisting the bent of civilization in our time', 'the blind drive onward of material and mechanical development'.[2] However, whereas in *Education and the University* the possibility still offers itself as capable of being achieved by formal, institutional means, by the devising of an appropriate curriculum, in later books the university as it is in practice all but prohibits what as ideal it should nurture. What needed to be achieved could be achieved there alone, but such achievement could only be unofficial and opportunistic. As Mulhern has suggested, the grounds for the greater hopefulness of *Education and the University* lay partly in the spirit of reform generated by the Second World War.[3] The need for change was felt at large and the situation was sufficiently fluid to make it possible that an intervention might be effective. At the same time the universities of the 1940s, particularly, as Leavis made clear, the ancient universities, seemed, in their perpetuation of a tradition which was also a tacit agreement in standards, to offer the kind of continuity necessary to guide a society that otherwise 'had lost intelligence, memory and moral purpose' (EU, p. 23). Probably, too, the idealism of the war years recalled the memory of the heroic days of Cambridge English and suggested their return as a possibility. The university, it was true, was necessarily implicated in the shortcomings of society but there was still enough there to make it, with careful planning, an effective counter-force. By contrast, the expansion of education in the 1960s and 1970s, the creation of the Open University and the polytechnics, the attempts to democratise education, were all inimical to Leavis's idea of the university, manifestations of a technologico-Benthamite society, and symptoms of social disease. Increasingly he set the ideal against the actuality: 'The real university is a centre of consciousness and human responsibility for the civilized world; it is a creative centre of civilization', and:

> The university, in so far as it is more than a centre and nursery of the sciences, a technological institute, or a collocation of specialist departments, is the representative of that instinct [self-preservation], and the organ through which society has to make the sustained effort (one directed by collaborative intelligence and a full human responsibility) to keep those needs recognized and provide our civilization with memory and mature purpose.[4]

The concern throughout *Education and the University* is to devise an education that will counteract the prevailing social and cultural disintegration by producing graduates who are more than specialists, who share a common culture and a common concern with the society in which they live, and who will become part of a self-conscious and powerful educated public – the lack of which Leavis had deplored in *Mass Civilization and Minority Culture*. Although attempts to devise a syllabus are set to one side in later books, Leavis commends the same idea of the university: 'the university not merely as a place of learning, research and instruction, but as itself a nucleus (one of a number) of the greater public, the spiritual community the country needs as its mind and conscience'.[5]

Leavis, then, sees the university as the training ground of that small minority he describes in *Mass Civilization and Minority Culture* as being vital to the health of their culture, and whom he considered to be depleted and powerless in his own time. Leavis envisaged the English school as essential to this endeavour in all his writings, and that because in his eyes it afforded a training in a particular kind of thinking, described simply in *Education and the University* as a 'discipline of intelligence and sensibility' – although one should notice, that the apparent simplicity of the definition implies a large claim to undo in students of English the effects of the almost universal dissociation of sensibility.

Two American writers influenced Leavis in *Education and the University*: Brookes Otis, whom Leavis quoted as seeing the need for an educated class able to combat the divisive effects of specialisation because of the shared knowledge of its members; and, much more importantly, Alexander Meiklejohn who, in *The Experimental College*, described an attempt in Wisconsin to provide a coherent liberal education which would prepare its students to be good citizens. The book was published in 1932, and reviewed favourably by Leavis in the same year under the title of 'An American Lead'.[6] Leavis uses a passage from Meiklejohn on the importance of education to society as an epigraph to the first chapter of *Education and the University*, which he begins with a quotation from his own earlier review. In defining and arguing for the kind of education he believed necessary to provide a defence against the conditions of modern life, an education 'bringing into relation a diversity of fields of knowledge and thought' (EU, p. 9), he rejects a variety of possibilities. The reasons for their repudiation are important. He condemns Great Books of Civilisation courses on the grounds that they teach humanist doctrine, disembodied ideas unrooted in any context of language and history (he makes a similar criticism of Pound's list of 'the books a man needs to know in order to "get his bearings" '(EU, p. 110)). Despite his sympathy for the experiment Meiklejohn describes, an interdisciplinary study of two contrasting cultures, Ancient Greek and present-day American, he concludes that in the end the course is too fragmented, giving its students no real knowledge of working within one academic discipline. Classics, the traditional liberal education at the ancient universities, is dismissed because its studies of the past lack a proper inwardness and give rise to rules of good taste rather than real understanding.

During this process of rejection, English literature is put in place by a series of associations and substitutions. A liberal education is treated as synonymous with a humane education, but a humane education is the study of a humane tradition, and 'the relation of "literary tradition" to "humane tradition" is plainly not the mere external one of parallel' (EU, p. 17) (and we may recall here his treatment of language as a metonymy for culture in 'Mass Civilization and Minority Culture', FC, p. 15). To study literature, then, is to study a vital part of a humane tradition (by implication the most vital part if we keep in mind Leavis's belief in the importance of the great writer to his society); but the study of one's own literature has an inwardness that the study of no other can possess; we discover our rootedness in the past by it, and in doing so become capable of creating a human future. At the same time, because the literary tradition is part of the humane tradition, because every literary work issues from a particular, concrete society, the study of literature leads outside itself into other disciplines. The literary student, therefore, will act as a liaison between subjects, bringing his own trained understanding to them.

It is of the essence of Leavis's proposed discipline that it should be present-centred, but this raises the question of the relation of literature to religious belief, the question of how the study of what is a part of the Christian tradition is to be conducted in a predominantly secularised world. Leavis insists on the need to bracket off belief, to see cultural values 'as human and separable from any particular frame or basis'. 'Literary criticism must, in this sense, always be humanist' (EU, p. 19). As we shall see, his position undergoes something of a sea-change in his later writing, for whereas at this point the humanistic approach is deemed to be necessary *historically*, the suggestion later is that the approach is necessary because of the nature of its object; for the thought which literature embodies is necessarily heuristic.

After this call for a new kind of liberal education Leavis narrows his focus to concentrate exclusively on English studies; on what he considers to be its essence, and on practical suggestions for the reform of Part 2 of the Cambridge English Tripos. He is concerned perhaps above all with the kind of student English studies should produce, and with defining the characteristics of that small, self-conscious – properly conscious – minority who are the guardians of minority culture in a machine civilisation:

> . . . we want to produce a mind that knows what precision and specialist knowledge are . . . has a maturity of outlook . . . and has been trained in . . . a scrupulously sensitive yet enterprising use of intelligence, that is of its nature not specialized but cannot be expected without special training – a mind energetic and resourceful, that will apply itself to the problems of civilization, and eagerly continue to improve its equipment and explore fresh approaches. (EU, pp. 58–9)

In this desideratum the moral and the intellectual are almost inextricably blended, but soon the moral assumes pre-eminence; the object is neither to train 'the scholar nor the academic "star"', '. . . but a mind equipped to carry on for itself; trained to work in the conditions in which it will have to work if it is to carry on at all; having sufficient knowledge, experience, self-reliance and staying power for undertaking, and persisting in, sustained enquiries' (EU, p. 60). This is a glamorising, yet strangely insubstantial character-sketch – what is the force of that long second clause beginning 'trained to work'?

Such firm and lonely minds as Leavis imagines are of course the end products of the humane education he has sketched as desirable, and in defining it he concerns himself with both method and content. After dismissing various moves to make English more rigorous he describes the 'essential discipline of an English School' as literary-critical, a training in 'intelligence and sensibility'. As usual his language has a strong moral flavour; 'sensitiveness', 'precision of response' modulate to 'a delicate integrity of intelligence', 'pertinacity', 'delicacy'. Interpretation and evaluation are necessary components of literary criticism in Leavis's eyes. Just as these activities are seen as issuing from the central activity of practical criticism, so literary studies are said to 'lead constantly outside themselves' and, most unusually in that period of hard-edged subjects, any education focusing entirely on the literary is condemned as inherently unsatisfactory. Leavis's sense of the subject as moving out from a centre, both in method and in content, is perhaps the distinctive feature of his definition, and of his suggestions for a new course. His search for an inward coherence, for a necessary and inevitable order, is very much part of his organicist frame of reference, and in this respect his proposal contrasts with the experimental courses described by Meiklejohn in which students were required to compare carefully related facets of contemporary American and Ancient Greek culture. In Leavis's eyes, such an education, whatever its merits, was doomed to externality and fragmentation, for no discipline could be mastered adequately in the time available. By contrast, the non-specialised, but highly trained English student he envisaged would be capable of recognising and using the specialist skills of others. Above all, the continuity between the native literary tradition and the life of its students he perceived to be vital, for 'A study of the literature of their own language and country' is 'the most intimate kind of study . . . of a concrete tradition' (EU, p. 19).

Leavis's suggestions for the reform of Part 2 of the English Tripos are aimed at making it a centre of excellence attracting a small élite of the highest calibre. Ideally its students would have read a subject other than English for Part 1, but would come to Part 2 acquainted with the major English writers from Chaucer to the present day (the aim of Part 1 and a necessary preparation).

His concrete proposals fall into three categories, concerning examinations, the curriculum, and teaching methods, with the first being given initial prominence, since what students learn is in fact largely determined by methods of assessment. Leavis is revolutionary in the changes he suggests, wanting to substitute for conventional three-hour essay papers, which he saw as privileging the opportunist and journalistic, a mixture of course-work and practical criticism papers which would test the students' capacity to read and evaluate rather than to memorise.

Moving from assessment to teaching, Leavis is scathing of the Cambridge system of lectures and weekly supervisions – at worst poor, at best directed towards good examination results, and therefore not giving students adequate guidance in preparing their work. Again following Meiklejohn, Leavis suggests seminars requiring preparation and planned reading. As happens at times, his preoccupation with order, and good reading habits gives the unfortunate and unintended impression that most reading is something of a chore. Is it self-evidently 'absurd that last year's schoolboy should be flung into a wilderness of books . . .'? Perhaps it is, or could be seen to be, but 'flung', 'wilderness'? Sadly he conveys no sense that such an unguided foray might be exciting to the intellectually alert and voracious.

Leavis's tendency toward directiveness – superficially so much at odds with his stress on the need to foster independence – emerges again in his first suggestion for the curriculum; that the existing Tripos might be modified to substitute for an optional special period paper a compulsory study of the seventeenth century as a 'key passage in the history of civilisation' embodying the transition from medieval society to capitalism. The terms in which the scope of the study is described make it clear that whether or not students would be studying a period, they would inevitably be taught the doctrines of the dissociation of sensibility and the loss of the organic community:

> . . . crucial issues . . . are decided in a spirit going against the tradition of centuries – the principle of toleration is established along with that of 'business is business'; the notion of society as an organism gives way to that of society as a joint-stock company; science launches decisively on its triumphant accelerating advance . . . the study of the Seventeenth Century is a study of the modern world

> . . . it involves an approach to the characteristic problems of the
> modern world that answers admirably to our requirements.   (EU,
> p. 49)

There seems to be much that is tendentious here; not least the
ahistoricity of what is declared to be a historical study, for this approach elides the changes wrought over three hundred years and
reifies curiously both the seventeenth century and the Middle Ages.
It is only by constituting both as entities that the former can be contrasted with the latter in order for it to be identified with the twentieth. Thus one continuity is established solely through denying
another, that between the sixteenth and seventeenth centuries.

Leavis's structuring of his literary map around the idea of the
dissociation of sensibility causes difficulties for him in his treatment of the Romantics, and his adherence to doctrine within a
proposed syllabus seems not only to have similar disadvantages,
but to raise yet again the question of belief, and the related question of academic freedom (it is perhaps not for nothing that in the
passage just quoted 'toleration' is presented as part of the despised
new age). While it is a truism that all syllabuses emerge from
preconceptions, ideologies and beliefs, it is notable that Leavis's
proposed object of study hardly seems to allow of any questioning
or modification. Students are not to ask, or, apparently, to be
concerned with, the question of whether the notion of society as an
organism persisted in the face of the posited new consciousness,
but rather, seem to be expected to take the phenomenon for
granted and to occupy themselves with its effects and manifestations. Here academic freedom seems to reduce itself to finding new
ways of agreeing with Leavis's diagnosis of society. The élite to be
trained in Leavis's idea of a university is to be distinguished by
shared moral and social values as much as by qualities of independence, sensitivity, and maturity, for it is only within the framework of such agreement that Leavis's reading of the past (which is
necessarily a reading of the present) can assume the status of self-
evident fact he wants to confer on it. The question of the extent to
which values are shared within our society is of crucial importance
in Leavis's thinking, but here it is not addressed as a question.

Despite its dogmatic approach, the study Leavis suggests is
wide-ranging and surprisingly modern, for although the movement he envisages is from a literary centre outwards, the non-

literary functions as more than inert 'background'. For example, in 'attempting to explain the decisive appearance of modern prose in the first decade of the Restoration, a student would find himself invoking something like the whole history of the century, political, economic, social and intellectual' (EU, pp. 53–4). The pieces of work Leavis suggests as additional to this – one on the causes of the Civil War, another on the new science, and a third on the relations between popular and sophisticated culture – seem to bring the course closer to a component in a modern History of Ideas or Cultural Studies degree than one in the traditional single discipline courses common at the time of writing.

Although Leavis's proposed course on the seventeenth century is clearly central to his scheme of things, his other proposals suggest a similar unconventionality without such a firm doctrinal commitment: students would be expected to produce work on Dante, and on some aspect of French literature, and there would be a viva voce examination at the end of the course. This breadth of reference, together with his assumption that students would need to consult teachers from other disciplines, tempts one to wonder whether some of the notorious hostility Leavis's work aroused among scholars was to do with the threat posed by the largeness of its expectations, for he seems to demand of students a greater knowledge of context than is always evident in conventionally scholarly works. However, the overt causes of intellectual disagreement were Leavis's present-centredness and his insistence on evaluation. Here time seems to have vindicated him, and what was controversial now seems self-evident, for the naïve objectivism that believed one could enter the past and capture an original response to a work has been all but routed, together with the notion that values can be by-passed, and facts gathered outside their frame.

However, this is a curriculum for Part 2 students, and Leavis, despite paying lip-service to the need to relate intensive to extensive studies, is at best vague, at worst contradictory about how this is to be done. He assumes that Part 2 students 'should be qualified literary critics' (EU, p. 60). However, he has already envisaged the ideal student as having undertaken some other course of study in Part 1, and as having gained the required background informally, perhaps at school. But if this were to be the case then either his proposals for a training in practical criticism in Part 1 are unnecessary, or his proposed 'practical' reforms for Part 2 are *im*practical – or he assumes that training in practical criticism will go in tandem with the extra-literary studies of Part 2, which is certainly not suggested. These criticisms might seem carping, but after all, Leavis *is* proposing what he considers to be a practical reform.

Leavis seeks to install the discipline he considers to be essential to English, not only by direct definition and demonstration, but by means of a powerful polemic designed to expose the shortcomings of other rival approaches. Although he does not deny a place to literary history and scholarship, the thrust of his attack on current practices is to suggest that their inadequacies are a necessary feature of literary history as it is commonly conceived rather than the accidental outcome of inadequate teaching (although he leaves one in no doubt of his opinion of most of his colleagues). His emphasis is all on the need for concreteness, for demonstration, for the student to experience literature at first hand, for:

> . . . there is no more futile study than that which ends with mere knowledge *about* literature. If literature is worth study, then the test of its having been so will be the ability to read literature intelligently, and apart from this ability an accumulation of knowledge is so much lumber. (EU, pp. 67–8)

He then defines the capacity to read intelligently as the ability to evaluate a text, to be able to say 'why it should be worth study'. Literary history, then, is not to be conceived of as a framework into which students will fit individual instances as they meet them, but rather as the outcome of the students' reading, the pattern of correspondences and priorities which will emerge from first-hand experience. To some extent Leavis sets up an antithesis between the notion of the subject as a skill and that of it as knowledge about an object, rather as one might contrast Mathematics and History. Although all subjects require both skill and knowledge, the relations between the two are different in different disciplines. This antithesis is more a matter of rhetoric than reality however, for Leavis accepts that 'Sureness of judgement . . . implies width of experience', and acknowledges 'an unending problem of adjusting, in the student's work, the relations of intensive to extensive' (EU, p. 69). However, his attack upon the scholarly and uncritical, and his insistence that intelligence is prior to useful knowledge allow him to evade further traffic with the problems implicit in his position, not least of which, perhaps, is the extent to which the careful direction he assumes students to need gives them, no less than a skeletal literary history would, a preconceived framework into which to fit their so carefully guided responses. But Leavis's stress is on practical criticism, and we need to look at his attempts to define it:

> Analysis . . . is the process by which we seek to attain a complete reading of a poem – a reading that approaches as nearly as possible to the perfect reading . . . suggestions that it can be anything in the nature of a laboratory-method misrepresent it entirely. We can have the poem only by an inner kind of possession; it is 'there' for analysis only in so far as we are responding appropriately to the words on the page. In pointing to them (and there is nothing else to point to) what we are doing is to bring into sharp focus, in turn, this, that and the other detail, juncture or relation in our total response; or . . . what we are doing is to dwell with a deliberate, considering responsiveness on this, that or the other node or focal point in the complete organization that the poem is, in so far as we have it. Analysis is not a dissection of something that is already and passively there. What we call analysis is . . . a constructive or creative process. It is a more deliberate following-through of that process of creation in response to the poet's words which reading is. It is a re-creation in which, by a considering attentiveness, we ensure a more than ordinary faithfulness and completeness. (EU, p. 70)

Although there are clarifications and some changes of emphasis in his later works, this is an understanding of the activity of practical criticism, or 'judgement and analysis' as he soon came to call it, to which Leavis substantially adhered throughout his writing, even to the extent of using many of the same phrases : 'a more deliberate following through . . .', 'a more than ordinary faithfulness . . .'.[7] Perhaps the simplest point to make is that the activity of practical criticism depends on the notion of a poem as an organisation, an entity, so that our understanding of 'nodes' or 'focal points' is to be held in relation to the whole, and conversely the whole is to be fully realised by attention to its parts. In contrast to a deconstructive approach Leavis's is organicist, and interpretation is held in check by the notion of poem-as-entity. Leavis's conception of analysis emerges from this idea of the poem as, paradoxically, something of a process of synthesis; it is neither 'a laboratory-

method' nor 'a dissection of something that is already and pas-
sively there', for its purpose is to recreate for readers the process of
creation, to deliver the poem over to them so that they have it by
'an inner kind of possession'. To this extent Leavis's description
seems to resemble some forms of present-day readership theory
which define the text as the product of an interchange between the
reader and the marks on the page, as the reader strives to pattern
and make sense of what he or she reads. However, Leavis com-
bines beliefs about the creative role of the reader with the notion
that there is one right reading to be worked towards, and speaks of
'a complete reading', 'the perfect reading' and 'faithfulness' to
what is there only in so far as we respond 'appropriately'. Superficially, at least, there seems to be something of a contradiction in
his thinking, stemming from his need for shared standards. If,
following Bell, we take Leavis's work to depend on a
phenomenological approach, we can perhaps say that the poem is
there in so far as the reader creates it, and the reader's reading is
'complete' and 'faithful' in so far as others agree with him or her.
Such an interpretation of his position accords with Leavis's insistence on the importance of demonstration, by means of which students are to be led from the obvious to the more subtle judgement.
It accords, too, with the question and response which he regarded as
paradigmatic of practical criticism and which is so securely associated with his name: 'This is so, isn't it?', and 'Yes, but . . .' Although in practice he seems at times to have treated his collaborators
as very junior partners, the creation or recreation of a poem is
always a co-operative venture of this kind in Leavis's eyes: ' . . . our
business is to establish the poem and meet in it', he declares in
English Literature in Our Time and the University (p. 48).

  Part of Leavis's explication of practical criticism takes the form
of demonstration, a demonstration to enforce how little the activity is an automatic application of technical terms. He chooses
the term 'realisation' to make his point. In his scheme of things
'realisation' is a kind of co-ordinate of '(re)creation', for where the
critic creates or recreates the poem, it is through the poem that the
poet 'realises' an experience or state of being. He describes the way
in which the word might be used of a passage from *Macbeth*:

> One might, by way of emphasising that 'realization' is not offered
> as a technical term, an instrument of precision, put it this way: it is

in the incomplete realization of the metaphors that the realizing gift of the poet and the 'realized' quality of the passage are manifested. However we apply the term, what we have to consider is always a whole of some complexity: what we have to look for are the signs of something grasped and held, something presented in an ordering of words, and not merely thought of or gestured towards. (EU, p. 78)

Whatever the complexities of using it, 'realisation' is instituted in this passage as being of primary importance, and collocates with 'grasped and held' and 'presented'.[8] This stated priority might profitably be considered in the light of the observation of the deconstructionist critic Paul de Man that much modern criticism privileges the symbol as a trope over allegory, for the symbol is taken as the moment of fusion, the point at which poet and experience are identified with one another. (Kermode's point that the doctrine of a dissociation of sensibility provided symbolist poetry with its justification also helps enforce the extent to which Leavis's criticism is allied to a modernist poetic):

Whereas the symbol postulates the possibility of an identity or identification, allegory designates primarily a distance in relation to its own origin, and, renouncing the nostalgia and the desire to coincide, it establishes its language in the void of this temporal difference. In so doing, it prevents the self from an illusory identification with the not-self.[9]

It is not that Leavis privileges symbolism explicitly, for he is cautious in his use of such critical terms, it is rather that this 'grasp' of experience on the part of a writer signifies for him something of a healing of sensibility in which we as readers are able to participate. Curiously, too, the poet's 'grasp' of experience is a means by which language may be said to efface itself by acting, not as an obvious mediator of the poet's experience, but as a kind of transparent medium by means of which poet and reader are able to aspire to the non-linguistic experience – hence, perhaps, Leavis's dislike of poetry that is merely musical or decorative. In *Thought, Words and Creativity* he defines as true impersonality a state of affairs where: 'In the art the felt separation between the creatively used words and the piece of living they have the function of evoking is at a minimum' (TWC, p. 22).

There is a close connection between *Education and the University* and 'Judgement and Analysis', the middle section of *The Living Principle*, to the extent that some of the suggestions concerning teaching strategies that Leavis made in the former are expanded on, and, indeed, even some of the same material is returned to. Two of the sections, ' "Thought" and Emotional Quality' and 'Reality and Sincerity' repudiate in their very titles the notion that the discussion of literature can be conducted solely, or even primarily in terms of technique. Their content – extended demonstrations of the processes of Leavisian analysis and evaluation – emphasises the primacy of the moral. Within the whole of 'Judgement and Analysis' Leavis is concerned to define his procedures and his literary values ostensively, and the judgements he makes are in many ways an elaboration, a practical extension of, his version of literary history propounded in *New Bearings* and *Revaluation* which I shall discuss in the following chapter.

Although, on the whole, he tends to treat moral and literary criteria as inseparable, in practice he is unable to escape entirely from distinguishing between them. The distinction appears most notably, perhaps, in his comments on Shelley in *Revaluation* where the suggestion is that not all literary faults lie within the sphere of the moral: '. . . criticism of Shelley has something more to deal with than mere bad poetry; or rather, there are badnesses inviting the criticism that involves moral judgements' (R, p. 216). In ' "Thought" and Emotional Quality' the relations between the literary and the moral seem to vary a little in Leavis's discussions of good and bad poems; literary qualities such as concreteness, impersonality, realisation, which are the guarantors of thought, emotional strength and a proper honesty, are dwelt on in his discussion of good poems, while on the whole (though not invariably) the focus on bad poems is more exclusively moral since he lacks a set of literary terms designed to express adverse judgement that is entirely co-ordinate with his vocabulary of approbation. This is an unfortunate aspect of Leavis's work, since because of this lack his attacks seem to focus on poet rather than poem.

As we have already seen, in literary terms his stance is organicist, and features of a poem are criticised if they do not contribute to the whole (and we can see here how he conceives poetry and criticism to be co-ordinate activities, for in his idea of criticism, the interpretation of individual nodes must be subordinated to a whole interpretation). So images in Tennyson's 'Tears, Idle Tears' are criticised for being inert, for no 'new definitions or directions of feeling derive' from them, while the characteristic vice of metaphysical poetry is subtlety for its own sake. Both these judgements lead into another aspect of Leavis's demands of a poem – stressed perhaps more towards the end of his career – the presence of thought. He asks of a poem that it should have movement and direction, that it should take the reader with the writer into understanding the complexity of an emotional or historical event. Lionel Johnson's 'By the Statue of King Charles at Charing Cross' is compared unfavourably with Marvell's 'Horatian Ode'. Describing some of the shortcomings of the former, Leavis's comments have the kind of ruthless accuracy that is inseparable from real wit, and that won him so many enemies among his contemporaries:

> It must be plain at once that such impressiveness as Johnson's poem has is conditioned by an absence of thought. This is poetry from the 'soul', that nineteenth-century region of specialized poetical experience where nothing has sharp definition and where effects of 'profundity' and 'intensity' depend upon a lulling of the mind.   (LP, p. 84)

By contrast, Marvell's 'contemplating, relating and appraising mind' is 'unmistakeably there in the characteristic urbane poise of the ode' (LP, p. 86). 'Thought', then, is to be set against some species of feeling, and 'relating' and 'appraising' are two of its constituent activities, the latter suggesting the kind of distancing activity that Leavis praises in Lawrence's 'Piano', a capacity to stand back from emotion: 'He is here, and his emotion there. Again, the "glamour of childish days" is a *placing* phrase; it represents a surrender that his "manhood" is ashamed of' (LP, p. 78). The expression of emotion represents a danger in Leavis's scheme of things, even when he judges the expression to have been successful. His comments on 'Break, break, break' suggest that the poem has succeeded in despite of its emotional quality: '. . . the emotion . . . asserts itself in the plangency of tone and movement that is compelled upon us. We do not, however, this time feel moved to a dismissing judgement . . . we cannot doubt that behind the poem there is a genuinely personal urgency' (LP, p. 74). These comments lead into a discussion of the question of the standards by which a poem should be judged, the grounds for claiming that 'A slumber did my spirit seal' is finer than 'Break, break, break': ' "Inferior in kind" – by what standards? Here we come to the point at which literary criticism, as it must, enters overtly into questions of emotional hygiene and moral value – more generally . . . of spiritual health' (LP, p. 75). The language of these two passages is revealing. The medico-moral tone of 'emotional hygiene', 'spiritual health' conveys a fear of corruption which finds corroboration in 'the emotion . . . asserts itself' and 'the plangency . . . is compelled on us'.

As the title of another section, 'Reality and Sincerity', suggests, Leavis regards bad poems as having something of the function of false statements, offering the critic the temptation of collusion in a narcissistic exercise; 'Heraclitus' is convicted of 'self-cherishing emotionality' and 'wallowing complaisance', while the greatness of 'A slumber did my spirit seal' is bound up with Wordsworth's capacity to impersonalise an experience of suffering, to convey the feeling by recreating its occasion. In this section Leavis expands upon the 'challenge . . . to establish an order of preference among' Alexander Smith's 'Barbara', Emily Bronte's 'Cold in the Earth', and Thomas Hardy's 'After a Journey'. It is Hardy's poem that fulfills Leavis's strenuous requirements, and its stylistic features become marks of the poem's greater 'reality' which 'is to say . . . that it represents a profounder and completer sincerity' (LP, p. 129). Again the insistence is all upon the necessity for concreteness and precision, for to create the lost situation in its complexity is to recreate and acknowledge mood and feeling. That Leavis's judgement here is essentially moral and concerned with the poem as the expression of a historical sensibility emerges in his concluding statement: 'It is a case in which we know from the art what the man was like; we can be sure, that is, what personal qualities we should have found to admire in Hardy if we could have known him' (LP, p. 134).

Even if one accepts Leavis's position that literary values are constituted within the sphere of the moral, one might well feel that such a fierce concentration on the moral value of a work leaves out too much, focuses too narrowly. It is also human to laugh, to enjoy without judgement, and literature which induces these qualities seems to me to have some claim on our attention. At times Leavis's severity resembles that of the blind Jorges in Eco's *The Name of the*

Rose who refuses to accept that Christ was capable of laughter. More importantly, perhaps, such terms as 'sincerity' which refer to an inner state tend to lead away from literary criticism into a species of psychology.[10] Although many of the insights and observations in these chapters are compelling one needs to resist the effortless movement from literary to moral judgement.

It is in the sections 'Imagery and Movement' and 'Prose' that Leovis is at his most illuminating in *The Living Principle*, perhaps because these categories of thought do not invite exploration of the writer's psyche. In the first of these sections he demonstrates brilliantly by means of passages from *Macbeth* (discussed previously in *Education and the University*) that not all imagery is visual, and that metaphor is not compressed simile. What is at stake here is not the mere refutation of naïve definitions of complex figures of speech; Leavis argues that figures of speech are forms of precise thought rather than verbal ornament, the means by which complex and often contradictory emotions can be presented as a single state. The quality of Leavis's perceptions emerges in his comments on Macbeth's soliloquy, 'If it were done, when 'tis done . . .':

> He feels his 'intent' as something external to himself, a horse on which he finds himself mounted, but not as a purposeful rider whose will can spur it on. And then – a non-logical continuation of the sentence that nevertheless affects us as cogent and inevitable – we have the shift of imagery; logically non-sequential, but unquestionably right as completing the dramatically relevant perception and thought. What is developed is not merely his sense of the danger inherent in being 'mounted', but the equivocal perversity of his relation to the danger . . . (LP, p. 96)

This stress on the complexity of attitudes displayed in the soliloquy is later generalised into something approaching definitions of metaphor, and poetic concreteness:

> It is from some such complexity as this, involving the telescoping or focal co-incidence in the mind of contrasting or discrepant impressions or effects, that metaphor in general – live metaphor – seems to derive its life: life involves friction and tension – a sense of arrest – in some degree.
>
> And this generalization suggests a wider one. Whenever in poetry we come on places of especially striking 'concreteness' – places

> where the verse has such life and body that we hardly seem to be
> reading arrangements of words – we may expect analysis to yield
> notable instances of the co-presence in complex effects of the dis-
> parate, the conflicting or the contrasting.   (LP, p. 108)

Metaphor, then, the conveyor of discrepancy and complexity, language at its most highly charged, is also, paradoxically, the point at
which language effaces itself to issue in the real: 'The palpability of
"globed" – the word doesn't merely describe, or refer to, the
sensation, but gives a tactual image. It is as if one were actually
cupping the peony with one's hand' (LP, p. 110).

   However, Leavis does not take imagery as being the only source
of life and meaning and turns to 'movement' as a more appropriate
means of approaching some poetry. He insists, as so often, upon
the need for reading aloud in order to convey a poem's full meaning. Again, he is insistent that 'movement' is not a technical matter
and uses none of the language of prosody. Although he claims that
this kind of analysis is one 'where the pen is peculiarly at a disadvantage as compared with the voice' (LP, p. 116), the disadvantage
is more apparent than real since he refuses to treat rhythm and
inflexion in isolation from other features of the poem and, indeed,
takes movement as, in part at least, a function of vocabulary and
tone.

   He demonstrates that metaphor in prose, as a vehicle of attitudes and values, can be as integral to meaning, as functional, as
metaphor in poetry. Refusing any sharp, 'naïve' distinction between poetry and prose, he asserts that the business of this section
of his book is 'to bring out the force of my contention that the
intelligent study of creative literature entails the study of language
in its fullest use' (LP, p. 139). Once more we have an assertion of
the inseparability, on some occasions, of imagery and thought:
'Swift's imagery . . . strikes us as the thought itself; it seems to
assail us in the concrete without mediation' (LP, p. 138). Leavis's
assertion and demonstration of the continuity of prose with poetry
allows him to suggest what he states explicitly elsewhere, that from
the nineteenth century onwards the novel is the dominant source
of creativity.[11] Commenting on a passage from Conrad, he claims
that 'the English language that had adopted and naturalized him
was the language not only of Shakespeare, but, in the not distant
past, of Dickens' (LP, p. 143).

Although the connection between Leavis's suggestions for the teaching of practical criticism in *Education and the University* and these extended illustrations from *The Living Principle* is so close that the latter seem no more than a gloss on the former, there is a new stress on literature as 'thought', which is accompanied by a dismissal of Wittgensteinian philosophy as having any relevance to English studies, and an attack on philosophical notions of clarity.[12] Also significant is the focus on prose, which helps to emphasise the place of literature in the language – a pre-eminent place if we consider Leavis's comments on Conrad's adoption of English, for the suggestion is that it is literature, the literature of the past, that is constitutive of our common language. These new features are signs of a much more clearly articulated and theoretically based account of the importance of literature and English studies, and, indeed, of the functioning of a society. In *English Literature in Our Time and the University* Leavis begins to work toward what he completed in *The Living Principle* under the influence of Grene and Polanyi.

In both books Leavis continues to hold to an ideal of the English School as a liaison centre that would enable the university to function as a breeding ground of the educated public he deemed necessary to the continuance of a proper culture, and once more he sees a humane education as offering a necessary opposition to the dominant tendencies of society. The enemy has changed a little, however, for it is no longer the machine as such that engages his attention, but processes of thought – 'technologico-Benthamite enlightenment' – that he claims are oblivious to human needs. It is through its access to more adequate ways of thinking that English studies finds its justification.

In *English Literature in Our Time*, however, that justification is not yet fully worked out and the fundamental problem presents itself as a question of standards of judgement.[13] At first Leavis's position seems similar to his refusal in *Education and the University* to accept that his confrères were sufficiently exacting in their judgements and discriminations. 'The problem is to *have* an English School that truly deserves the respect of those who are acquainted with intellectual standards in their own fields', he declared then (ELOTU, p. 3).

Although a lack of adequate standards in the subject is necessarily connected with it, is one aspect of it, the essential problem he wrestles with is deeper. It is to do with the very nature of English as a subject; to do with what constitutes the subject's importance in the present, for 'The modes of thought distinctive of the field entail, as essential to – as essentially in and of – the thinking, kinds of judgement of quality and value that don't admit of demonstrative enforcement' (ELOTU, p. 3). The contrast is with Mathematics, and Leavis defines the act of judgement, the process by which standards are to be established within English Studies as collaborative. It is through the interplay of personal judgements that the very object of study is created, and 'Where the interest is widely enough spread, the outcome of the interplay will be something approaching a consensus as to what English Litera-ture, the truly living reality, is – for us' (ELOTU, p. 7). We do not, that is, operate on something already 'there', but create what is to be deemed English Literature for our time, just as Leavis, following the lead of T. S. Eliot and other modernists, collabo-rated with them in the 1930s to redefine the canon, for – and this is an essential point – 'English Literature must be different for every age' (ELOTU, p. 8).

Just as the canon is to be created by collaborative interplay, so each individual poem finds its existence by the same process. After defining practical criticism in terms almost indistinguishable from those he used in *Education and the University*, Leavis expands on his position in that book:

> What . . . we call analysis is a creative, or recreative, process. It's a more deliberate following-through of that process of creation in response to the poet's words . . . than any serious reading is . . . by a considering attentiveness, we ensure a more than ordin-ary faithfulness and fulness . . . when one is engaged in analysis one is engaged in discussion . . . a judgement has the form, 'This is so, isn't it?' One is engaged in discussion of . . .? – the poem which is there *for* discussion only in so far as those discussing have each recreated it.
>
> The discussion is an effort to establish the poem as something standing in a common world between those discussing, and thus to justify our habitual assumption that it does so stand. It's 'there' only when it's realized in separate minds, and yet it's not merely private. It's something in which minds can meet, and our business is to establish the poem and meet in it. Merely private, on the one hand, and on the other, public in the sense that it can be produced

in the laboratory, or tripped over – the poem is neither. . . . There is a third realm and the poem belongs to that. (ELOTU, p. 48)

As always, Leavis takes the poem to be, not marks on the page, but a re-enactment in the reader of the complex state the poet has realised by his words. What is new is that he has found a means of bridging the gap between public and private. He can still hold that 'A judgement is personal, or it is nothing', but now the paradigmatic question, 'This is so, isn't it?' is the means by which the literary work, and with it, the 'third realm' is established, for 'the establishing of a poem . . . is the establishing of a value' (ELOTU, p. 50). 'Value' and 'significance' are words which Leavis sees as closely tied, and, in his use of them, as inimical to 'a Benthamite and egalitarian world', for such use can never be the application of pre-existing criteria:

> . . . so far from valuing being a matter of bringing up a scale, a set of measures, or an array of fixed and definite criteria to the given work, every work that makes itself felt as a challenge evokes, or generates, in the critic a fresh realization of the grounds and nature of judgement. A truly great work is realized to *be* that because it so decidedly modifies – alters – the sense of value and significance that judges. (ELOTU, p. 50)

This description of the act of valuation takes us on to Leavis's new stress on the nature of thought in literature; a great writer is necessarily intelligent, but his intelligence – a fusion of intellect and sensibility – produces a distinctive kind of thought unlike that of the philosopher; a kind of thought that is creative, heuristic, taking him or her into new areas of experience and understanding (and here we might remember I. A. Richards's definition of the poet). In the creative and corrective process that English Studies ideally is, the critic as he or she traces and recreates the poet's thought is changed, and establishes with others, also changed, the work as work, and thus contributes to that growth in understanding that is the life of a culture.

The assertion of such a primacy within a society as little concerned with literature as ours finds its justification in Leavis's insistence on literature as 'a mode or manifestation of language' – language which he describes as 'very largely the essential life of a culture' (ELOTU, p. 49). And our language is continuous with the language of the great writers of the past, those undissociated, pre-Benthamite beings who have shaped it so that it can still express for us the needs our society denies. The new great writer is the one who, using this language, is able to restore us to the consciousness of those needs. She is also one who in her struggle with language exposes new needs for us. At the same time, the establishment of the literary work by the processes of criticism is also the establishment of the 'third realm', a realm of interpersonal judgements and values. 'Values', 'standards', 'needs', 'consciousness', 'creative-collaborative', 'third realm'. The new vocabulary, or old terms found in new collocations, is extended by yet other items, 'life', 'responsibility', 'the common world', 'the human world', 'nisus', '*ahnung*' as Leavis struggles to free his conception of a human society from the bewitchment of language, to allow his meaning to emerge through the gaps created by his qualifications. 'The common world', 'the human world', these phrases are closely linked with the idea of a 'third realm', for the world that Leavis seeks is a world of values and significance such as would be created if his ideal conception of the university could be realised – 'a nucleus (one of a number) of the greater public, the spiritual community the country needs as its mind and conscience' (ELOTU, p. 30). Characteristically the word 'spiritual' is glossed in the interests of greater precision as 'that association of knowledge and political purpose with non-material ends and other-than-quantitative standards . . .' (ELOTU, p. 30). The human world, then, is directly opposed to the 'objectivity' of the 'technologico-Benthamite', 'utilitarian', 'egalitarian' materialistic world of the 1960s.

'Nisus' and '*ahnung*' are regarded by Leavis as closely related to one another. He defines and defends his use of them in *The Living Principle*. 'Nisus' 'implies conscious, explicitly realized, and deliberate purpose', though without any connotation of 'ego, will and idea' (LP, pp. 62–3). Here Leavis invokes the Blakean distinction between identity and selfhood, so that a kind of impersonality is implied, a word perhaps avoided by him at this point in his career partly because of its capacity to get assimilated to ideas of 'objectivity', and partly because (the two reasons are not in the end completely separable) he has repudiated the Eliotic notion of impersonality by this time. On the whole 'nisus' is used as a critical term, first in relation to *Ash-Wednesday*, and then in an essay subsequent to *English Literature in Our Time*, in relation to Blake's poetry. '*Ahnung*' as Leavis explains it has something of the force of 'inkling', but is a more weighty word – 'anticipatory apprehension that carries the weight implicit in "foreboding" ' (LP, p. 63). In *English Literature in Our Time* Leavis describes his conception of the university as 'the answer to humanity's *ahnung* of its profound and desperate need' (ELOTU, p. 31).[14] Both words, it is important to notice, reach out toward the future, the one consciously, the other at a kind of preconscious level, and both are descriptive of that movement toward growth which, for Leavis, is a principle of life, and which is part of the human, creative, enterprise.

The vision Leavis preaches in *Education in Our Time*, attractive though it is, seems to me to have a fatal flaw, for in the end his concern with standards serves not to dissipate the problem but to make it more obvious. We are not, after all, presented with a process that is *simply* opposed to the quantifying, materialist mode of the time. It is rather that *within* this process differences in valuation are common, as Leavis himself recognises: 'We talk about "standards", in fact, at times when it is peculiarly hard to invoke standards with effect' (ELOTU, p. 56). This comment occurs immediately after Leavis has taken scholarly evaluations of Hemingway and Kingsley Amis as, respectively, 'great' and 'serious' to demonstrate 'a period marked by a collapse of standards'. The force of the comment is such as to preclude any possibility of the existence of that creative difference proper to criticism. But, in the face of such radical disagreement within the discipline it is hard to see how the object of study is to be established, and even harder to see how one unifying human world might be created. Because of his refusal of any kind of concession to those with whom he disagrees the activity Leavis proposes as the healer of the wound emerges as the brandishing of a sword and, finally, because of his intransigence, the values that he wants to establish as more than private remain more or less that. To reject the process by means of which values and standards are established in the sciences is one thing, but to declare standards to be immanent within the object of study is another, for such a declaration is in a strange tension with the idea of collaboration and consensus, or, rather, there is almost an aporia between the two. If the standards reside within the thing itself, then the notion of error as something external to, and ultimately defining consensus is present. Presumably even if the whole of the literary community had collaborated to install Hemingway's works as great literature (in Leavisian terms created them as such) Leavis, standing alone, would have regarded it as in error, and himself as the only inhabitant of the human world. But surely that is to be in self-contradiction?

The terms 'nisus' and '*ahnung*' recur in 'On Justifying One's Valuation of Blake', but the appearance of the names of Grene and Polanyi, those writers I discussed in Chapter 2, is new. Their work in its attack on Cartesian thought sorted well with Leavis's own ideas, and allowed him to arrive at a more coherent account of his position in *The Living Principle*. The value of Grene's ideas for Leavis is that they carry the implication that the thought proper to the creative writer and therefore, in Leavis's acceptation, to English Studies itself, is not a specialised mode of apprehension; rather, there is but one mode, and what distinguishes the great writer is the capacity to use that mode to the full. The collaborative interchange that establishes the poem, that establishes it as a value, is typical of all exchanges, for as Grene describes it, in the human world values are constitutive of facts, and values are instituted by the community. Our world, *all* our world is the product of creative collaboration. It is a world constituted by language, into which we are born, and it is only within the prior agreement of our language that we are able to disagree. This language which stretches back in time is a macrocosm of that tacit knowledge which each of us possesses (and part of our tacit knowledge is our language), the condition of our potentiality, Polanyi's 'protensive pull'. We are all, then, participators in creativity, and the role of the great writers is to make us conscious of this, to make us conscious of our humanity, which is our language:

> The nature of livingness in human life is manifest in language – manifest to those whose thought about language *is*, inseparably, thought about literary creation. They can't but realize more than notionally that a language is more than a means of expression; it is the heuristic conquest won out of representative experience, the upshot or precipitate of immemorial human living, and embodies values, distinctions, identifications, conclusions, promptings, cartographical hints and tested potentialities. It exemplifies the truth that life is growth and growth change, and the condition of these is

continuity. It takes the individual being . . . back to the dawn of
human consciousness, and beyond, and does this in fostering the
ahnung in him of what is not yet – the as yet unrealized, the
achieved discovery of which demands creative effort.   (LP, p. 44)

The final move has been made, and language is now taken to be
constitutive of our culture rather than a major part of it; the study
of literature established as central to the continuance of that culture. With this new orientation there appears a new definition of a
major writer, a criterion that is in some sense a reworking of the
notion of impersonality. Quoting, as so frequently in this period,
Blake's 'Tho' I call them Mine, I know that they are not Mine',
Leavis continues, 'One's criterion for calling an artist major is
whether his work prompts us to say it, emphatically and with the
profoundest conviction, *for* him, to put the words in his
mouth . . .' (LP, p. 44).

In *The Living Principle*, as in all his later books, whatever his
disclaimers, and however much he seeks to argue ostensively,
Leavis is trafficking in theory and philosophy. Given his interest in
Grene and Polanyi it is interesting to speculate on the reasons for
his violent denial of the usefulness of Wittgensteinian philosophy
to English, for, after all, Wittgenstein is no Cartesian, and, like
Leavis took language to be constitutive of human life. Wittgenstein's approach to standards, too, in *Lectures in Aesthetics*, and his
comments on exactness in *Philosophical Investigations* seem close to
Leavis's position. His famous definition of language as 'an agreement in a form of life' occurs, moreover, in the context of an
exploration of the extent to which language mediates between the
public and the private, and is itself an assertion of what Leavis
would term the 'third realm':

> 'So you are saying that human agreement decides what is true and
> what is false?' – It is what human beings *say* that is true and false;
> and they agree in the *language* they use. That is not agreement in
> opinions but in form of life'.[15]

Leavis himself explains his hostility by imputing a naïvety about
language to most Wittgensteinian philosophers, and by a suggestion that they have little interest in the human agency involved in
meaning, but such accusations, although they are made forcefully,

are extremely unspecific, and the real reason may have more to do with Wittgenstein's alleged contempt for literary criticism (' "Give up literary criticism!" – Wittgenstein' appears as an epigraph to *The Living Principle*) and his apparent lack of interest in literature as Leavis describes it in 'Memories of Wittgenstein'. The tone of this piece is a curious compound of admiration, disapproval and a kind of rivalry. Leavis ends with a nice story describing an abortive attempt to explain Empson's 'Legal Fiction' to the philosopher:

> At the third or fourth interruption of the same kind I shut the book, and said, 'I'm not playing.' 'It's perfectly plain that you don't understand the poem in the least,' he said. 'Give me the book.' I complied, and sure enough, without any difficulty, he went through the poem, explaining the analogical structure that I should have explained myself, if he had allowed me.[16]

Perhaps one could speculate on the importance of the different styles of the philosophers in determining Leavis's acceptance or rejection of them. Wittgenstein's spare, speculative, analytic; Grene's emotional, rhetorical, persuasive; above all, committed. Both she and Leavis write out of a desire to convince and convert, and both are holistic in their approach as they strive to create the desired end through their words.

Chapter Four

Literary 'Theory' and Constituting the Canon

Introduction

Leavis's hostility towards philosophy has been a recurring theme in previous chapters, and I have suggested in passing a variety of motives and reasons ranging from the intellectual to the purely personal. Leavis's attitudes are complex, and probably nowhere so strongly expressed as in those parts of his work where he engages in literary history and seeks to establish the grounds for his judgements. One of the most famous debates in which he engaged not only raises questions crucial to his practice, but illuminates the difficulties inherent in discussing his work with any kind of detachment.

In 1937 a letter from the distinguished literary historian, René Wellek, was published in *Scrutiny*. Wellek professed admiration for *Revaluation*, praising it as 'the first consistent attempt to re-write the history of English poetry from the twentieth century point of view'. However, he offered criticisms which he regarded as 'fundamental'. His first was that Leavis had not stated his assumptions with sufficient explicitness, nor defended them systematically. Culling Leavis's own phrases from *Revaluation*, Wellek then summarised what he took to be Leavis's assumptions about poetry, concluding, 'the only question I would ask you is to defend this position more abstractly and to become conscious that large ethical, philosophical, and, of course, ultimately, also aesthetic *choices* are involved'.[1]

Wellek saw his second criticism as related to his first: Leavis, who insisted that poetry should have 'a firm grip on the actual', was predisposed towards a position of philosophical realism and unsympathetic towards any idealist position, particularly such as were to be found in Romantic poetry. After seeking to show Leavis's misunderstanding of a number of passages of Romantic poetry he concluded: 'Your book . . . raises anew the question of the poet's "belief" and how far sympathy with this belief and comprehension of it are necessary for an appreciation of the poetry' (S5, p. 383).

Leavis's rather dusty answer sought to distinguish between the methods of the philosopher and the literary critic. Wellek's reaction to his book was a philosopher's, he claimed, and what Wellek asked of him was philosophy. He, Leavis, had produced literary criticism and, he suggested, something more precise than the generalisations Wellek had formulated to outline his position. He then went some way towards defining his approach and identifying the differences he saw between the two disciplines:

> The reading demanded by poetry is of a different kind from that demanded by philosophy. I should not find it easy to define the difference satisfactorily, but Dr. Wellek knows what it is and could give at least as good an account of it as I could. Philosophy, we say, is 'abstract' . . . and poetry 'concrete'. Words in poetry invite us not to 'think about' and judge, but to 'feel into' or 'become' – to realize a complex experience that is given in the words. They demand . . . a kind of responsiveness that is incompatible with the judicial, one-eye-on-the-standard approach suggested by Dr. Wellek's phrase: 'your "norm" with which you measure every poet'. The critic . . . is indeed concerned with evaluation, but to figure him as measuring with a norm which he brings up to the object and applies from the outside is to misrepresent the process. The critic's aim is, first, to realize as sensitively and completely as possible this or that which claims his attention; and a certain valuing is implicit in the realizing. As he matures in experience of the new thing he asks explicitly and implicitly: 'Where does this come? How does it stand in relation to . . .?' And the organization into which it settles as a constituent in becoming 'placed' is an organization of similarly

'placed' things, things that have found their bearings with regard to one another, and not a theoretical system or a system determined by abstract considerations.   (S6, pp. 60–1)

The doubleness of Leavis's gesture is ipportant here, for he suggests formulation's impossibility in the very process of formulation: 'I should not find it easy to define . . .', 'Philosophy', we say, is "abstract"', 'this or that', 'a certain valuing'. The quotation marks, negative constructions, qualifications combine to suggest that any positive statement would be unspeakably crude; that Leavis's meaning lies outside the ordinary net of words, the mesh of rational discourse, and can only be gestured towards or realised by some kind of direct re-enactment in the reader's mind: 'Dr. Wellek knows what it is'. His reply to Wellek's second criticism reiterates that literary criticism is something subtler than philosophy so that a writer's philosophical position can hold no proper interest for the critic:

'The romantic view of the world', a view common to Blake, Wordsworth, Shelley, and others – yes, I have heard of it; but what interest can it have for the literary critic? For the critic, the reader whose primary interest is in poetry, these three poets are so radically different, immediately and finally, from one another that the offer to assimilate them in a common philosophy can only suggest the irrelevance of the philosophical approach.   (S6, p. 64)

Leavis's dismissiveness, his insistence throughout the encounter on the inadequacy of generalisation and paraphrase brings the difficulty of trying to explicate his ideas into sharp focus; if one abstracts in Wellek's fashion then the very method implies an adversarial stance, for it is a method which Leavis has condemned as distorting and oversimplifying. However, to accept Leavis's approach entails accepting without examination the contention that 'philosophic' discourse is of no use in the discussion of literature; that what is needed is a 'realising', a 'feeling into' Leavis's thought. As Paul de Man, writing of Heidegger, puts it, in such a case 'Ultimately the ideal commentary would indeed become superfluous and merely allow the text to stand fully revealed'. Significantly de Man is discussing Heidegger's contention that foreknowledge is necessary for interpretation, and, as Bell has pointed out, Leavis's position bears marked resemblances to

Heidegger's.[2] What needs to be noticed, perhaps, is that Leavis makes no distinction between the interpretation of poetry and the interpretation of interpretation, and the appeal is to a shared practice and shared assumptions even where such a practice and such assumptions are in question: 'Dr. Wellek knows what it is'. His rhetoric, that is, attempts to preclude sympathetic detachment, or, indeed, reasoned opposition as a possible attitude for a reader. Not to be convinced is to have misunderstood, and the only possible moves seem to be to enter into his discourse or to reject it.

But it seems to me that Leavis cannot be criticised adequately from *within* his assumptions, for that would be to leave unexamined precisely the question at issue in his encounter with Wellek: the question of what *is* the appropriate mode of discourse for criticism. Leavis would claim his to be ostensive on every level; of the poem ('This is so, isn't it?'), of the nature of literary criticism, of the inadequacy of philosophy. This is a powerful rhetorical ploy, enabling the easy dismissal of dissent – 'Well, if you can't see it, there's not much point in going on . . .'. It is a ploy that needs to be resisted, however, for the polarised attitudes of submission or rejection are alike in suggesting that whether or not Leavis's position is acceptable it is coherent. Paradoxically, to reject Leavis is to accept his dualistic construction of the intellectual world, is to slip meekly into the place assigned for non-believers.

It seems possible to prise open what Leavis in his debate with Wellek wants to present as a monolithic stance, and to show that it has more than one strand; to suggest, too, that Leavis is not so much substituting one mode of discourse for another as operating within, and *mis*using, the one he is ostensibly rejecting. First, what exactly is the 'philosophy' and its methods that he rejects so thoroughly? Leavis suggests it as something specialised and abstract – as a separate academic discipline. But Wellek's request that Leavis should make his assumptions explicit and defend them systematically hardly classifies him as a philosopher. The requirement seems to be that Leavis should conform to the conventions of rational discourse within which it is possible to discuss, rather than to merely assert, the truth or falsity of different positions.

For Wellek, Leavis's unexamined stance (the fact that it *is* unexamined) renders him incapable of recognising that a way of looking at the world with which he disagrees may be perfectly coherent – may be philosophically respectable. However, he does not claim that a coherent philosophical position ensures good poetry. Leavis, on the other hand, seeks to suggest that Wellek's demand for conceptual clarity about critical practice entails a corresponding emphasis on 'ideas' in poetry. He conflates, that is, the writing of criticism with the writing of poetry. This position seems open to objection, for however convincing Leavis's arguments are that poetry is not susceptible to philosophical analysis, or reducible to paraphrase (and who would disagree with him?), this does not in fact imply that criticism is to be written and read in the same way as poetry. One might, as Wellek does, accept the validity of most of *Revaluation*; accept, that is, the methods of literary criticism as they are applied to texts, but still feel that a different order of discourse is necessary in order to discuss more general issues. Attempts to define a poet or to delineate the relations between literature and society are part of the stuff of English as a subject area, but such attempts engage the limited discourse of literary criticism with other discourses. *Revaluation* is not just a series of literary critical essays, but an attempt to articulate T. S. Eliot's ideas about the canon, about the relation of past to present literature, about the relation of literature to society into a coherent theory, and to rewrite literary history in accordance with that theory. The responses appropriate to understanding poetry hardly seem to have a bearing on such an enterprise. Does it, as theory, demand that we 'feel into' or 'become' it? Are we presented with 'a complex experience'? I don't think so. To notice this elision of the distinction between different kinds of discourse is, I think, to register that Leavis, for all his eloquence, has not really met Wellek's first objection. However well-grounded his criticisms of Wellek's manner of expression may be, they do not establish the justice of his own approach. But it is precisely Leavis's seeming rejection of normal rational discourse as 'philosophy' that obscures this.

It is this rejection that allows Leavis to obfuscate, too, the issue of the poet's beliefs by misinterpreting Wellek's meaning in such statements as 'I cannot see why the argument of Canto II of *The Prelude* could not be paraphrased', and when he holds that passages Leavis judges harshly are coherent from the standpoint of idealism. Wellek's position is not that paraphraseable, coherent ideas make good poetry, but that Leavis's preconceptions lead him to misrepresent and – in the case of Shelley – undervalue some poems:

> I am not sure whether this intellectual system in Shelley's poetry
> says anything in favour of its value as poetry, but I think it should
> meet a good deal of the criticism against him which seems to me to
> exaggerate the 'confusion' of his style because it underrates the
> thought implied.   (S5, pp. 382–3)

Wellek does not imply here that the whole meaning of a poem is
paraphraseable, only that in some of the cases discussed by Leavis
the poet's *argument* is, and since poets make statements in their
work and their use of language is continuous with other uses this
seems a perfectly acceptable contention. Leavis suggests, however,
not only that Wellek believes the passages he discusses to be completely paraphraseable, but that he judges the quality of the poetry
entirely by the coherence of the philosophy. He seems to imply,
too, that poetry and philosophy are separable: '. . . I had heard of
and read about Wordsworth's thought, which, indeed, has received a great deal of notice, but my business was with Wordsworth's poetry; I never proposed, and do not propose now, to
consider him as a philosophic thinker' (S6, p. 67). The cool,
dismissive tone signals Leavis's refusal to engage in debate; in a
sense, the tone is all there is of the argument. It has to be, because
Leavis's case depends on a kind of feint, for after separating
philosophic thought from poetic intelligence he places the qualities
in opposition to one another, suggesting them as mutually contradictory. So, although Wordsworth's philosophising is deemed to
be of no value his intelligence is not denied. Moreover, both here
and in *Revaluation* poetic intelligence is treated as intelligence *tout
court*, so that, while acknowledging his philosophical interests
Leavis can claim in *Revaluation*, 'The effect of Shelley's eloquence
is to hand poetry over to a sensibility that has no more dealings
with intelligence than it can help' (R, p. 210). After cataloguing
Shelley's intellectual pursuits Leavis concludes, 'But there is
nothing grasped in the poetry – no object offered for contemplation, no realized presence to persuade or move us by what it is' (R,
p. 210). This passage illustrates precisely Wellek's point about the
relevance of a poet's 'belief' to critical valuation of the work. If one
accepts that Shelley conceived the world 'as a phenomenal flux
behind which the unreachable absolute is only dimly perceived',
then Shelley's 'lack of intelligence' seems to emerge as a different
conception of reality from that of Leavis.

The points I have been trying to make here are precise, and

limited in their scope. I am not suggesting, for instance, that Leavis's failure to acknowledge Shelley's philosophical beliefs as relevant to the practice of criticism invalidates the judgements he makes. Neither am I suggesting that Wellek's readings act as correctives to those of Leavis, for Leavis seems to me a much better reader than Wellek; nor do I think that a one-way application of pre-existent standards to poems is desirable. It is rather that, however convincingly Leavis seems to rebut him on details, he does not properly address Wellek's central contentions. His reply, that is, did not establish literary criticism as a mode of discourse separable from what Leavis would call philosophy, but which I think is no more than rational argument. Rather than using language with the kind of precision proper to literary criticism Leavis deploys it to obfuscate, to blur distinctions that need to be made. Crucially we find him evading Wellek's question about the influence of the poet's belief on critical valuation.

If Leavis seems to evade the issues Wellek poses, one can assume it was not because they were invisible to him. He is an extremely subtle thinker. His evasion, I believe, comes down to notions of a common pursuit, shared standards, a mutual reality. Without any notion of the transcendental, except in so far as it may be said to inhere in language, Leavis with his need for order has to believe in it there. Language, that is, has to embody shared values, has to be agreement in a form of life. Moreover, his authoritarian temperament leads him to interpret very rigidly what such agreement and such a sharing of values might mean. In rejecting any kind of relativism he has to take his realist philosophical stance, not as a *position*, but as representing the actuality of life. His judgements will then be authoritative because at bottom they will not *be* judgements – rather they will be an exposing of what was always already there, for '. . . the organization into which [the thing] settles as a constituent in becoming "placed" is an organization of similarly "placed" things, things that have found their bearings with regard to one another, and not a theoretical system' (S5, pp. 60–1). Thus, the need for Leavis's discourse to be persuasive, ostensive rather than argumentative and theoretical. What is at stake for him is, of course, English culture, for relativism is in itself a sign of breakdown, a sign that the old agreements are passing.

This is, of course, only one aspect of Leavis's rejection of theory and philosophy. When he engages, not with theoretical issues, but with the detail of specific texts then his concern is to find a style answering to the object of his attention, a medium adequate to its task, a way of speaking that will not reduce literature to prose meaning or any other false simplicity.

The distinction I have attempted here between what one might call Leavis's theoretical and practical literary discourses is a means of refusing the polarities of submission or rejection of his rhetoric demands. It is an insistence that to explicate his literary theories, to treat them *as* theories is not to misunderstand his position, nor, necessarily to distort it, but to submit it to the rules of a common discourse in which he believes.

The Poetic Canon

In *New Bearings in English Poetry* (1932) and *Revaluation* (1936) Leavis adopted and expanded I. A. Richards's definition of the poet and the poet's relation to society, rewrote English literary history, and in doing so provided his own account of the practice of criticism. These books, that is, together with *Education and the University*, constitute a claim to define the content and values, the methods and justification of English as a discipline. Much, though not all, of Leavis's later criticism, whether its primary concern is with the explication and valuation of specific texts or with demonstrating critical method, depends upon the assumptions formed in this period.

Although Leavis claims to eschew the abstract and the academic he yet seems to mould and synthesise some of the insights of his contemporaries into an articulated pattern or, at the very least, to encourage his readers into such an articulation. It is because of this that I have chosen to use the word 'theory' in the title of this chapter. The quotation marks within which I have so carefully enclosed it are an acknowledgement, not only that Leavis himself would have rejected such a description, but that finally the pattern strains or breaks at different points when it is pressed. It is, however, by a kind of legerdemain, by his rhetorical embrace of the concrete and the specific that Leavis's generalisations are given weight and take on the appearance of forming a coherent position.

New Bearings and *Revaluation* are notable for their redrawing of the map of English literature. Although Leavis's claim that the 'considerations' of the former had been 'commonplaces for some years' is not without truth, it is his work that acquired something like general acceptance for them, and by presenting them coherently made them new. The two books need to be taken together, and were intended to be complementary; indeed, those essays which were later to make up *Revaluation* began to appear in *Scrutiny* almost immediately after the publication of *New Bearings*. Leavis stressed in his introduction to *Revaluation* that 'the planning of the one book was involved in the planning of the other'. A few lines later, in commenting on 'the business of the critic', he expands on the nature of the essential relation between, or interpenetration of, past and present that he posits. What he has to say here has obvious bearing on his assertion in his cultural criticism of the need for continuity:

> It must not be assumed that the account of the past given here is merely ancillary to a sovereign interest in what is being written today . . . the critic . . . endeavours to see the poetry of the present as continuation and development; that is, as the decisive, the most significant, contemporary life of tradition. He endeavours, where the poetry of the past is concerned, to realize to the full the implications of the truism that its life is in the present or nowhere . . . His aim, to offer a third proposition, is to define, and to order in terms of its own implicit organization, a kind of ideal and impersonal living memory. (R, pp. 1–2)

The movement in this passage from the unexceptionable, if overly optimistic (is 'development' always to be posited?) is characteristic of Leavis. It is also characteristic that his second proposition, which he takes as self-evident, has an unstated connection to his controversy with F. W. Bateson over the relation of criticism to scholarship. The controversy began with his review in 1935 of Bateson's version of literary history, *English Poetry and the English Language* and continued in the pages of *Scrutiny*. Leavis argued strongly against Bateson's attempt to differentiate sharply between criticism and scholarship and to allow each its separate, autonomous sphere, for, as we have already seen, criticism was foundational in Leavis's eyes, the very means by which the object of study was to be constituted.[3] So, while it may indeed be a truism that the literature of the past 'has its life in the present or nowhere', the proposition that the critic should 'realize to the full' the implications of that truism constitutes a claim, particularly controversial at the time of writing, for the primacy of criticism over scholarship as the organising principle in the study of English. Such a claim entails not only that we should recognise the need for judgement, but also the inescapability of our own partiality, that we can respond to the poetry of the past only as readers in the present.

Leavis's third proposition not only sorts oddly with his second, but courts self-contradiction. The critic is 'to define and order in terms of its own implicit organization, a kind of ideal and impersonal living memory'. This self-contradiction is perhaps a measure of the need for order that is such a pressure in Leavis's early work: it is not enough for the critic to undertake the ordering, to impose a pattern, or, indeed to expose a pre-existent order. Order itself (admittedly implicit) must be ordered. This indecision between defining the critic's task as the exposure of order or its creation is perhaps also an attempt to validate as 'out there', by a lapse into the objectivism he so consciously rejected, what to him had such obvious and palpable existence. 'Ideal' and 'impersonal'also insist that the order he perceives has an existence independent of its being perceived.

The inspiration for the re-ordering of the canon in *New Bearings* and *Revaluation* is T. S. Eliot, and in his preface to the former book, Leavis defines it as 'largely an acknowledgement, vicarious as well as personal, of indebtedness to a certain critic and poet' (NBEP, p. 11). His central debts are to Eliot's definition of the canon, and his idea of tradition in 'Tradition and the Individual Talent'(also important is Eliot's notion of poetic impersonality in this essay, an idea that Leavis was to abandon later), and his 'theory', formulated in 'The Metaphysical Poets', that 'In the seventeenth century a dissociation of sensibility set in'. (Eliot, *Selected Essays*, p. 288).

Eliot defines the canon, not as a constantly expanding collection of disparate works, but as an order of related texts, with each work finding its meaning in relation to the others. With the addition of a new work the pattern so formed shifts, and with that shift the value and meaning of each individual work is also affected:

> The existing monuments form an ideal order among themselves, which is modified by the introduction of the new (the really new) work of art among them. The existing order is complete before the new work arrives; for order to persist after the supervention of

novelty, the *whole* existing order must be, if ever so slightly, altered; and so the relations, proportions, values of each work of art
toward the whole are readjusted; and this is conformity between
the old and the new.[4]

Part of the attractiveness of Eliot's insistence on the canon as an
order may well have lain in the opportunity it offered to exclude
from consideration that flood of new works that Leavis so deplored
in *Mass Civilization and Minority Culture* as signifying invasion by
the forces of mass-production. The kind of connection between
past and present postulated by Eliot is also important, for to describe the present as altering the past is to see the past, not as
something dead and inert, but as living and changing its value and
meaning in its interactions with the present. Tradition is thus both
constantly coming into being, and that which governs its own new
manifestation. Given that culture, language and tradition are such
close homologies in Leavis's thought as to be almost interchange-
able, Eliot's formulation is closely linked with Leavis's insistence
on continuity as a condition of growth within a culture.

In the end, however, it is not Eliot's criticism alone that Leavis
declares to be of central importance to contemporary culture, but
the combination of his criticism and his poetry. 'He has made a
new start and established new bearings', Leavis concludes at the
end of the first chapter of *New Bearings* (NBEP, p. 28), gracefully
attributing to Eliot the changed map he elineates in that book, and
in *Revaluation* the compliment is reiterated and reinforced as
Eliot's dictum is granted the status of fact when Leavis, proclaim-
ing Milton's dislodgement from the canon, invokes Eliot's poetry
as cause: 'The irresistible argument was, of course, Mr Eliot's
creative achievement; it gave his few critical asides . . . their final-
ity, and made it unnecessary to elaborate a case' (R, p. 42). Eliot is
defined as the producer of that really new work that alters our
apprehension of the poetry of the past, and causes us to relate and
value its different components in new ways. For Leavis, it is
Eliot's work that provides a warrant for rejecting the dominant
poetic of the late nineteenth and early twentieth centuries:

> Poetry, it was assumed, must be the direct expression of simple emo-
> tions, and these of a limited class: the tender, the exalted, the poign-
> ant, and, in general, the sympathetic . . . Wit, play of intellect,

stress of cerebral muscle had no place: they could only hinder the
reader's being 'moved' – the correct poetical response.   (NBEP, p. 16)

Such poetry in its concentration on feeling alone was unable to
explore the complexities of life, and thus the operation of intelligence was barred from poetry, so that the intelligent were either
discouraged from poetic practice or, if they wrote poetry, expressed their intelligence in other spheres.

Conversely it is in his criticism that Eliot himself justifies his
poetic practice by presenting it as a return to a poetic in which
intellect and feeling were fused. As we have seen, according to
Eliot such poetry disappeared in the seventeenth century when
something 'happened to the mind of England' and a 'dissociation
of sensibility set in'. As I noticed in Chapter 2, the idea of a
historically located change in sensibility was not Eliot's alone, but
shared by T. E. Hulme and W. B. Yeats among others. Frank
Kermode in his chapter on the dissociated sensibility in *Romantic
Image* has commented on the difficulty of deciding precisely when
such a loss took place (both Hulme and Yeats dated it earlier than
did Eliot); under pressure, an undissociated sensibility emerges as
being as elusive an entity as an organic society, remaining stub-
bornly just beyond one's grasp. However, Kermode stresses the
value of the notion as an enabling fiction for symbolist poetry
which sought immediacy and extolled the image as an embodiment
of otherwise inexpressible complexities of meaning.

The notion is central to Leavis's criticism, and not least,
perhaps, in the justification it might seem to provide for his style
of critical discourse; for his rejection in the debate with Wellek of
what he regarded as a language appropriate to philosophy in favour of a language which was concrete and particular, and which
allowed poetry to body forth its meaning.

One of the obvious attractions for Leavis of the theory of a
dissociation of sensibility is its resemblance to the idea of the loss
of the organic society. At a glance it might seem to function as the
individual equivalent to that universal social doom. However, it
was Yeats and not Eliot who insisted on a logical connection
between Unity of Being and Unity of Culture. Leavis's lack of
interest in Yeats's ideas may have been because he dated the
advent of the dissociation of sensibility earlier than did Eliot. Yeats
also castigated urban mercantilism rather than the advent of the

machine as the source of modern ills, a view unlikely to appeal to one of Leavis's antecedents.[5] Perhaps more importantly, although Eliot's version of the event restricts itself, or can be restricted, to the sphere of the narrowly cultural (Eliot himself links it with the victory of puritanism), it has the advantage of being less carefully worked out than that of Yeats, and is therefore more easily accommodated to Leavis's own thinking. Despite the apparent precision of dating which locates the dissociation in the seventeenth century, in almost the same breath Eliot declares that this shift in the quality of experience 'is something which had happened to the mind of England between the time of Donne or Lord Herbert of Cherbury and the time of Tennyson and Browning'. It is something that 'set in', rather than the precisely accomplished fact it appears to be in other contexts, and is therefore quite easy to assimilate without too much thought to the notion of the loss of the organic community. Eliot's version of the idea is helpful precisely because it *is* vague, and what he has to say functions primarily as a description of what poetry ought to be like rather than as an historical account of English literature. This is apparent in his movement from a description of the way in which his archetypal undissociated poet, Donne, thinks, to his famous prescription for all poets:

> When a poet's mind is perfectly equipped for its work, it is constantly amalgamating disparate experience; the ordinary man's experience is chaotic, irregular, fragmentary. The latter falls in love, or reads Spinoza, and these two experiences have nothing to do with each other, or with the noise of the typewriter or the smell of cooking; in the mind of the poet these experiences are always forming new wholes. (Eliot, *Selected Essays*, p. 287)

If the dissociation of sensibility is to be defined as an historical event, and one 'affecting the mind of England', then Eliot's position seems inescapably contradictory since it is impossible to see how he could suppose that he and other twentieth-century poets were absolved from the fate of those of the seventeenth century and their successors. Since Eliot is a poet forging a justification for a new poetic rather than an academic writing literary history the contradictoriness of his position is not too important. For Leavis, however, it must be a factor to be reckoned with, since he produces two major books which rewrite literary history using Eliot's ideas. To a point, his high estimate of the figure of The Poet – an expansion and elaboration of Richards's definition which he quoted in *Mass Civilization and Minority Culture* – suggests that he may be able to avoid Eliot's predicament:

> The potentialities of human experience in any age are realized only by a tiny minority, and the important poet is important because he belongs to this . . . his power of making words express what he feels is indistinguishable from his awareness of what he feels. He is unusually sensitive, unusually aware, more sincere and more himself than the ordinary man can be. He knows what he feels and knows what he is interested in. He is a poet because his interest in his experience is not separable from his interest in words; because, that is, of his habit of seeking by the evocative use of words to sharpen his awareness of his ways of feeling, so making these communicable. And poetry can communicate the actual quality of experience with a subtlety and precision unapproachable by any other means.   (NBEP, p. 19)

Leavis's definition of the significant poet differs from that of Eliot in its stress on the poet's possession of qualities of a kind which, on the whole, we would be inclined to class as moral virtues, albeit virtues which are closely related and quite narrowly restricted; sensitivity, awareness, sincerity, individuality (and this last seems to gain the status of virtue by the company it keeps). It is also worth noticing that individuality is something to be attained only by rare beings, so that in Leavis's scheme of things humanity is suggested as something to be aspired to rather than securely possessed.

Even more important to Leavis's picture is the interpenetration, the fusion of language and awareness within the poet. It is not so much that the poet is better able to express his feelings than others, rather, it is that his very use of language contributes to his awareness. His search for the right words is, in fact, a self-searching, an exploration. It is through this exploration-by-language, too, that the poet is able to break down the post-seventeenth-century insulation of feeling from intellect (or so, I think, Leavis implies), for it is 'by the *evocative* use of words' that the poet seeks 'to *sharpen* his *awareness* of his ways of *feeling*' [my italics].

The third important aspect of Leavis's definition is that he presents the poet as representative of his age, as realising the potentialities of that age. However much he or she may surpass their contemporaries, they cannot transcend history, or not, at least, by evading implication in their own time. As representative, the poet realises what is possible at a particular moment, and in so doing is able to extend the range of possibilities for others by extending the boundaries of the language of the time, by making explicit and realised what before was only implicit and potential.

The activity of poet as poet, then, is necessarily heuristic; as much to do with the creation of meaning as with its communication. It is because of this capacity to create, to realise new states of being, that the poet is potentially able to overcome a dissociation of sensibility, to attain, that is, something approaching a proper individuality. At the same time, however, because the poet is rooted in a particular time and place, his or her movement toward such individuality may be incomplete or abrupted; and, of course, some periods are more inimical than others to the development and recognition (and the two activities are closely related) of authentic poets. Although the psychological and moral powers Leavis attributes to poets go some way to clearing up the apparent self-contradiction in Eliot's position, his high estimate of their capacities raises a new question: if poets, by definition, have the capacity to overcome their dissociation, why is it that on Eliot's and Leavis's reading so few poets since Donne have managed to do so? Leavis's answer to this unacknowledged question lies in his estimate of Milton's poetry, and in his account of the nature of poetic convention.

Although in his rejection of Milton Leavis was defined by many as a lone and eccentric figure, it should be pointed out that at the time of writing *New Bearings* and *Revaluation* he was in good company. He himself refers to Eliot's critical asides, and to Middleton Murry's criticisms in *The Problem of Style*. Although Eliot's first sustained, and very critical, essay on Milton did not appear until 1936, the year in which *Revaluation* was published, his comments in 'The Metaphysical Poets' and 'John Dryden' are less than favourable for he claimed that the dissociation of sensibility was aggravated by the influence of Milton and Dryden, and that out of their influence arose 'the sentimental age' in which thought and feeling were obstinately separated. In the latter essay Eliot not only defined Milton as 'our greatest master of the *artificial* style', but lapsed into something approaching the satirical with his comment that Milton 'has elected a perch from which he cannot afford to fall, and from which he is in danger of slipping'. Murry's criticisms anticipate both Eliot's and Leavis's sustained attacks on Milton's relation to, and effect on, the English language, and consequently on its poetry: 'Milton was a great artist in language; he, too, won a victory over the English tongue, but I do not know that he greatly enriched it, and I have felt many times in reading *Paradise Lost* and *Samson Agonistes* that he all but killed it'.[6]

In *Revaluation* Leavis too mounts his main attack on Milton's language; the drift of his criticisms is always toward showing the detachment of language from feeling, which for him includes sensory experience. Milton 'exhibits a feeling *for* words rather than a capacity for feeling *through* words'(and in this he does not conform to Leavis's definition of the poet) and 'commonly the pattern, the stylized gesture and movement, has no particular expressive work to do' (R, p. 46). This lack of expressiveness, Leavis argues, is to do with the 'remoteness of Milton's medium from any English that was ever spoken', from 'speech that belongs to the emotional and sensory texture of actual living and is in resonance with the nervous system . . . the Grand Style barred Milton from essential expressive resources of English that he had once commanded' (R, p. 51). Leavis's criticisms are made from an organicist, expressivist point of view demanding of literature that it should be a bodying forth of a complex of emotional and physical feelings and impulses ('embody' is a favoured critical term in Leavis's vocabulary). His stress on the centrality of speech in conveying 'the sensory texture of actual living', on speech's 'resonance with the nervous system' (one notes here the way in which certain aspects of I. A. Richards's thought are in the process of being assimilated into Leavis's own scheme of things) is one that persists throughout his criticism, and is as important for the critic as for the poet. Leavis saw reading aloud as a way of enforcing his judgements, for reading aloud is a re-enactment, a recreation of the poet's complex state: 'It is impossible to enforce a judgement about rhythm by written analysis', he generalises in his note on *Samson Agonistes* (R, p. 64). The spoken word, for both poet and critic, is essential to convey full meaning. Significantly, the pejorative adjectives he uses of Milton's verse are 'mechanical', 'stiff', 'lifeless'.

In Leavis's judgement, then, the remoteness of Milton's poetry from the rhythms of speech entails that it should be thin in texture and crude in sensibility. The charge of crudeness brings in a moral dimension, and Leavis's criticisms move from poetry to man, or at least to man as he is constructed by the poetry, providing an incidental gloss on what Leavis means by 'intelligence', a word which in his usage extends beyond the mere operation of the intellect: 'His strength is of the kind that we indicate when, distinguishing between intelligence and character, we lay the stress on the latter . . . He has "character", moral grandeur, moral force; but he is . . . disastrously single-minded and simple-minded' (R, p. 58). As the analysis continues Leavis's tone becomes increasingly moralistic, and Milton is convicted of 'a dominating sense of righteousness', a 'complete incapacity to question', and 'a guileless unawareness of the subtleties of egotism' (R, p. 58).

That Leavis was not alone in his estimate of Milton suggests that the latter's dethronement was felt to be necessary as a modernist poetic came to be established. The conflict was between antithetical sets of values, and Leavis's detailed criticisms express more clearly than those of Murry and Eliot the values implicit in the poetics of modernism. Interestingly, the inexorable drive toward the moral emerges in this context as having as much to do with the high value placed on the recreation of complex sensory, emotional, and intellectual states as on Richards's psychological theories. Indeed, the latter's theories might themselves be seen as a description of the new poetic rather than as a prescription for poetry of all persuasions.

To emphasise Milton's shortcomings is not, however, to account for the destructive effect he is envisaged as having had on subsequent poetry; not, that is, if Leavis's (and not Leavis's alone) high estimate of The Poet is to be accepted. It is here that notions of poetic convention and preconceptions of the poetic offer the possibility of explanation although both problems and solutions remain implicit and therefore difficult either to challenge or to expound without the risk of distortion. It seems, however, that a model of development supplements that of revolution, and that history, abolished by the notion of the dissociation of sensibility (which necessarily makes all history since the seventeenth century the manifestation of one characteristic), is allowed to return.

On Leavis's account every age has preconceptions about the

poetic. These are largely unconscious, and the more powerful for being so. When these preconceptions result in poetic conventions that have lost touch with the reality they ostensibly define then they hamper poetic creativity and need to be overthrown. Leavis argues that the malaise he detects in the poetry of the forty or fifty years previous to his writing can be traced back to preconceptions of the poetic prevalent in the Romantic era. Such preconceptions, first formulated by Joseph Warton in 1756, excluded complexity and the play of intelligence as characteristics of pure poetry, privileging instead the sublime and the pathetic. The all-too-representative Milton plays the dual role of instigator and beneficiary of this preconception, for Warton establishes the line of descent within the canon from Spenser through Shakespeare to Milton, and by this grouping foregrounds certain qualities in the first two poets which are consonant with a Miltonic connection while excluding others which are not, and in this way lends their authority to the Miltonic conception of the poetic. In one aspect the adoption of this poetic has to be seen as a severe limitation since it issues from a dissociated sensibility. However, the conventions to which it gave rise were such as enabled the Romantic poets to break out of the Augustan social ethic and explore more individual states of feeling and being; but then nineteenth-century society in its turn produced new challenges which the prevailing preconceptions were unable to meet so that its poetry grew increasingly remote from the realities of life, and took refuge in dream and the creation of dream landscapes. So it became divorced from the creative intelligence of the period, either because the intelligent did not write it or because they had no means of writing it intelligently. The alleged incapacity of nineteenth-century poetic conventions to confront the reality of nineteenth-century society was held by Leavis to continue and intensify in the earlier twentieth century, and he has nothing but scorn for most practitioners and critics – hence the flat, deliberately provocative opening sentence of *New Bearings*, 'Poetry matters little to the modern world'. For him, the modern interpretation of the Victorian mode 'manifests itself . . . in a complacent debility . . . and technical liberation . . . takes the form of loose, careless, unconvinced craftsmanship' (NBEP, pp. 25–6). Within this environment, 'To make a fresh start in poetry . . . is a desperate matter', and Eliot's role is seen as that of the liberator, the poet who can alter our preconception of the past and redeem the time. More or less implicit in *New Bearings* is the assumption, central to Leavis's scheme of things, and voiced with great force in *Mass Civilization and Minority Culture*, that in order for poetry to flourish it must have an intelligent and knowledgeable audience, for without such an audience the wrong valuations are made, and the best poetry, if not unappreciated, is appreciated for the wrong qualities.

It is in the context of the ideas I have just sketched – ideas about the nature and function of the poet, tradition and the canon, poetic convention, the dissociation of sensibility – that Leavis's judgements of individual poets, and the relations he sees between different poets, are grounded. Already certain criteria have emerged: the need for poetry to engage with reality, for it to fuse intelligence and feeling, to be a means of self-exploration. Such assumptions find their elaboration, and further articulation, not as generalised statements, but within the particularity of the critical practice.

In his chapter in *New Bearings* on the state of poetry at the end of the First World War, Leavis names Yeats, Hardy and de la Mare as poets 'in general acceptance who really were considerable poets' (NBEP, p. 29), and therefore worthy of attention. Despite his adherence to Pater and aestheticism, and his prediliction for the dreamy world of the Celtic Twilight in his early work, Yeats is singled out for high praise; this is partly because Leavis saw his identification with an Irish tradition as rescuing his dream world from the realm of the purely private and merely literary; his work, that is, has links with a wider, extra-literary culture. Characteristically, Leavis's analysis moves between the literary, the moral, and the psychological. Paradoxically Yeats's early aestheticism is to some extent redeemed by 'a naïvely romantic, wholehearted practical energy' which makes something new of the convention within which the poet seeks to confine himself (NBEP, p. 32). Yeats is praised both for his honesty and his power of mimesis in his acceptance of reality in *The Green Helmet* and subsequent poems, where his verse 'belongs to the actual, working world' and is described as being 'in the idiom and movement of modern speech'. His poetic development is defined, in medico-moral terms: 'It is like an awakening out of drugs, a disintoxication; the daylight seems thin and cruel' (NBEP, p. 41). Surprisingly, given the high praise Leavis bestows on Yeats's poetry, character and intelligence – he describes him as having 'a magnificent mind and less than the ordinary man's capacity for self-deception' (NBEP, p. 40) – he discusses the poet in terms of waste, of dissipation of energy, holding that 'His poetry is little more than a marginal comment on the main activities of his life' (NBEP, p. 44), and cites Yeats's own formulation of the dissociation of sensibility to prove his point. The final judgement seems perverse, not merely because of Leavis's reiterated high praise, but also in the light of Yeats's very considerable oeuvre, and his almost obsessive revisions of his work. Quite clearly *he* did not regard his poetry as a marginal activity. In Leavis's contradictory attitude we seem to have theory and particular observation at war with each other, and despite all Leavis's insistence on the primacy of the particular observation, theory triumphs. The specific case is made to submit to the procrustian general rule. A lot is at stake, though. The brilliantly intelligent, energetic and honest, though ultimately failed poet can function as a measure of what has been lost, and the emptiness of our civilisation for 'if the poetic tradition of the nineteenth century had been less completely unlike the Metaphysical tradition Mr Yeats might have spent less of his power outside poetry' (NBEP, p. 42). The message is clear, if not quite clearly stated: Yeats, with all his gifts, with all his concern for Unity of Being and an undissociated sensibility, fails in the end, or puts his real energies elsewhere because the poetic conventions within which he works are dominated by dissociation.

The statement I have just quoted suggests an even more pressing reason for Leavis's valuation, for to have given Yeats's poetry its due and proper praise would have been to discredit his (Leavis's) assertion that the poetic tradition inherited from the Romantics was incapable of revitalisation and of speaking to us of our condition; but to discredit *that* assertion would also call into doubt the whole idea of a dissociation of sensibility. Again, to recognise Yeats as an important and central *modern* poet could well involve a different valuation of Eliot's poetry, for the tendency would be to look for connections between the two. In that case, Eliot's relation with the past might be conceived as something more complex than mere repudiation, but then this would have made of him not precisely the poet whom Leavis at this point admired so much. Leavis himself, after a virtual silence on Yeats until the publication of *Lectures in America* (1969), betrays his unease with the poet, though not, ostensibly, for the reasons I suggest. In the significantly titled 'Yeats: The Problem and the Challenge' he suggests the need to come to 'a bold and precise' estimate of the poet, but produces a rather muffled and evasive account, padded out with reminders of the time limits within which he has to operate, and with a rather long autobiographical description of his encounters with the early Yeats. Within this account the poet's significant oeuvre is almost confined to three poems; the Byzantium poems and 'Among Schoolchildren'. Works before the publication of *The Tower* are seen to belong within the Victorian tradition, those after to be distinctively modern. The suggestion is of a significant break, but there is also recognition of continuity. With hindsight 'one saw that there had been a development into such command of expression as implied, for consummation and *raison d'être*, a modern major poetry' (NBEP, p. 62). The possibility that Victorian conventions could be remade seems to be accepted here, but what is granted is removed, partly by the paucity of works deemed to be significant, and by a final implication that in the end Yeats is most important as a symptom, for 'Yeats's career poses the insistent questions of the place, part and possibility of the major artist in modern civilization' (NBEP, p. 81).

Leavis seems to feel himself on safer ground with de la Mare and Hardy, the poets with whom Yeats is linked in *New Bearings*. His estimate of the poetry of de la Mare is couched in almost exclusively moral terms, for despite his claims for its subtlety and its status as exquisite minor poetry he represents it as something devious: 'The apparent recognition is not the frankness it pretends to be but an insidious enhancement of the spell, which is more potent to soothe and lull when it seems to be doing the opposite' (NBEP, p. 49). As a consequence of such moral surrender, 'the dream takes on a nightmare quality; and the unwholesomeness of the fantasy habit is, implicitly and explicitly, admitted' in the later work (NBEP, p. 50).

Leavis presents Hardy as something of a sport, as a soon to be extinct relic of the organic society: 'Hardy was a countryman, and his brooding mind stayed itself habitually upon the simple pieties, the quiet rhythms, and the immemorial ritual of rustic life' (NBEP, p. 55). As such, and as a writer within the Victorian tradition, he was unable to offer any kind of model for the urban and modern. His naïvety and 'pre-critical innocence' betrays itself in the very small proportion of his work that has value. Once more, Leavis's estimate is fundamentally moral:

> Hardy's greatness lies in the integrity with which he accepted the conclusion, enforced, he believed, by science, that nature is indifferent to human values, in the completeness of his recognition, and in the purity and adequacy of his response. He was betrayed into no heroic postures. (NBEP, pp. 52–3)

Whereas in his treatment of Yeats, de la Mare and Hardy, Leavis tended to emphasise the disabling convention available to these poets, he brings into play the destructive qualities of modern society in his discussion of others, who on the whole are given short shrift. Rupert Brooke is described with acerbic wit as having 'energised the Garden-Suburb ethos with a certain original talent and the vigour of a prolonged adolescence. His verse . . . has something that is rather like Keats's vulgarity with a Public School accent' (NBEP, p. 57).[7] Edmund Blunden and Edward Thomas are praised as authentic, if minor poets. Interestingly, the latter is seen as limited by reason of the very fidelity with which he displays modern limitation – he had 'a representative modern sensibility' (NBEP, p. 61).

The survey of post First World War poetry functions as an introduction to the three major poets of modernism in Leavis's scheme of things; Eliot, Pound and, with a fine disregard for historical realities, Hopkins who, although not published until 1918, had died in 1889. It is within the chapters on these poets that Leavis conveys what he values in poetry. Despite his insistence that great poetry creates its own criteria, and his stress on the crudity of attempting to define other than ostensively what is of value in it, certain preoccupations recur with remarkable frequency.

T. S. Eliot is praised almost unconditionally, for in Leavis's acceptation, his poetry 'expresses freely a modern sensibility' and 'the ways of feeling, the modes of experience of one fully alive in his own age', so 'Portrait of a Lady' is praised not only for its 'flexibility' and 'control', for verse that is both 'very strict and precise' and free and varied, but also for capturing 'the idiom and cadence of modern speech' (NBEP, p. 67). At the same time, the sustained comparison of Eliot's verse with that of the seventeenth century makes a claim for it as being more than purely mimetic.

When Leavis applies Eliot's own formulation of metaphysical poetry to 'Gerontion' – 'Sensation became word, and word sensation'
– the assumption is that our modern, dissociated world is presented to us filtered through the undissociated sensibility of the
poet. The point is enforced in the comparison of Eliot's practice
with that of Milton. Milton's words 'have little substance or muscular quality', whereas in Eliot's poetry 'the whole body of words
seems to be used' (NBEP, p. 71). This stress on the physicality of
language, which is part and parcel of his insistence on the relation
of poetry to speech, is characteristic of Leavis, as we have already
seen. Paradoxically, his stress on the inextricability of the physical
from the mental is one of the causes of his later revulsion from
Eliot. At this point however, he is able to see Eliot's poetry as
illustrating his contention that 'A man's most vivid emotional and
sensuous experience is inevitably bound up with the language that
he actually speaks' (NBEP, p. 71).

An assumption central to both *New Bearings* and *Revaluation* is
the need for the important poet both to be of his age and to
transcend it. In *Revaluation* Ben Jonson is held to achieve such
transcendence by the particular form his classicism takes, and in
Eliot's case it is by his use of the device of the persona that Leavis
sees him performing this function. 'Gerontion' is singled out for
high praise, and the persona of the old man seen as central to its
attainment of 'a really dramatic detachment' (NBEP, p. 72). The
terms in which the poem is praised suggest the depth of Leavis's
concern that poetry should interpret its age: 'projecting himself, as
it were, into a comprehensive and representative human consciousness, the poet contemplates human life and asks what it all
comes to' (NBEP, p. 72). It is such contemplation that gives
'Gerontion' 'the impersonality of great poetry'.

Eliot's use of personae was important to Leavis for another
reason, as the word 'impersonality' implies, for at this stage in his
criticism he accepted Eliot's notion of the impersonality of art, of
the distinction to be made between 'the man who suffers and the
mind which creates'.[8] However, his comments on *The Waste Land*
already suggest an underlying unease with the notion. In Leavis's
eyes that poem is at the outer edges of impersonality; 'it would be
difficult to imagine a completer transcendence of the individual
self', he claims, and describes the poem as 'an effort to focus an
inclusive human consciousness' (NBEP, p. 80). The terms in

which he describes the subject of the poem, however, suggest that such an attempt at inclusiveness might lead to a too close mimesis, a reproduction of chaos, rather than an understanding of it:

> The traditions and cultures have mingled, and the historical imagination makes the past contemporary; no one tradition can digest so great a variety of materials, and the result is a break-down of forms and the irrevocable loss of that sense of absoluteness which seems necessary to a robust culture.   (NBEP, p. 78)

Ash-Wednesday and 'Marina' were poems that Leavis consistently admired throughout his long career, and his attitude toward them, particularly the former, raises interestingly the problem of belief identified by Wellek in his criticisms of *Revaluation*. The terms of praise which Leavis, the free-thinker, uses of *Ash-Wednesday* and the *Ariel Poems* are important; he describes the poetry as particularly modern in its concerns, and remarkable for 'the strange and difficult regions of experience that it explores'; 'the modes of feeling, apprehension, and expression are such as we can find nowhere earlier', he claims (NBEP, p. 109). Even more important to notice is his conflation of form and content: 'For the poet "technique" was the problem of sincerity' (NBEP, p. 99), and he gives a fine account of Eliot's movement toward a new understanding in *Ash-Wednesday*, toward a non-paraphraseable reality:

> He had to achieve a paradoxical precision-in-vagueness; to persuade the elusive intuition to define itself, without any forcing, among the equivocations of 'the dream-crossed twilight' . . . the repetitive effects . . . suggest a kind of delicate tentativeness. The poetry is itself an effort at resolving diverse impulses, recognitions, and needs.   (NBEP, p. 99)

Such an account of the poem seems to establish Eliot as, in I. A. Richards's phrase, 'the point at which the growth of the mind shows itself', and to reinforce the idea that great poetry is almost necessarily heuristic. It seems, above all, to privilege form, form in the sense of praxis, over content, and at this stage Leavis, Richards and Eliot all adhered to this position. It was not so much the business of poetry to teach doctrine as to enact states of being. However, content cannot be so simply dismissed, as Leavis recognises in his next chapter when he takes issue with Eliot's lack of concern over the content of Pound's *Cantos*. The difference here between Leavis's position and Eliot's is that Eliot implies that a separation between the two is possible, that there is no necessary connection between them, whereas Leavis takes a completely organicist stance; if technique is an instrument for sincerity then form and content are inseparable. The unexpected difficulty with this position, however, is that to collapse the distinction between form and content is in fact ultimately to do away with, or at least seriously undermine, the importance of form, and to make content the determinant of acceptance or non-acceptance, as Leavis was eventually to do with *Four Quartets*, with Blake's prophetic books, and with Lawrence's novels. The process by which this state of affairs comes to pass is somewhat paradoxical, for Leavis's and Richards's position seems to begin by privileging form; what is of value is exploration, a wrestling with the complexities of belief – that is, with praxis. The implication is that there is no room in this scheme for the poetry of belief or statement. Given Leavis's insistence, however, that poetry is to engage with the realities of life, then the demand for poetry to be heuristic is a statement about the way things are. The realities of life, that is, as Leavis understands them, preclude any simple, achieved belief, and so poetry that is not exploratory in form, poetry that seeks to affirm, is finally untrue to life, and because of that, the less poetry. The logic of Leavis's position here works itself out later in his career until content finally becomes of central importance in his submission to Lawrence.

Leavis's estimate of Pound is couched in terms, both favourable and unfavourable, that have become familiar. He writes, in relation to *Hugh Selwyn Mauberley*, of 'a pressure of experience, an impulsion from deep within', and his expressionist stance is further revealed in his description of the verse, which is 'extraordinarily subtle, and its subtlety is the subtlety of the sensibility that it expresses' (NBEP, p. 115). *Mauberley* is praised, too, for its reflection of modern culture and its impersonality which Leavis describes as that of great poetry. Limiting judgements on Pound (and Leavis rejects Eliot's high estimate of the poet), concern his aestheticism – 'Mr Pound's main concern has always been art' – and Leavis's mocking tone contains a strong undercurrent of chauvinism. Pound's devotion to the aesthetic is described as being 'accompanied by intense seriousness: Mr Pound is not an

American for nothing' (NBEP, p. 117). Leavis's concern with Pound's nationality (and with Eliot's when that poet lapsed from favour) is part and parcel of his demonising of America as the epitome of a rootless society, and his criticisms of Pound's *How to Read* (appearing both in *Scrutiny*, and as an appendix to *Education and the University*) emphasise how little Pound's proposals for a syllabus are rooted in any culture.[9] Pound's ultimate limitation in Leavis's eyes, however, is that he is in danger of succumbing to the world he portrays. Such a succumbing is described as a moral shortcoming for 'To compel significant art out of that plight needed the seriousness, the spiritual and moral intensity, and the resolute intelligence that are behind *The Waste Land*' (NBEP, p. 129).

What Leavis has to say both of Gerard Manley Hopkins's poetry and of that poet's relations with Robert Bridges illuminates what might seem to be little more than quirks and prejudices elsewhere in his writing. In dealing with Hopkins Leavis is more than usually in the grip of the organic, so in commenting on Hopkins's insistence that his poetry needs to be read with the ear, he adds, 'and with the brains and the body' (NBEP, p. 136); his stress throughout is on both the physicality of the poetry and the need for the critic's intelligence to match that of the poet. Hopkins's difficulty is a matter of his use of language, for 'every word in one of his important poems is doing a great deal more work than almost any word in a poem of Robert Bridges' (NBEP, p. 134). Leavis sees Hopkins's distortions of the language to which Bridges objected so much as a kind of creativity, a sign of growth, and suggests that his innovations are inseparable from 'his own direct interest in the English language as a living thing' (NBEP, p. 139). His stress is all on the materiality of the language, and the point is enforced by frequent comparisons between Hopkins's poetry and Shakespeare's. Hopkins is also declared to be decisively at odds with any Miltonic poetic.

One of the features that Leavis admires in the poet is his lonely, isolated stand, his capacity to insist, despite the criticisms of Dixon and Bridges, that his poetic practice had validity. Leavis saw that capacity as being strongly allied with the exploratory quality of his poetry: 'This skill is most unmistakably that of a great poet when it is at the service of a more immediately personal urgency, when it expresses not religious exaltation, but inner debate' (NBEP,

p. 147). Leavis, with all the partisan generosity we might expect of
him, castigated Bridges for his condescension toward Hopkins; he
is seen as the dead hand who attempted to suppress the poet, first
by his incomprehension when Hopkins needed his understanding,
and then by limiting public recognition of his poems through
delaying publishing them, by his alterations to them, and by his
comments on them. The indictment is savage, but the attack is
more than personal, for Bridges's adverse judgements are seen to
stem from his classicism. Classics, the senior partner of English
within the university, was the object of Leavis's scorn. He saw
Classics, the signifier of culture at that time, the source of 'correctness' with its rules of prosody and grammar, as fundamentally
alien; its rules were not rooted in the English language, but imposed upon it, and therefore demanded no more effort than the
learning. The ambience of classicism, being composed of a concern
with correctness, comprehensibility and decorum, being unrooted
in the culture, was unable either to recognise the new or to produce it. (It must be stressed that Leavis was speaking of the
classicism of his time for, as we shall see, he held a quite different
view of the Classicism of some of his favoured poets).

For Leavis the modernist revolution was established because
Eliot the essential modernist, had the support of his predecessor,
Hopkins, the one Victorian poet from whom development was
possible, and his lesser contemporary, Pound. These three, despite
the smallness of the minority who could appreciate them, seemed
to guarantee a future for poetry. The Eliotic achievement,
however, entailed a rewriting of the past, beginning in *Revaluation*
with his bid 'to define, and to order in terms of its own implicit
organization, a kind of ideal and impersonal living memory' (R,
p. 2). Both his arrangement of poets, the relations he sees between
them, and those he chooses to exclude from discussion, shed further light on his critical priorities, and expose problematic areas in
his practice.

Leavis's reordering of the past in *Revaluation* is perhaps primarily notable for his exclusions. Declaring his aim to be 'strict
economy' rather than 'exhaustiveness' he begins his account with
the seventeenth century, 'because I can do all that I want to do
without going back earlier' (R, p. 4), but even then his account of
the progress of poesy is far from complete. It is easy to accept some
of his claims that exclusions are strategic; he omits Donne and

Dryden because enough has been done on them, and Shakespeare because he is too big. Spenser's importance is acknowledged, but he 'is too simple a fact to need examining afresh' (R, p. 5), and his relations with Milton are said to be sufficiently conveyed in Leavis's asides. Given that in *New Bearings* Leavis has identified the vitiating line of descent as passing from Spenser through Shakespeare to Milton, and given Spenser's presumably secure habitation of an undissociated sensibility, the omission smacks of some disingenuousness, particularly since Spenser, in contrast to Shakespeare, never figures as more than a kind of marker buoy in the tracing of a tradition. Could it be possible that Leavis's coupling of him with Milton would, under examination, become the downfall of the theory of the dissociation of sensibility as an historical event?

Leavis's exclusion of Tennyson and the Pre-Raphaelites is upon grounds other than strategy. It is rather that their verse, not offering 'any very interesting local life for inspection' is not a particularly suitable subject for 'the critical method of this book' (R, p. 5). This judgement is, of course, the obverse of the praise we have met in *New Bearings* for poetry that embodies complexities of experience, for poetry which uses the whole body of words; but its negative formulation opens the possibility, dismissed by Leavis, that his method may indeed be limited in a damaging way. After all, the poetry of Chaucer and Langland, to which he pays a rather superficial lip service, frequently gains its effects by other means which are not always susceptible to a Leavisian analysis.

Leavis's method of ordering what he *does* deem worthy of discussion is co-ordinate with his critical values, for he stresses his reliance on the concrete, on the exemplary, in the communication of his arguments; he also suggests that the organisation of his material emerges from the various subjcts themselves, and from their relations with one another.

A chapter, 'The Line of Wit' (essentially a review of *The Oxford Book of Seventeenth Century Verse*), is followed by chapters on Milton and Pope, and chapters on Wordsworth, Shelley and Keats follow the next chapter, 'The Augustan Tradition'. The two general chapters are said to provide a context and background for the chapters on specific authors, but there is no such context for the Romantic poets whom Leavis declares to be essentially unconnected with one another. This declaration throws some light on his idea of the 'concrete'. His use of the word is quite distinctive, and, used of critical method implies, as we have seen, a process of exemplification, a reference back to the poem. But 'concrete', applied to a poem, or some feature of a poem, is (more often than not) an epithet of approval. In both uses the sense of the word is something like 'closeness to the thing delineated'. What is *not* implied is any attempt to anchor the poetry of the Romantics in any kind of historical materiality. The attachments that Leavis considers worth discussion are purely formal (we are reminded of his classification of Hopkins as a modern poet), and not to do with the implication of the poets in a shared world, or their confrontation of the same events. This practical neglect of history goes with the cerebral quality I have already noticed as distinguishing Leavis's idea of culture, but it seems to weaken his assertion of the necessity for rootedness in the sense he gives the word and his insistence in *Education and the University* on the need to go beyond the literary and into the study of history and related subjects.

In his first chapter, 'The Line of Wit', Leavis challenges the Spenser–Shakespeare–Milton configuration he saw as so harmful by outlining an alternative genealogy where Shakespeare is associated with a line beginning with Donne and Ben Jonson and moving through Carew and Marvell to Pope. This genealogy not only marginalises the Tennysonian connection, but, by associating Pope with the Metaphysical tradition, frees him from his customary association with Dryden, and therefore with prose and the social ethic of the Augustans. 'Elegy to the memory of an Unfortunate Lady' becomes an important text here, for Leavis is able to stress Pope's capacity for emotional response through it. Crucial to the new configuration is not only Pope's association with Metaphysical wit, but also with the classicism of Ben Jonson. Leavis's comments on Jonson are an important locus within the whole body of his criticism, for they spell out a means by which the individual poet may be able to transcend the limitations of even an overwhelming social ethic and enter into 'an ideal community' (R, p. 19) through his naturalisation of poets of the past. Eliot's definition of tradition is a ghostly presence, felt even in the detail of the phrasing:

Jonson's effort was to feel Catullus, and the others he cultivated, as contemporary with himself; or rather, to achieve an English mode

that should express a sense of contemporaneity with them . . . In it
the English poet, who remains not the less English and of his own
time, enters into an ideal community, conceived of as something
with which contemporary life and manners may and should have
close relations.   (R, p. 19)

As always with Leavis, the stress is on the need for the poet or
critic to work out of his or her own experience, to make – and the
ambiguity here is important – the past present. As so often, despite
Leavis's hatred of theory, connections can be made with theories
popular at the time. The insistence of the philosopher, Hans-
Georg Gadamer on the need for prejudice in the process of understanding the past seems to have affiliations with the Leavisian-
Eliotic position. Gadamer's notion that we may understand the
past only by means of our preconceptions, and that such understanding is not the recapturing of an objective state of affairs, but a
fusing of horizons, parallels Leavis's rejection of the empiricist
position held by many of his contemporaries.[10] At the same time it
needs to be stressed that Leavis's enterprise is almost the reverse
of Gidamer's, for Jonson's classicism, defined as the product of a
literary sensibility operating on the past, is seen in part as a gateway into the life and manners of the present. Through it the poet
is able to attain an *English* mode, 'consciously urbane, mature and
civilized' (R, p. 19). As Leavis defines it, Jonson's classicism,
translated into the idioms of English, and suggesting the possibility of making an art out of living, is set in opposition to
Milton's which is characterised by its concern for mellifluousness,
and its pleasure in words and grammatical constructions alien to
English. Fittingly, Pope is placed with Jonson and separated from
Dryden and other Augustan poets. Dryden 'is the voice of his age
and may be said to have, in that sense, responsibility' (R, p. 33); he
has, however, no resistance to the powerful social ethic of his day,
no vantage point such as the classicism of Jonson and Pope, and so
surrenders to the ethic completely, and in doing so, confirms and
strengthens it.

Although the dissociation of sensibility is invoked as a phenomenon to explain the development of poetry, there is no attempt to
explain the phenomenon itself. Leavis's list of features that ought
to be brought into play – 'Social, economic and political history,
the Royal Society, Hobbes . . .' – does not suggest deep thought.

However, one factor, the decay of court culture, is insisted upon, and accounted for by the deracination entailed by the Interregnum, by its, at first, forcible separation from country-house culture in 'the period of disruption, exile and "travels"'. Leavis continues:

> The cheaper things remind us forcibly that to indicate the background of Restoration poetry we must couple with the Court, not as earlier, the country house, but the coffee-house, and that the coffee-house is on intimate terms with the Green Room.   (R, p. 34)

One feels Jonson's 'To Penshurst' behind this observation, a poem which in its very writing is a rich symbol, since it creates in opposition to those houses 'built to envious show' the ideal society which it celebrates. Penshurst, an ideal to set against a less hospitable reality even in Jonson's day, by Dryden's time has been lost *as* ideal in Leavis's scheme of things, and the physical deracination of the Court attended by a moral and cultural deracination of which Rochester's isolated individualism is evidence. It is worth noticing how, in this account, notions of an undissociated sensibility and an organic society reinforce one another by association, without any causal connection being established between them.

Leavis's chapters on Pope and on the Augustan tradition insist both on the poet's implication with his society, and on his transcendence of it. Leavis sees Pope's wit as a reconciliation of the Metaphysical with the polite, and argues that he is as much the last poet of the seventeenth century as the first of the eighteenth (R, p. 71). It seems to be by virtue of his membership of an older tradition that, in the quality of his insight, Pope is deemed to transcend the purely social mode of Augustanism and invest it with a moral, even a religious force, for 'When Pope contemplates the bases and essential conditions of Augustan culture his imagination fires to a creative glow that produces what is poetry even by Romantic standards. His contemplation is religious in its seriousness' (R, p. 83). There is a move toward theorising the relationship between literary convention and social reality when Leavis claims that 'The development was in English life, and the "correctness" of Pope's literary form derives its strength from a social code and a civilization' (R, p. 76).

Despite the forthrightness of his opening, what Leavis has to say of the Augustan period as a whole is curiously elusive. However, his initial claim that the rejection of nineteenth-century poetic values 'has not rehabilitated the eighteenth' encourages an attempt to capture his drift in the vulgar positives he takes care to eschew. The chapter attacks the *Oxford Book of Eighteenth Century Verse* as representing in its selection a weak by-line rather than that poetry which shows the strength of the period; it shows, that is, permutations on 'the various Miltonic strains – blank-verse and those derivative from the minor poems' (R, p. 105). The implication is that this by-line is the poetry favoured by the Augustans themselves who, cut off from the past, as Pope (seemingly alone) was not, created a society with values belonging to the 'realm of manners' and 'a polite social mode' (R, p. 113). Revealingly, Leavis speaks of the favoured poetry as being directed 'to the "outer ear" – to an attention that expects to dwell upon the social surface' (R, p. 113). Whatever the value of the social, and Leavis sees considerable value in the Augustan construction of it, it is to be distinguished from the moral which is inseparably linked with the internal, the intuitive, the physical. The Augustan limitation, the lack of a positive moral sense, shows itself in Swift's writing: 'In the absence of the superficial Augustan urbanity the Augustan assurance lies exposed as a spiritual poverty, its hollowness brought out by Swift's very force' (R, p. 110). Linked with Leavis's mistrust of what he saw as the purely social mode of most Augustan poetry is his disagreement with T. S. Eliot's assertion that poetry should 'have the virtues of good prose', for to privilege prose is to privilege the social, the reign of 'Reason', logic and common sense (R, p. 123); in effect the assertion can be seen as a denial of the heuristic, for what can be said clearly and grammatically is the already-thought, the familiar and the accepted.

For Leavis the important poetic line in the eighteenth century passes through the Metaphysical non-Miltonic Pope to Johnson who, seemingly paradoxically, achieves the moral through his very literariness. The paradox, however, is seeming only, for Johnson's 'feeling for a literary order', like Pope's membership of an earlier tradition, is the means by which he is able to transcend the merely social. Some of the terms in which Leavis praises Johnson seem to suggest a departure from his previously expressed values by his acceptance of Johnsonian generalisation. However, such generalisation is suggested, by a submerged metaphor, 'weight', to be anchored in experience, to proceed from the concrete. Crabbe, the final recipient of Leavis's praise as being in the right relation to Augustanism, is seen as a late-comer, his sensibility belonging 'to an order that those who were most alive to the age . . . had ceased to find sympathetic' (R, p. 128).

The new leaders were the Romantics, and Leavis discusses the work of Wordsworth, Shelley and Keats in his final chapters. Despite his explanation of his practice, Leavis's neglect of the background to their work, and his resistance to seeing any relations between the poets, seems to undermine the claims made elsewhere for the importance of the mutual interaction between poets and their audiences. It is, perhaps, partly because Wordsworth and Shelley are treated so much in the void that Leavis's criticism takes on an even stronger than usual psychological-moral emphasis.

Leavis's 'revaluation' of Wordsworth consists of an attack on the conventional scholarly estimate of him as either a philosophical poet or a nature poet, neither of which estimates, according to Leavis, can be satisfactory to those who 'really' read him, 'Who read him as they read contemporary literature'. Instead, Leavis praises Wordsworth's 'preoccupation with sanity and spontaneity', a preoccupation which he sees as being invested with a religious force. By contrast, the use of Hartleian philosophy in his poetry 'had not the value he meant it to have'. Leavis describes as 'unfortunate' the connotations of the phrase, ' "poet of Nature" . . . suggesting as it does a vaguely pantheistic religion-substitute' (R, p. 164). He remarks sharply 'Wordsworth's preoccupation was with a distinctively human naturalness, with sanity and spiritual health, and his interest in mountains was subsidiary' (R, p. 165). To my mind this view contains revealing inconsistencies and distortions: given the high value he places on critical intelligence, can he really find Wordsworth so admirable if he believes him to be misguided in the valuation of his own work, and can such a mistaken valuation produce a consistency and stability likely to be found admirable? Why is it necessary to associate an interest in nature with pantheism? Is implication with the natural world to be so easily dismissed as 'an interest in mountains'? These defects suggest a need to rewrite Wordsworth according to Leavisian principles and help to account for the absence of context in

Leavis's treatment of the poetry, for intellectual and physical contexts need to be obliterated if Wordsworth is to be drawn into the fold.

Leavis's attempts to show how little Wordsworth is a philosophical poet are lengthy, but not particularly effective, and at times the poetic baby seems in danger of being poured out with the philosophical bathwater. To describe the verse as giving 'the effect of a subtle, pervasive and almost irresistible dissuasion from effort' (R, p. 155) is to run the risk of recalling similar comments which in other contexts function as severely limiting judgements.[11] There is also much recourse to long quotation, though without the telling attention to significant detail that makes Leavis at his best so compelling, and which, in other contexts, would be used to justify a characteristically firm judgement about the rival merits of two versions of a passage from *The Prelude*; 'No one is likely to dispute that the later version is decidedly the more satisfactory'.[12] Instead, the first version is rejected because it *is* philosophical, and its phraseology 'technical' – 'the parts afterwards omitted merely incite to an attention that the argument will not bear' (R, p. 158). However, Leavis makes no attempt to show how the argument *is* weak, and Wordsworth's consequent revisions are attributed to his 'poet's touch', as distinguished from his intellectual acumen. In his comments on another passage from *The Prelude*, Leavis's determined assaults on Wordsworth's philosophical capacities lead him, first to throw doubt on the poet's sincerity, and then into what looks like a strange misreading in order to prove either that Wordsworth was not interested in thinking logically, or was unable to argue:

> By an innocently insidious trick Wordsworth . . . will appear to be preoccupied with a scrupulous nicety of statement, with a judicial weighing of alternative possibilities, while making it more difficult to check the argument from which he will emerge, as it were inevitably, with a far from inevitable conclusion'. (R, p. 162)

In the passage in question (1805–6 version, Book 2, 396–418) Wordsworth, having described his preference for associative, anthropomorphising thought which he regards as 'more poetic' than 'analytic industry', continues:

Coercing all things into sympathy,
To unorganic natures I transferr'd
My own enjoyments, or, the power of truth
Coming in revelation, I convers'd
With things that really are, I, at this time
Saw blessings spread around me like a sea.
Thus did my days pass on, and now at length
From Nature . . .
I had receiv'd so much that all my thoughts
Were steep'd in feeling . . .

Although it is difficult to tell, presumably Leavis wants 'thus' to mean 'consequently', 'therefore', and so to confer an argumentative structure on the passage in order to quarrel with it. But 'thus' surely means 'in this way', 'like this' and Wordsworth is describing, and not causally accounting for, a state of affairs. His stress is upon the richness of his life at that point rather than on the causes of that richness which, he speculates, could stem from revelation of truths external to him, or from his anthropomorphising habits. The implication is that the cause is not particularly important. Why is it that Leavis's reading of the passage is directed toward undermining Wordsworth's capacity for philosophical thought, and what is it about his philosophical thought that provokes Leavis's hostility? In this particular case it cannot be in its capacity as a mode of argument, for the mode is simply not there. Much of the content of the passage, too, seems likely to be congenial to Leavis, for Wordsworth's earlier account of the creative process as the 'observation of affinities/ In objects where no brotherhood exists/ To common minds' is consonant with both Richards's and Eliot's formulations. Yet again the objection to 'philosophy' suggests itself as a refusal of any kind of relativism. Wordsworth's stance – cerebral, detached from the experiences he recounts – presents itself as a danger. It is a stance that can be justly described as philosophical, for the poet takes cognizance of the existence of different views of reality, and in this particular passage is not prepared to adjudicate between them. Such relativism, inherent in philosophical practice, is inimical to Leavis, for despite his recognition that different societies have different values, implicit in his writing is the sense that beyond these differences there is a morality that is finally shared by and demonstrable to the favoured minority. I think this is why he displays a mistrust of the capacity of words to express states of feeling with sufficient precision, for they gesture toward a reality that ultimately transcends them, and one which the sensitive can feel on their pulses. Ultimately, the test for great poetry is physical, sensational – hence the centrality of 'embody', 'enact' as critical terms. To separate poetic from philosophical language is to assert the former as a master code, as one capable of speaking of that which lies beyond and contains philosophy, whereas to bring together the poetic and the philosophic in the manner of the Romantics is to articulate in cerebral terms some of Leavis's own positions, and in doing so, define them as *positions* rather than the touchstone of reality.

Leavis's insistence on the inappropriateness of describing Wordsworth as a 'poet of Nature' is in one important aspect a justifiable refusal to countenance large talk about the poet's pantheism, but in view of his concern with rootedness and with the organic community, it is surprising that Leavis makes little attempt to explore and redefine the label. He insists instead upon the poet's profound moral preoccupations, as though these precluded any implication in the physical, natural world. Although Leavis acknowledges that Wordsworth's best poetry springs from his contact with his childhood and youth, and describes him as lapsing into the Anglican, public poet when that contact has been lost, he seems not to grasp the centrality of the physical environment to those early experiences. Yet the apprehension of the natural world (which is a moral apprehension at the same time) in a poem like 'Nutting' is integral to the mode of experience conveyed, just as 'Michael' shows physical and moral rootedness as not to be ultimately separable in Wordsworth's understanding. It is as if Leavis's, the town-dweller's, belief in the importance of the rural and the organic is ultimately cerebral, and not grounded in experience, as is suggested by his frequent quotation of the constantly peripatetic Lawrence (who was so contemptuous of Eastwood and, indeed, England), 'Thank God I am rooted as the tree is rooted'. Significantly Leavis describes Wordsworth as being 'rooted', not in a physical landscape, but in a cultural tradition, 'Wordsworth's roots were deep in the eighteenth century' (R, p. 174).

Leavis's attempts to enforce Wordsworth's importance as a moral poet seem curiously unsuccessful, partly because he tends to quote from the letters rather than the poetry, and partly because his biographical bias is so strong. He begins by contrasting Wordsworth with Lawrence and Shelley in order to emphasise Wordsworth's distinctive qualities, and, picking up Shelley's description of the poet in 'Peter Bell the Third' as 'a kind of moral eunuch', takes the absence of sexuality in his work as a way in to understanding 'an aspect of Wordsworth's importance' (R, p. 169). He links this absence to Wordsworth's understanding of spontaneity, elucidated by quotation from the letters and the *Preface* which are glossed in order to separate the quality from any association with the primitive and instinctual. Wordsworth's is 'the spontaneity supervening upon complex development, a spontaneity engaging an advanced and delicate organization. He stands for a distinctly human naturalness; one, that is, consummating a discipline, moral and other' (R, p. 170). Wordsworth's importance, then, lies in his capacity to subsume sponteneity without loss under other aspects of life, to see it as an outcome of, rather than an aberration from, past patterns. Sexuality, in this reading, can then be contained within an order, may, indeed, be ignored as irrelevant to some important purposes, and 'The absence both of the specifically sexual in any recognizable form . . . serves to emphasize . . . the significance of this achieved naturalness' (R, pp. 170–1).

Leavis's account of Wordsworth's development (or decline) is predominantly biographical-psychological. He takes as self-evident his estimate of the later poetry, and proceeds to account causally for what he judges to be its quality. On his account, Wordsworth's detached poise is hard-won and precarious, for his 'course had not been steady', he had known extremities of feeling. While his emotional pain drove him back to the experiences of childhood and youth, 'the hiding-places of my power', he was able to produce great poetry, but as time passed and his need for order grew stronger he lost touch with that significant past and became a 'Miltonizing' public poet. Arising from this account, and contributing to it, are Leavis's constructions of the poetry. The description of the Wanderer in Book 1 of *The Excursion* which emphasises the character's 'equipoise' is 'fairly obviously, very much in the nature of an idealized self-portrait' (R, p. 178); the 'disturbing' 'poignancy' of *Margaret; or, The Ruined Cottage* is associated with Wordsworth's memories of his affair with Annette. At the same time, Leavis veers toward seeing Wordsworth's 'problem' as general as well as personal: 'if (and how shall they not?) the sensitive and imaginative freely let their "hearts lie open" to the suffering of the world, how are they to retain any health or faith for living?' (R, p. 178). Suggesting as it does Leavis's identification with what he conceives to be some aspect of Wordsworth the man, the comment is revealing, for such identification may have its connections with his treatment of the poetry.

Leavis's judgement of Shelley is notoriously and devastatingly hostile, and raises, as Wellek saw, the question of the effect of the critic's beliefs upon his judgement, although perhaps not so simply and centrally as Wellek believed. Quoting and commenting on Eliot's confession that he found Shelley, once a favoured poet, unreadable, Leavis insists that this unreadability is not to do with Shelley's being out of fashion, neither is it to be accounted for by his beliefs, as Eliot suggests.[13] Leavis asserts that beliefs are beside the point, although his dismissive phrase, 'idealistic ardours and fervours', suggests that they cannot be entirely ignored: '. . . when one dissents from persons who, sympathizing with Shelley's re-volutionary doctrines, and with his idealistic ardours and fervours – with his "beliefs", exalt him as a poet, it is strictly the "poetry" one is criticizing' (R, p. 204). The quotation marks around 'poet-ry' suggest that the alternative to doctrine is not to be recourse to any simple formalism. Rather, they leave the way open for a fresh definition of what attention to the poetry might involve. Leavis begins by suggesting that what is characteristic of the best poetry is also characteristic of the worst; there is 'a general tendency of the images to forget the status of the metaphor or simile that intro-duced them', which is part of an 'essential trait', Shelley's 'weak grasp on the actual'. As Leavis describes it, the poetry 'depends for its success on inducing . . . a kind of attention that doesn't bring the critical intelligence into play' (R, p. 207). These comments are literary critical; at the same time they are capable of gaining a moral dimension in an enlarged context, and do so as Leavis moves inevitably toward the moral and psychological characteristics es-sential to his idea of the poet. Interestingly, because this is new, he distinguishes between literary criticism and moral judgement, seeing Shelley's poetry as demanding 'The transition from the lighter concerns of literary criticism to the diagnosis of radical disabilities and perversions, such as call for moral comment' (R, p. 216). The implication is that Shelley is a special case in his provocation of moral judgement. Literary and moral criticism in this case cohere and support one another, and perhaps this is what makes the essay one of Leavis's most successful and influential. It is also notable that in his use of Wordsworth as a standard of comparison Leavis seems to come closer than he has previously done to demonstrating the literary qualities of that poet.

One of Leavis's central concerns is with Shelley's lack of capacity to order his perceptions and material (and here we may remember the horror Leavis expresses at what he conceives to be a social world in which the customary patterns and landmarks have disappeared), hence his mistrust of, even when they are successful, those images that 'forget the status of the metaphor or simile which introduced them' (R, p. 206). He links this literary phenomenon with Shelley's notion of spontaneity as it emerges from the poet's definitions of 'inspiration' in *A Defence of Poetry*, and contrasts Shelley's insistence on its momentary nature with Wordsworth's anchoring it within the whole order of a life. Spontaneity is thus claimed to be divorced from intelligence in Shelley's poetry, and this divorce is responsible for his 'weak grasp on the actual'; 'there is nothing grasped in the poetry – no object offered for contemplation, no realized presence to persuade and move us by what it is', he claims (R, p. 210). By contrast, we have 'the sureness with which Wordsworth grasps the world of common perception' (R, p. 212). However, it is clear from later comments that Leavis sees Wordsworth's grasp as extending both to 'the world as perceived' and to 'inner experience' (R, p. 214). Leavis's realist position might seem to be less simple, then, than Wellek claimed. His position is not entirely consistent, though, for later he differentiates Keats from Shelley by noting the former's 'strong grasp upon actualities – upon things outside himself' (R, p. 261). The 'actual' in this use is confined to being some external, definable entity, and there is no suggestion that it could include any inner state.[14] Leavis's complaint that there is nothing 'to *persuade* and *move* us by what it is' [my italics] seems to be precisely focused on poetic capability, as is his contrasting comment on Wordsworth, who 'seems always to be presenting an object . . . and *the emotion seems to derive from what is presented*' (R, p. 214) [my italics]. In other words, Wordsworth, unlike Shelley, is able to find an objective correlative to convey his emotion. Shelley 'at his best or worst, offers the emotion in itself, unattached, in the void' (R, p. 214). At the same time, the judgement does not confine itself to

use or non-use of an objective correlative, but makes some allowance for the direct expression of emotion – Wordsworth is able
to 'grasp surely . . . inner experience' – but this is by virtue of his
capacity to place it within the order of his life. It is through this
concentration upon the literary that Leavis moves toward his
sharply moral judgements of Shelley, while still maintaining touch
with the poetry. A physical revulsion seems to underly what can
only be called the savagery of his judgements, a recoil from the
erotic and the emotional. Shelley's fascination with 'emotion in the
void' gives rise to a habitual 'fondled vocabulary' betraying
'viciousness and corruption' (R, p. 215). The emphasis is all on
Shelley's self-indulgence which is as much a moral as a poetic
concern – 'corruption' is one of Leavis's favoured words here –
and Shelley's refusal of thought is described as 'sinister' as Leavis
focuses on the poet's 'ability to accept the grosser, the truly corrupt gratifications that have just been indicated' (R, p. 221). The
reiterated moral judgement is that Shelley in nearly all circumstances is his own hero/heroine, indulging in corrupt fantasising,
and that such moral inadequacy gives rise to bad poetry and worse
drama, for it precludes any sense of the dramatic, any capacity to
allow objects or characters an independent existence. Hence the
failure, in Leavis's eyes, of *The Cenci*. The play is unedifying
fantasy which, because of its lack of grip on an emotionally realised
situation, produces verse replete with echoes and plagiarisms from
Shakespeare and Webster.

As with Wordsworth, Leavis offers a psychological and literary
account of the poet. Shelley's inadequacies come from his being
undirected and unloved as a child so that, 'driven in on himself he
nourished the inner life of adolescence on the trashy fantasies and
cheap excitements of the Terror school' (R, p. 227). The literary
tradition in which he began to write was unfavourable in the stress
it placed on emotion, and the repression and injustice of society
'must, in its effect on a spirit of Shelley's sensitive humanity and
idealising bent, be allowed to account for a great deal' (R, p. 228).
In the light of this last comment, the terms in which Leavis praises
'England in 1819', 'The Mask of Anarchy' and 'The Triumph of
Life' seem to suggest a somewhat cursory interest in the influence
of contemporary politics on Shelley's work.

Apart from this last lacuna, Leavis's essay on Shelley seems to
be an almost exemplary demonstration of a revaluation strictly

dependent upon those principles he adhered to at the time. Within its scope he is able to hold the literary and the moral together, and to show their interdependence without collapsing the one into the other. Although at times there are suggestions, as Wellek alleges, that he confuses distaste for Shelley's beliefs with distaste for his poetry, he most frequently justifies his low estimate of the poetry on less tendentious grounds.

After removing Keats from the hands of the biographers and insisting that 'the chief relevant discipline' is the literary critical, Leavis's revaluation is intent on rescuing him from the category of aesthete into which the Victorian poet and critic, Arthur Symons, had placed him. Leavis's energies are directed toward showing that, despite Keats's luxuriance, his revelling in sensation, he had finally too firm a grip on life, too much vitality, and a moral strength too strong for him to remain a mere aesthete. Taking issue with Symons's criticism that 'Ode to a Nightingale' lacked structure, Leavis distinguishes between structure and organic form, and compares the poem to Shelley's 'Skylark', to the latter's disadvantage, bringing out the movement in the poem from one part to another, and setting individual felicities within the context of the whole work. The familiar Leavisian virtues – 'concreteness', 'realization', 'sureness of grasp', 'complex organism', which are contrasted with 'poetical outpourings' and 'ecstatic "intensity"' – recall the opposition set up between Wordsworth and Shelley in the previous chapter, and in Leavis's reading of the Ode the literary qualities he extols are those which impel Keats away from his original revelling in luxury into the somewhat cold light of reality. The terms in which Leavis praises Keats's achievement are significantly similar to those he used of Yeats in *New Bearings*. In both cases the poetic mode to be escaped from is described as a drug, and the poetic progress must move through the 'thin unreality of the disintoxicated, unbeglamoured moments that the addict dreads' (R, p. 248). In both cases, too, the poet is seen as having the capacity to conquer his addiction by virtue of his vitality, a vitality which is at war with his overt purposes. Organic form has its tentacular connections with the human order, the order of a whole life previously attributed to Wordsworth, and, like Wordsworth, Keats is implicated in a real world. Of Keats's 'tactual effects' in his 'Ode on Melancholy' Leavis comments, 'they express, not merely the voluptuary's itch to be fingering, but that

strong grasp upon actualities – upon things outside himself, that
firm sense of the solid world, which makes Keats so different from
Shelley' (R, pp. 261–2). Leavis sees Keats's 'grasp upon actualities' as manifesting itself in the critical intelligence shown in the
letters and 'in the perfection attained within a limiting aestheticism' in the 'Ode to Autumn' (R, p. 264). Necessarily the achievement is moral as well as literary and 'remarkable intelligence and
character are implied in that attainment' (R, p. 264).

By contrast, whatever the qualities of the earlier 'Ode to a
Nightingale' and 'Ode on a Grecian Urn', their limitations, Leavis
suggests, can be discerned in Keats's influence on nineteenth-
century aestheticism and its preoccupation with fantasy and ritual
– and Leavis's language here conveys not merely a distaste for
aestheticism but for Catholicism too, as though the Huguenot
blood which Leavis acknowledged was stirred: 'There is a sacred
hush, and an effect of candles or of light through stained glass, of
swinging censers and of rites before a veiled altar' (R, p. 256).
Such an atavistic response may be not irrelevant to his later attitude toward Eliot.

What supervenes between the two earlier Odes and the 'Ode to
Autumn' is Keats's attempt at the revised *Hyperion* with its new
induction which alone, in Leavis's judgement, shows a new life.
However, the terms in which he praises the induction are surprising, for he describes the verse as having 'an evenly distributed
weight – a settled and quite unspringy balance', even 'a kind of
inertness' (R, p. 269). The criterion which Leavis uses here is the
expressiveness of the verse, the expressiveness of a profoundly
moral state of being which has been achieved through great intellectual and moral discipline, so that the poetry, although impelled
by Keats's pain, attains 'the profoundest kind of impersonality' (R,
p. 271). Part of the discipline, the moral growth, Leavis stresses in
his quotation of Keats's letters is the poet's rejection of Milton in
order that English should be 'kept up', and his recognition that
Miltonic poetry is 'the verse of art'. For Leavis, the poet's development takes on the aspect of a Yeatsian withering into the
truth, a truth that is both artistic and moral. Fittingly *Revaluation*
ends where *New Bearings* started, with the dethronement of
Milton, though with no conclusion to draw the threads together.

It is worth returning at this point to Wellek's criticism that
nowhere in *Revaluation* does Leavis state his ideal of poetry, and

Leavis's subsequent refusal to accept that he has one. Wellek, abstracting from Leavis's own writing, produced the following:

> . . . your poetry must be in serious relation to actuality, it must have a firm grasp of the actual, of the object, it must be in relation to life, it must not be cut off from direct vulgar living, it should not be personal in the sense of indulging in personal dreams and fantasies, there should be no emotion for its own sake in it, no afflatus, no mere generous emotionality, no luxury in pain or joy, but also no sensuous poverty, but a sharp, concrete realization, a sensuous particularity. The language of your poetry must not be cut off from speech . . .[15]

Despite Leavis's recurring praise for all these features he is still able to reject them as the 'norms' Wellek wishes him to acknowledge, and it seems to me that he is right in doing so, for at times he praises what is dissonant with one or the other of them. However, he is wrong to declare that he has no preconceived position. His position, of course, is not ostensibly about poetry, but about the nature of the poet, about the poet's need to have, or to strive toward, an undissociated sensibility, and to be, while implicated in society, yet detached from it. But a body of poetry constructs its poet, no less than the poet constructs *it*; it constructs a persona or, if one prefers, a persona is abstracted, detached from, the amalgam of qualities that make up the historic individual. The poet who appears in the poetry, then, is an amalgam of what we might call literary modes and devices. When these modes and devices allow us to infer a creator who fuses intelligence and feeling, or one who by the operation of wit is able to maintain a detached yet serious stance toward his or her reality, Leavis is able to discuss the poetry in the appropriate literary critical terms and to show its strengths, but with such poetic conventions as those of the Romantics and late Victorians his preoccupations cause him difficulties, for he takes the poetic persona as the whole person.[16] This difficulty is not particularly apparent in his discussion of Shelley because his dislike is such that the inadequacies of the poet can be demonstrated from what he considers to be the inadequacies of the poetry. His approach remains literary critical. However, the violence of his moral repugnance is an indication of his concern with poet rather than with poem. It is also attributable to the account he gives in his reply to Wellek of what is involved in reading a poem, 'Words in poetry invite us not to "think about" and judge, but to "feel into" or "become" – to realize a complex experience that is given in the words' (S5, p. 60). To read a poem is to enter into the experience of another person, to have that experience enacted within oneself, and it is because of this that a poet can be described as corrupting. The difficulties inherent in Leavis's position become more obvious in his dealings with the poets whom he admires or acknowledges to be outstanding, but who write within a convention he rejects; he has comparatively little to say of Yeats; and Wordsworth and Keats, both of whom he admires, are treated, not as poets – not, that is, primarily in terms of their poetry, but as men whose lives are relevant to their poetic creation. The poetry is thus treated primarily as a record of psychological and moral struggle rather than as art form making use of a given set of conventions. Leavis sees the conventions of Romanticism as such that the poets must be detached from full participation in them (Wordsworth is seen as belonging to the eighteenth century because of 'his essential sanity and normality') or able to transcend them by virtue of their moral strength. Ultimately, it seems, one cannot be a good Romantic poet, although moral worth may allow one to throw off Romanticism's shackles.

It is notable, too, that the scheme by which Leavis organises the canon does not at this point take prose into account. This omission probably has more than one cause. Remarking in 'How to Teach Reading' (EU, p. 125) that 'criticism of the novel has hardly yet begun' Leavis registered the difficulty of applying the methods of practical criticism to a form of writing so much more diffuse than poetry. Perhaps more importantly, the novel, that latecomer to literature, seemed to have no place within a schema of literary history based on the hypothesis of a seventeenth-century dissociation of sensibility. As we shall see, Leavis found in his later writing both a critical method that satisfied him, and a theoretical place for 'the incomparable achievement' of the novel, defining it as the dominant form in post-Romantic literature, and tracing a line of descent 'running from Blake . . . through Dickens to D. H. Lawrence' (LP, p. 101).

The map of English poetry which Leavis constructed in *New Bearings* and *Revaluation* was expanded and qualified in some of the essays in *The Common Pursuit* (1952), a collection of miscellaneous pieces and reviews covering a period of nearly twenty years, and including some of Leavis's most famous and influential work. The book contains two pieces on Hopkins; one on the letters, the other on the poetry. The latter, with its stress on Hopkins as a Victorian poet, shifts the focus of the earlier *New Bearings* usefully. It also raises, yet again, the question of the importance of a poet's belief to a critic's appreciation of the poetry: 'Hopkins is the devotional poet of a dogmatic Christianity. For the literary critic there are consequent difficulties and delicacies' (CP, p. 48). In this particular context Leavis is able to admit that a poet's alien belief poses him a problem but, it is important to notice, the situation is saved because of the form taken by that belief, a form which itself can count as a belief in which Leavis shares, for the philosophy of Duns Scotus 'lays a peculiar stress on the particular and actual, in its full concreteness and individuality, as the focus of the real' (CP, p. 48). Hopkins, like his chosen master, is concerned with the individuality of things. He celebrates his faith, that is, through a realisation of the physical world. There is also a group of pieces on eighteenth-century writers. A fine essay on Pope's *Dunciad* places the poet once again in the Metaphysical tradition. In 'Johnson and Augustanism' Leavis suggests obliquely and tantalisingly a sense of identification with the earlier doctor. Mentioning the 'abnormality' of Johnson's character, he says of Johnson's 'so-called "dogmatism" ', 'I myself, when I hear this dogmatism spoken of, recall his own distinction: "what I have here not dogmatically but deliberately written . . ." ' (CP, p. 100). The phrase, ' . . . not dogmatically but deliberately . . .' appears as the epigraph to the first chapter of his previous book, *The Great Tradition*. The essay 'Johnson as a Poet' is an impressive demonstration of Leavis's capacity to accept his own dictum that great writers create their own criteria for judgement, for despite his emphasis on complexity, and on enactment of meaning he is able to describe 'The Vanity of Human Wishes' as great, although it is 'a poetry of statement, exposition and reflection' (CP, p. 118). It is worth noticing, however, that Johnson is conceived of as in some sense departing from the reader's expectations. There may not be, in a strong sense, rules or norms which govern our poetic judgements, nevertheless norms, expectations, preferences help to constitute those judgements.

An important essay, 'The Irony of Swift', which in its concern with prose, eludes my present categorisation, may perhaps be mentioned here as having a subject belonging historically with those I have just mentioned. As well as providing a luminous account of the intricacies of Swift's writing the essay is of interest because of Leavis's evaluation of him as both 'a great English writer' and one who provides 'the most remarkable expression of negative feelings and attitudes that literature can offer – the spectacle of creative powers . . . exhibited consistently in negation and rejection' (CP, p. 86). The juxtaposition of its two terms, greatness and negativity, is one which Leavis finds increasingly problematic in his later writing, particularly in *Thought, Words and Creativity* where, as we have seen, he gives the word 'creativity' an almost literal force; the work of the great writer is heuristic, it has a protensive pull – it *makes* meaning rather than destroys it. Since Leavis comes to equate this process of meaning-making with a distinctive intelligence, it is significant that even as early as 1934 he concludes the essay with the comment, 'We shall not find Swift remarkable for intelligence if we think of Blake' (CP, p. 87).

Also in *The Common Pursuit* is a group of essays about Shakespearean drama which formed part of an attack in *Scrutiny* upon the largely character-based explication of Shakespeare of which A. C. Bradley was the leading proponent. The attack was led by L. C. Knights in an essay, *How Many Children had Lady Macbeth?* Knights insisted that 'character' was something created by the reader in response to written or spoken words, and not a pre-existent entity having some kind of life beyond the text.[17] 'A Shakespeare play is a dramatic poem' was the critical formula, and the phrase, 'dramatic poem', was later used by Leavis to describe the novels he admired (he also attacked the notion that the novel was primarily concerned with the creation of lively characters).[18] Although Leavis is dismissive of Bradley and other writers whom he feels to be radically mistaken, his essays on *Othello*, on *Measure for Measure*, and on the late plays take the form of a debate with his fellow Scrutineers and function primarily as 'Yes, but . . .' responses of the kind he regarded as crucial to criticism. So, although he attacks Bradley and other critics in 'Diabolic Intellect and the Noble Hero: or The Sentimentalist's *Othello*' (1937) for their acceptance of Othello as a man 'not easily jealous' and their consequent overstating of the importance of Iago, he incidentally provides a gloss on, and corrective to, L. C. Knights's dismissal of character.[19] Commenting on the 'generally recognized peculiarity' of the play, he continues 'even *Othello* . . . is poetic drama, a dramatic poem, and not a psychological novel written in dramatic form and draped in poetry, but relevant discussion of its tragic significance will nevertheless be mainly a matter of character analysis' (CP, p. 136). He then produces a character analysis rooted in the language assigned to Othello, and described by G. Wilson Knight as the 'Othello music'.[20]

Leavis's foundational assumption that organic form derives from and testifies to a 'commanding significance' exhibits itself in 'The Criticism of Shakespeare's Late Plays' (1942) as defining his concern to illuminate a variety of Shakespearean modes. On Leavis's assumption, although *Cymbeline* and *The Winter's Tale* share romantic, fairy-tale features, it is not genre or form that would allow us to see the plays in relation to one another, but a shared significance. Without this significance, the formal resemblance is mere semblance. So, in *The Winter's Tale* 'What looked like romantic fairy-tale characteristics turn out to be the conditions of a profundity and generality of theme' (CP, p. 175), whereas in *Cymbeline* 'The romantic theme remains merely romantic' (CP, p. 176). Again, what might seem to count as the greater technical perfection of *The Tempest*, the elimination of the long time-gap to be found in *The Winter's Tale*, entails a loss and limitation, for 'With the absence of the time-gap goes also an absence of that depth and richness of significance given . . . by the concrete presence of time in its rhythmic processes, and by the association of human growth, decay and rebirth with the vital rhythms of nature at large' (CP, p. 180). Leavis's stress on the play as dramatic poem; on the importance of poetry as embodying, and making concrete, meaning; on poetry as creating character, find more general expression in 'Tragedy and the "Medium" ' (1944) in which, ostensibly taking issue with George Santayana's 'Tragic Philosophy', he attempts to define the nature of dramatic thinking.[21]

Leavis and the Novel

By the time *The Common Pursuit* was published in 1952, Leavis's attention was focused predominantly on the novel. *The Great Tradition* (1948) contained essays published in *Scrutiny* between 1937 and 1941, and after the publication of this book articles on D. H. Lawrence began to appear. These were to issue in the publication of *D. H. Lawrence: Novelist* in 1955. Although Leavis's shift of emphasis was not complete – he published on Blake, Yeats, Montale, and (repeatedly) on Eliot, and was working on Wordsworth in his last years – his new preoccupation with the novel was implicated with the place he came to assign it on the cultural map.[22]

In *The Great Tradition* his concern on the whole seems to be to construct for the novel a system of affiliations analogous with and parallel to but separate from the one he had constructed for English poetry, although his comments on the Dickens of *Hard Times* – 'there is surely no greater master of English except Shakespeare' – and his description of novels as 'dramatic poems' leave the way open for cross-genre connections.

With *D. H. Lawrence: Novelist*, however, the novel is thoroughly incorporated into Leavis's scheme of literary history, with the advantage that such incorporation allows for the possibility of postulating significant new movement. It allows, that is, for the possibility of history after the seventeenth-century dissociation of sensibility, for:

> In these great novelists . . . we have the successors of Shakespeare; for in the nineteenth century and later the strength – the poetic and creative strength – of the English language goes into prose fiction. In comparison the formal poetry is a marginal affair.   (DHLN, p. 18)

Presumably the novel in the hands of its greatest practitioners is seen by Leavis as holding together emotion and intelligence in a way no longer possible for poets. Whereas post-seventeenth-century notions of the poetic with their stress on poetry as the expression of emotion entailed that the best poets would always be in the position of writing against the grain, the novel by its very form, which is in essence an interplay of various characters, offers the possibility of providing stances which distance and qualify that of the major character. The kind of equilibrium Leavis saw as being characteristic of metaphysical poetry, with its play of one emotional position against another within the same fictive psyche, is now to be achieved through the interaction of different psyches. This displacement of emphasis from poetry to prose fiction is bound up with the displacement of T. S. Eliot by D. H. Lawrence, and a growing animus against Eliot the man makes itself felt in the limitations Leavis increasingly finds in the poetry. The difficulties his one-time mentor posed for him were various: he was at home in the social world that Leavis despised; he had, in Leavis's view, surrendered to the Establishment in his British Academy lecture on Milton in 1947 in which he distanced himself from his own former position and, consequently, from Leavis's which was an elaboration of his.[23] He was also a practising Christian, and worse to an instinctive, if non-doctrinal protestant, an Anglo-Catholic. Above all, perhaps, Eliot had remained blind to the genius of D. H. Lawrence whom Leavis came to venerate, if not to idolise. Whether one agrees with his judgement of the respective merits of the two writers, the tone in which he compares them is frequently distasteful. Although Leavis's observations on Eliot in *D. H. Lawrence: Novelist* have an unpleasant edge to them, they remain within the bounds of the legitimate:

> . . . the achievement of T. S. Eliot, remarkable as it was, did not reverse the relation [between poetry and the novel]. This is a truth that adds an irony to the insistent part played by Eliot in retarding the recognition of Lawrence. (DHLN, p. 18)

However, Leavis's comments on the two writers in *Thought, Words and Creativity* transgress the boundaries of literary criticism and move into a kind of oblique character assassination on the one hand (Eliot lacks the moral qualities Leavis defines in Lawrence), and naïve hero-worship on the other:

> . . . I want to stress . . . the ease with which he [Lawrence] got on with all kinds of casually encountered people. He got on with them so easily because he was spontaneously interested in them, and in a way that was not only inoffensive but irresistible: they were humanity and life, and *he* was obviously without pretensions or designs. This characteristic was the secret of his dramatic power . . . Eliot had no dramatic power and no ease. You can reduce his limitations to those two lacks – which themselves are closely associated. (TWC, p. 32)

More important to notice than either the mythologising bent which seems to obliterate all difference of belief and temperament in those 'people' who were 'humanity and life', or the unpleasantness of these remarks, is the tendency they betray – increasingly frequent in Leavis's later writing – to confuse and conflate writers with their works, and art with life.

However, within the pages of *The Great Tradition* Lawrence and Eliot co-exist as presences; Lawrence as the last of the great novelists, and Eliot as a critical influence. P. J. M. Robertson has described the book as straining at its seams to accommodate the 'classical' Leavis of the earlier essays with a new leaning toward the 'romanticism' of Lawrence and points to discrepancies between the criteria of the first and last chapter on the one hand, and the middle sections on the other.[24] Up to a point this seems sound. However, in the introductory chapter, 'The Great Tradition', Eliot's is primarily the critical voice one hears. Leavis's comments on tradition substantially paraphrase Eliot's:

> . . . Jane Austen . . . exemplifies beautifully the relations of 'the individual talent' to tradition. If the influences bearing on her hadn't comprised something fairly to be called tradition she couldn't have found herself and her true direction; but her relation to tradition is a creative one. She not only makes tradition for those coming after, but her achievement has for us a retroactive effect . . .   (GT, p. 5)

The definition is that of *New Bearings* and *Revaluation* and, as in those books, the tradition is to be discerned through its significant members. Once again Leavis insists that literary history is essentially evaluative, and argues that, because of the popularity of the nineteenth-century novel, 'it is well to start by distinguishing the few really great' writers who, like the great poets, 'change the possibilities of the art for practitioners and readers' (GT, p. 2). There is, perhaps, a shift of emphasis from that of the earlier books in Leavis's continuation of his definition: ' . . . they are significant in terms of the human awareness they promote; awareness of the possibilities of life' (GT, p. 2). Such phrasing suggests the possibility of a more direct intervention of literature into individual lives than the rather more guarded pronouncement in *New Bearings* that great poets experience more consciously than others, and convey those experiences *to* others. This is perhaps the first sign of Leavis's movement toward seeing certain texts as, if not exactly enacted doctrine, at the least offering 'normative' views of life.

This dual stress on the impact great literature has on life as well as art is of a piece with Leavis's conviction that to be great a literary work must have significant life for us as well as for its contemporaries. Accordingly, he distinguishes between writers and works that fit both parts of his definition and those which offer us no possibilities of life, but which opened new artistic possibilities to their successors. Fielding and Richardson have no part in the Great Tradition for, although they helped to make Jane Austen's art possible, they have no life in the present. They are important historically, but neither is 'one of the significant few' (GT, p. 3).

It is striking how few the significant are. Jane Austen and D. H. Lawrence, the first and latest members of the group are not discussed, and Lawrence is not mentioned in the opening list. The rest are the George Eliot of *Middlemarch* and those parts of *Daniel Deronda* to which Gwendolen Harleth is central;[25] the earlier rather than the later Henry James, and the Conrad of *Nostromo*, *The Secret Agent*, *Under Western Eyes*, *Chance* and *Victory*. Dickens is almost entirely excluded – 'the genius was that of a great entertainer, and he had for the most part no profounder responsibility as a creative artist than this description suggests' (GT, p. 19). *Hard Times*, the great exception, is discussed in 'An Analytic Note' almost at the end of the book. Although Leavis is insistent that his emphasis on the very greatest is not intended to dismiss other writers and works as unworthy of attention, his prediction that he will be taken by his readers to do that very thing seems to gain credibility from the terms in which he writes of them: 'Fielding's attitudes . . . are . . . not such as to produce an effect of anything but monotony' (GT, p. 4). Although *Clarissa* is 'a really impressive work' 'the demand he [Richardson] makes on the reader's time is . . . prohibitive (though I don't know that I wouldn't sooner read through *Clarissa* again than *A la recherche du temps perdu*' (GT, p. 4).

His overt concern, however, is with the 'great tradition of the English novel' which he defines as that 'to which what is great in English fiction belongs' (GT, p. 7). The tradition, that is, is to be seen in terms of individual, discrete works and authors. When Leavis comes to define what it is they have in common that would merit use of the word 'tradition' we find once again that the moral is the foundational category, for 'they are all distinguished by a vital capacity for experience, a kind of reverent openness before life, and a marked moral intensity' (GT, p. 9). Form is defined, not in any aesthetic or Flaubertian sense, but as issuing from the writer's moral preoccupations (following Lawrence, Leavis throughout the book treats the formalism of the novels of Flaubert as fundamentally opposed to life). The 'formal perfection of *Emma* . . . can be appreciated only in terms of the moral preoccupations that characterize the novelist's peculiar interest in life' (GT, p. 8). The tradition is tradition, then, by virtue of a specific kind of moral force. It is also a tradition by virtue of the fact that its members knew and learned from each other's work; what they learned Leavis describes as 'the hardest kind of "influence" to define' since in great writers such learning entails the forging of their own originality.

Leavis's organicist, expressive notion of form, together with his sense of the novel as being inescapably implicated in life, leads to a criticism of the novel which is unrelated to normal considerations of genre. To define the novel as dramatic poem is to conflate it with Shakespearean drama and, indirectly, with poetry of the approved variety. There are really only two categories of literature for Leavis: the good and the bad, and those in the former group share the same characteristics: emotions are 'placed' in some way – brought, that is, into conjunction with thought; and themes and subjects are *embodied* in a rich and vital language. Form in this acceptation is ungeneralisable, for the form of each great work will be individual, will be a function of the writer's complex perception of life.

This practical dismissal of the relevance of genre precludes any discussion of narrative devices such as point of view, for these in Leavis's scheme of things are irrelevant to the evaluation of a work, being merely descriptive of technicalities. In his criticism the crucial test of a novel lies in the relation of author to character. In *Middlemarch* and *The Mill on the Floss*, Dorothea and Maggie function respectively as, at times, two close dream surrogates of their author, the vehicles of her unexamined and self-indulgent fantasies. If we accept this criterion, then we cannot easily counter Leavis's assertion that the adjectival insistence of parts of *Heart of Darkness* betrays a lack of authorial grasp by arguing that it is to Marlow, the narrator-actor, rather than to Conrad that this over-insistence belongs. Contrasting *Typhoon* with *Heart of Darkness*, Leavis seems to attribute the relative success he claims for the former to the absence of Marlow 'who is both more and less than a character and always something other than just a master-mariner' (GT, pp. 184–5). How little sustained argument is part of Leavis's practice shows itself in this last comment, for the presence of Marlow as narrator is hardly noticed in the lengthy discussion of the alleged weakness of *Heart of Darkness*; it is noticed, in fact in connection with the tale's predominant success, which is at least partly attributed to 'that specific and concretely realized point of view' (GT, p. 183). But *that*, of course, links with the sailor in Conrad. It is through this link that Leavis is able to conflate Marlow with Conrad, for Marlow, the 'technical function', by virtue of his 'dramatic status in the action', allows 'the author the freedom of a presence that . . . constitutes a temptation' (GT, p. 189). The maintenance of a proper distance between author and character is crucial, but the distance is an *emotional* distance, so Leavis is able to praise strong and overt authorial intervention such as George Eliot's. He describes approvingly as 'one of the distinctive characteristics of her mature style' (GT, p. 103), 'a kind of psychological notation' which accompanies dialogue and action in *Daniel Deronda*. At the other end of the scale he praises *The Awkward Age* – 'nearly all dialogue' – for its author's capacity to convey character through style, noticing wryly that this novel is unusual among James's later works in allowing its characters their own voices rather than giving them 'the author's own late style' (GT, p. 170).

As always, concreteness is a value in Leavis's eyes, so George Eliot is praised for 'the fulness and reality' of her picture of country-house society in *Daniel Deronda*, Conrad for the 'irresistible reality' of Sulaco in *Nostromo*, his 'supreme triumph in the evocation of exotic life and colour' (GT, p. 190). Such concreteness is presented at times as a function of experience, so that it is Conrad's service as a seaman that enables him to write about the Merchant Service 'from the inside'. Put like this the statement has all the irresistibility of tautology, but what Leavis means by 'experience' is not so simple as statements such as this would suggest for, while he pays tribute to the realism in *Adam Bede* of George Eliot's 'mellow presentation of rustic life (as [she] recalled it from her childhood)', he comments adversely on the lack of 'any pressure from her profounder experience' in the novel. Significant experience, then, seems to be not so much a matter of the registration of sensory and emotional impressions as the placing and understanding of events; it is a shaping activity rather than the description of whatever has befallen the passive recipient. Such an emphasis, although this may not be immediately apparent, is continuous with Leavis's rejection of one of the conventional criteria of realism: the psychological exploration of character as foundational to the novel. Quoting T. S. Eliot's dictum that a ' "living character" is not necessarily "true to life" ', he likens Conrad's *Nostromo* to Elizabethan drama, locating the impressiveness of Conrad's characterisation in 'the vivid reality of the things we are made to see and hear' rather than 'in any sustained analytic exhibition of the inner complexities of the individual psyche' (GT, p. 196). George Eliot, too, in *Silas Marner*, 'that charming minor masterpiece', transgresses the normal requirements of realism. The book has, 'in its solid way, something of the fairy-tale'. At the same time Leavis declares that the moral fable is dependent for its success on its realisation 'in terms of a substantial real world' (GT, p. 46). *Hard Times*, like *Silas Marner*, is classified as moral fable, and its lack of recognition attributed to its flouting of the normal criteria of characterisation. Leavis claims that the different modes of the novel, the different conventions it invokes at different moments, are reconciled by 'the astonishing and irresistible richness of life that characterizes the book everywhere' (GT, p. 234). Out of this richness Dickens challenges our normal sense of the real and makes us see our world differently. His art is poetic in its power of evocation.

The concreteness of *Hard Times*, it is important to notice, is not linked with the replication of an already known world. Rather, a new world, a new reality, is conjured into being through the agency of the word. Dickens's language is crucial to the success of the novel, and 'The final stress may fall on Dickens's command of word, phrase, rhythm and image: in ease and range there is surely no greater master of English except Shakespeare. This comes back to saying that Dickens is a great poet' (GT, p. 246). Such a judgement is at odds with Leavis's overall limiting estimate of Dickens which he makes earlier in the book, for a writer's revelation of himself as a great poet, even if in only one work, seems to preclude his other works being defined as no more than entertainment. If language is all-important to Dickens's achievement, then, on Leavis's own assumptions, that achievement can hardly be confined so exclusively to one work. Perhaps this inconsistency is to do with the way in which Leavis in *The Great Tradition* is still in the process of exploring his view that a poetic use of language is essentially heuristic, and that language is constitutive of both living and fictive reality.

However, Dickens is not just a master of language, but of

English, that English which is continuous with the language of Shakespeare. The specificity of Leavis's stress is important, marking the extent to which he seems to invest English with a superior creative capacity. Thus, in *D. H. Lawrence:Novelist* he remarks of D. H. Lawrence, 'he seems to me to be plainly one of the greatest masters of what is certainly one of the greatest of languages' (DHLN, p. 26). Emphasising that English was the necessary, the inevitable medium for what Conrad wanted to do, Leavis declared his earlier description of Conrad's use of English as a 'choice' to be inadequate, continuing, 'We might go farther and say that Conrad chose to write his novels in English for the reasons that led him to become a British Master Mariner' (GT, p. 17).[26]

For Leavis, the concreteness of English as a language not only gives it a peculiar status as a medium for creativity; that concreteness seems, too, to relate to the distinctive moral tradition of its literature as he has defined it. It is not that he makes the connection in any direct way; it is rather to be inferred from his tendency to make concreteness a precondition of moral significance, as in the case of *Silas Marner*. Just as Conrad's choice of English is entailed by the concreteness of the language, so the concreteness of his writing is the guarantee of its moral significance. Consequently, while Leavis acknowledges that *Nostromo* is discussible and praiseworthy in terms of Flaubertian notions of form, he sees it as transcending such notions, and its very shape is necessarily connected with Conrad's moral intensity: 'His organization is devoted to exhibiting in the concrete a representative set of radical attitudes, so ordered as to bring out the significance of each in relation to a total sense of human life' (GT, p. 30). Conversely, as is the case with Shelley's poetry, a lack of concreteness is to be associated with more reprehensible qualities. Observing that Henry James's late style 'involves for him . . . a kind of attention that doesn't favour his realizing his theme . . . as full-bodied life', Leavis continues, 'The relation between deficiency of this order . . . and the kind of moral unsatisfactoriness that we have observed in *The Golden Bowl* should be fairly plain' (GT, p. 168). The 'moral unsatisfactoriness' he identifies could be defined as a conflict in valuation between James and his readers. In Leavis's judgement the Ververs, two of the central characters in the novel, whom James treats sympathetically, are manipulative, and as ready to buy human beings as *objets d'art*. If James had made them more concrete, more real, the suggestion is, he too would have seen that they were to be disapproved of. The high value Leavis places on concreteness seems to connect, then, with his notion of teaching as a kind of showing, a demonstration of that which, once it is seen, becomes obvious. Both concreteness in writing and 'showing' in criticism assume an underlying configuration of shared values that are normative once they are exposed.

Despite all his stress on the materiality of the worlds his novelists, at their best, create, and despite his insistence that the tradition he traces is an *English* tradition, as in other aspects of his writing there is something cerebral and unanchored about the pattern Leavis constructs. He does not, on the whole – despite comments on their circumstances – give one any sense of the novelists as writing out of specific cultural and social formations. Then, too, two of the three writers treated at length are not in fact English, and are, as Leavis acknowledges obliquely, as much a product of the French tradition of the novel as the English. As he shows, Flaubert is a potent influence on both James and Conrad. At this point a paradox begins to make itself felt, for these two pre-eminent members of the tradition are so by virtue of their de-racination – James from 'that refined civilization of the old European America' (GT, p. 11) which had almost disappeared, and Conrad from Poland and his first language. They earn their pre-dominance within the ostensibly so-rooted tradition precisely because they *are* deracinated, for it is in part through their deracination that they are able to speak to our condition, to reveal us to ourselves. Commenting on the intensity with which Conrad treats the theme of isolation, Leavis remarks:

> But then a state of something like deracination is common today among those to whom the question of who the great novelists are is likely to matter. Conrad is representative in the way genius is, which is not the way of those writers in whom journalist-critics acclaim the Zeitgeist'.   (GT, p. 22)

This final qualification returns us to his discussion of modern poets in *New Bearings*, and his insistence there on the need of the great writer to do more than merely reproduce the anxieties of his time. The movement of great writing is always for Leavis a sense-making, a shaping movement taking the reader into new areas of understanding.

D. H. Lawrence and Later Criticism

Leavis begins his introduction to *D. H. Lawrence: Novelist* by associating the book with *The Great Tradition*, and the later book can be seen as a continuation of the earlier in that Lawrence is described there as the latest in the line of significant English novelists. However, Leavis himself suggests that it is different in 'feel', attributing this to 'the nearness – in more than one sense – of Lawrence' (DHLN, p. 9). That nearness emerges as not merely closeness in time. There is an emotional commitment rather different from that of the previous book. Accompanying this, there is, too, an attack on T. S. Eliot which seems to mark the end of his significant influence as a critic. In P. J. M. Robertson's way of putting it (which he takes from Leavis) Leavis has moved from Eliot's classicism to Lawrence's romanticism, and almost uniquely in his writing repudiates a previous piece of work, his essay of 1930 on Lawrence,[27] commenting, '. . . when I look at it now I cannot judge that my sense of being critically qualified was well-grounded' (DHLN, p. 9). In fact Leavis's position in this early essay, despite all the praise he bestowed on Lawrence, is not too dissimilar to that of Eliot's in *After Strange Gods*[28] (a work, incidentally, that Eliot refused to have reprinted) which Leavis was to attack so strongly in *D. H. Lawrence:Novelist*. His criticism of Lawrence's 'mechanical' vocabulary seems not too distant from Eliot's charges of bad writing, and he blames Lawrence's 'fanatical concern for the "essential"' for his 'limited' range. He finds 'something repellent about' Lawrence's attitude to sex, and speaks of 'the terrible monotony' of the religion in his later works, seeing it 'as a symptom; a refuge from the general malady rather than a cure' (FC, p. 111). There is, too, a different order of valuation between Leavis's earlier and later criticism, for in the former *The Rainbow* and *Women in Love* are judged to be inferior to 'the splendid artistic maturity of *Lady Chatterley's Lover*' (FC, p. 131), (a book he later refused to defend at the famous obscenity trial of 1960 on the grounds that it was bad).[29]

In *D. H. Lawrence: Novelist*, by contrast, *The Rainbow* and *Women in Love* are claimed to be Lawrence's 'two greatest works', and accompanying this change of valuation is a train of attendant judgements which radically alters the picture of Lawrence that Leavis drew earlier. He is now 'one of the great masters of comedy', and, 'As for anger, no sensitive and highly vital man was ever less given to it' (DHLN, p. 13). He was 'by far the best critic of his day' and 'supreme intelligence' was 'the mark of his genius' (DHLN, p. 14). His 'un-Flaubertian attitude towards life' is 'the reverence that, in its responsiveness, is courage and vitality' (DHLN, p. 128). Characteristically, works are praised for their centrality to our condition. Thus *St Mawr*, with 'a creative and technical originality more remarkable than that of *The Waste Land*' gives us what feels like 'a representative view of the civilized world' (DHLN, p. 225), and in *The Fox*, the 'fox-motive . . . is remarkable for its inevitability of truth and the economy and precision of its art' (DHLN, p. 258). The book ends by reiterating what has been an important theme throughout (and one to become central to *Thought, Words and Creativity*) the primacy of Lawrence's intelligence to his art. Interestingly, Leavis cites, to support this judgement, not a creative work but *Psychoanalysis and the Unconscious*, which he decribes as displaying 'the intelligence of the creative artist' (DHLN, p. 310).

The disparity between earlier and later judgements of Lawrence is striking, and particularly so in one as retentive of his valuations as Leavis so frequently is. In his introduction to the later book he himself suggests that his earlier view was partly a product of the unfavourable critical climate of the time when it was written, and clearly this climate cannot be discounted. By Leavis's own account, the truths we arrive at are collaborative, and we cannot step too far outside accepted values. At the same time, the vehemence of the later book, a vehemence not only visible in Leavis's support of Lawrence, but in his attacks on those he considers to have been his detractors, suggests impulses to be at work that are perhaps not adequately to be described by such a formulation as his having moved from a classical to a romantic position. The difficulty of such terms seems to me two-fold. First of all, whatever his acceptance of T. S. Eliot's critical assumptions, Leavis's conception of the great writer, as it was formulated by I. A. Richards, was essentially romantic, so that in fact there is not quite the kind of tension between the earlier and later phases of his work that the terms suggest. Secondly, the terms seem to imply, to my mind misleadingly, that Leavis's change of position was purely literary. To claim that this is not the case is to embark on an enterprise of some difficulty, for such a claim seems to involve me in making distinctions between the literary and the extra-literary that Leavis himself usually rejected.

However, even on Leavis's own terms there is a fissure in his treatment of Lawrence in *D. H. Lawrence: Novelist*, a dissonance between his treatment of Lawrence-the-man and Lawrence-the-writer, despite his attempts to assert that the two are one and the same. Lawrence the man is exalted into a prophet figure endowed with charismatic qualities and the capacity to minister to our sick civilisation, while Lawrence the writer, although extraordinarily highly valued, is yet allowed to have lapses, and the writing is intermittently appraised with some detachment. The distinction I am attempting is not sharp and clear-cut, for, as Leavis remarks in his early essay, Lawrence's 'art bears a peculiarly close relation to the man'. However, in that early essay, while recognising his assumption of the prophetic mantle in the works following *The Rainbow*, Leavis is still far from accepting Lawrence as a prophet for *him* – 'his writings are far from constituting presumptive validation of a cult' (FC, p. 127). Revealingly, however, some of his comments on *Lady Chatterley's Lover* suggest that Lawrence's art is limited by its inability to provide answers for life. Having described the art as 'beautifully poised and sure', he continues, 'criticism must take the form of the question: How comprehensive or generally valid is this solution?' (FC, p. 131). In the early work, then, writer an prophet/man seem to be held together, and on the whole the man is inferred from the work without being given overriding prominence, even though there is a rather disquieting quest for 'solutions'.

In the later book man and work seem to spring loose from one another, not only in Leavis's differing valuations of the two, but in the way in which the work seems to function at times as almost the raw material for a biography of Lawrence. The very titles of the earlier chapters suggest some such bias, for we have 'Lawrence and Art', 'Lawrence and Class', 'Lawrence and Tradition', and the first of these is largely concerned with the way in which Lawrence transmutes his own life into his work. 'A desperate personal urgency . . . provided theme and impulsion for *Sons and Lovers*', we are told (DHLN, p. 31), and Leavis goes on to ask a few pages later, '. . . what relation does Aaron bear to Lawrence himself?' This kind of approach is, of course, continuous with that of *The Great Tradition* in which Leavis takes the maintainance of a proper distance between character and writer as one of the hall-marks of success. However, at times he conceives *Aaron's Rod* as a direct reporting of Lawrence's experience, both fantasy and real; so, 'in Lilly we have a self-questioning, or experimental self-testing, on the part of Lawrence', and 'Rawdon Lilly and Tanny in their cottage . . . are unmistakably Lawrence and Frieda, and the chapter, we cannot doubt, registers the actual living relation between them' (DHLN, p. 36). The biographical tendency is pervasive; the marriage between Lawrence and Frieda is seen as a type of the relation projected between Hannele and Hepburn in *The Captain's Doll*. It is not that Leavis is uncritical of the works. He is often shrewd and interesting in his exposure of Lawrence's weaknesses, but the stress seems to me to be too dangerously on Lawrence the man as raw material for the work rather than on the works themselves, or even Lawrence as the works construct him.

Having said this, however, it is important to register that Leavis differentiates his own enterprise from that of Middleton Murry, whose interest in Lawrence he defines as being emphatically biographical, and centred on Lawrence's relations with his mother. While allowing that there are 'peculiar difficulties', Leavis claims Lawrence as 'a case for literary criticism', (DHLN, p. 146) and distinguishes a variety of relations between life and works, some of which he saw as inviting a biographical approach. Thus:

> *The Rainbow* exemplifies in a special way the peculiar Lawrentian genius: the extraordinary power of the impersonalizing intelligence to maintain, while the artist, in an intensely personal exploratory way, is actually living the experience that goes into the art, the conditions that make creative impersonality possible. (DHLN, p. 143)

However, it is not merely that Leavis sees such an approach as a function of the form of a work, although form would, on some occasions come into it. Much more important is the question of the work's quality, so that for Murry to declare himself and Katherine Mansfield to be prototypes for Gerald and Gudrun[30] is to say nothing about *Women in Love*; the book may be discussed only as art-form: '. . . the original treatment of life he was now proposing required a formidable originality of method and style' (DHLN, p. 148). The successful work renders biography superfluous, but biography in the less successful is able to describe the reasons for the lack of success. This position seems familiar and comfortable, particularly when it is taken with Leavis's assertion that 'Murry's perverse, tortured and hate-possessed Lawrence is not the whole truth, or the most important part of it' and his counter-claim of 'the serenely triumphant reign of intelligence' in some of Lawrence's works (DHLN, p. 147). What we seem to be offered is a notion of impersonality close to Eliot's, and the word 'impersonality' is used by Leavis in his next paragraph. A clear distinction is made between Lawrence the man in his daily life and Lawrence the writer as he is constructed, or constructs himself, within his work.

However, Leavis's position seems to be rather more complex than this and to envisage a transmutation of art into life corresponding to that of life into art. From what he knows of him from his works, and from biographies and memoirs, Leavis constructs a fictional (whatever the truth of the detail) Lawrence who is a hero for our times. The story Leavis tells is of a man at home with all classes of people, vitally interested in all around him; 'spontaneous', alert, 'responsible', with a 'reverence for life'. The plot is the movement from psychic suppression to liberation through the act of writing. *Sons and Lovers* is an 'emancipating triumph of intelligence' which enables Lawrence to overcome to some extent 'the too-close relation established with him by his mother' (DHLN, p. 46). Out of this misfortune – 'What, for a genius, *is* misfortune?' Leavis exclaims – he is subsequently able to create in all its impersonality the relation between the child Ursula and her father in *The Rainbow*. Moreover, the intelligence which Lawrence uses to escape his own plight is such as to give him 'diagnostic insight' into the ills of our civilisation; his preoccupations are 'hygienic', 'normative'. The space between the artist who creates and the man who suffers has closed, and the prophet has been born. This prophet is necessarily a fiction. It is a fiction, moreover, to which its author is rather too close (we remember his comment on 'the nearness – in more than one sense – of Lawrence'), occupying a place in Leavis's psyche analogous to that which he ascribes to Dorothea or Maggie Tulliver in George Eliot's, as is betrayed by his extensive comparison of Vronsky and Anna with Lawrence and Frieda in 'Anna Karenina'.[31] It is a closeness that shows itself in Leavis's adoption of a vocabulary answering to that of

Lawrence, a vocabulary heavily value-laden and somewhat fervid, in which events and people are variously 'wonderful', 'profound', 'vital', 'irresistible', 'spontaneous' and 'affirmative'.

Leavis's tendency to hero-worship Lawrence produces a criticism that is strangely mixed. As he claims, Leavis does indeed engage in literary criticism, and in some of his best in places, bringing out Lawrence's capacity to portray pre-conscious states, his symbolism, his methods of shaping his novels. 'Truth' and 'reality' are words which appear frequently, and words that perform a valuable critical function, for it is a condition of the success of such writing as Lawrence's that it should take us up into its world and convince us while we are reading. However, there is a distinction to be made between the 'truth' and 'reality' we attribute to a work of fiction, and the truth to be attributed to a prophet, and Leavis's conflation of the two, as for instance in his juxtaposition of passages from *Psychoanalysis and the Unconscious* with a discussion of Gerald Crich's character and role in *Women in Love*, serves to make Gerald symptomatic and exemplary outside the confines of the novel. Such a tendency also betrays itself in some of the favoured vocabulary I mentioned earlier. Words like 'normative', 'diagnostic' and 'hygienic' seem to me to be uneasy members of the literary/critical lexicon. When Leavis presents us with relationships and emotions which we are to take as normative and self-validating because of the power of Lawrence's writing then, to borrow Frank Kermode's terminology, an enabling fiction is being invested with all the dangerous, potentially destructive power of myth.[32]

In a footnote in *The Great Tradition* (GT, p. 10), and again, later in the book, Leavis describes James as belonging to an American as well as to an English tradition. The decisive figures in this other tradition were the originary figure, Hawthorne, to whom James was indebted in his early work, James himself, and Melville. Around the time he was producing those essays on Lawrence which were later to become *D. H. Lawrence: Novelist* Leavis also produced some work on this new topic. In 1952 'The Americanness of American Literature', a review of five volumes of American literary history written by Van Wyk Brooks, appeared in an American periodical, *Commentary*, and in the same year he contributed an introduction to the American critic Marius Bewley's *The Complex Fate*. In 1955 he wrote an introduction to the Zodiac Press edition of Mark Twain's *Pudd'nhead Wilson*. A review of letters and essays of Ezra Pound, which has some relevance to these other pieces appeared in *Scrutiny* in 1951.[33]

Both the review in *Commentary* and the introduction to *The Complex Fate* attack American attempts to define a literary tradition independent of English origins, the 'idea that the true American tradition derives from the West' away from 'the Anglicizing dominance of New England and the East' (AK, p. 146). Instead, Leavis endorses Bewley's identification of the significant tradition as residing in Cooper, Hawthorne, Melville and James (adding on his own account Mark Twain to Bewley's list), as opposed to 'the collocation of Whitman, Dreiser, Scott Fitzgerald, and Hemingway' (AK, p. 154). The issue here is continuity, of course, and Leavis's and Bewley's great American writers are placed with their English counterparts as 'the successors of Shakespeare' (AK, p. 145). It is axiomatic for Leavis that the necessary condition for good writing is a mature and flexible language. It is also axiomatic that America, with its waves of immigrants, is a Spenglerian megapolis in which culture cannot flourish. So it is that Dreiser 'represents the consequences of the later influxes from Europe and the sudden polyglot agglomeration of big raw cities, and may with some point be said to belong to the culturally dispossessed' (AK, p. 155). Because of his felt need for rootedness in the past Leavis stresses the sophistication of Twain's writing, dwelling on his literary antecedents and refusing attempts to locate him in the American frontier tradition. Americanness of the kind he and Bewley object to is described, somewhat paradoxically, as provincial, and the American experience is used increasingly to account for writerly inadequacies. So 'the admirable American energy and disinterestedness and generosity that were his [Pound's] virtues carried with them certain attendant disabilities' (AK, pp. 163-4). The major 'disability' Leavis identifies is Pound's incapacity to understand with any inwardness the constitutive role of language to a culture. This shows itself in Pound's attitude to foreign literature and in the violence of some of his writing, and is suggested finally to be continuous with the brutality of his anti-semitism (AK, pp. 163-4). In 'The Americanness of American Literature' Leavis suggests that Pound has an inadequate conception of culture 'as something apart and aloof', and connects this with his representing 'something very significantly American'; and 'the nature and manner of the dislike' of Lawrence which Leavis attributes to Eliot is put down to the fact that he 'was after all, a fellow-countryman of Pound' (AK, pp. 150–1).

If approval of Lawrence has by this time become a touchstone of critical integrity, the Laurentian attainment of psychic health through writing, as it has been defined in *D. H. Lawrence: Novelist*, finds its Transatlantic parallel in Mark Twain, 'For in his supreme creation the complex and troubled Mark Twain did achieve a wholeness' (AK, p. 122). Like Lawrence's, Twain's work is praised in terms which emphasise it as the product of the man, and as criticism of life; as 'inspired creative possession, the voice of deeply reflective maturity – of a life's experience brooded on by an earnest spirit and a fine intelligence' (AK, p. 122). *Huckleberry Finn* conveys 'poised humanity', and the novel is 'a profound study of civilized man' (AK, p. 124).

This tendency to treat works of literature as Holy Writ and their authors as prophet figures grows ever stronger in Leavis's later work, and Dickens and Blake join Lawrence as teachers for our time. *Dickens the Novelist*, produced in 1970 in collaboration with Q. D. Leavis, contains chapters by Leavis on *Dombey and Son* and *Little Dorrit*, as well as the essay on *Hard Times* which appeared in *The Great Tradition*. Unlike *D. H. Lawrence: Novelist*, the book contains no retraction of Leavis's earlier judgement of Dickens. The preface announces with an aplomb startling to those familiar with his estimate of Dickens as, above all, an entertainer, 'We should like to make it impossible . . . for any intellectual . . . to tell us with the familiar easy assurance that Dickens of course was a genius, but that his line was entertainment' (DN, p. 9). With characteristic acerbity it also dismisses American criticism 'from Edmund Wilson onwards as being in general wrong-headed, ill-informed . . . and essentially misdirecting' (DN, p. 10). The preface insists, too, on the importance of Leavis's conception of the novel as a dramatic poem, at first 'Received . . . with ridicule', but later seen as 'effecting a revolution in Dickens criticism' (DN, p. 11).

In common with other novelists whom Leavis has praised, Dickens is described as an heir of Shakespeare, but in his case the observation is given a kind of sociological, factual force. Shakespeare was 'a popular institution' 'in Dickens's formative period', and a 'potent fact . . . not only in his own life, but in the life of the English people for whom he wrote' (DN, p. 55). In stressing

Dickens's popularity, the closeness existing between him and his audience, Leavis gestures toward the existence of a sustaining culture for the writer, now all but lost. It is because of this culture, it seems to be suggested, that 'Dickens was in the fullest sense a great national artist' (DN, p. 55). What that title implies is defined further: 'His genius responded with inexhaustible vitality to the new, the unprecedented conditions of a rapidly developing civilization. In catering for the tastes and needs of a nation-wide public he found congenial employment for his powers' (DN, p. 55).

The stress on Dickens's relation to Shakespeare is in essence a stress on language, on Dickens's language as poetry. Leavis speaks of 'the inexhaustibly wonderful poetic life of his prose', of 'the poetic conception of his art' (DN, p. 53). Throughout the chapters there is an unobtrusive attention paid to the imagery and symbolism of the novels – 'The evocation of the Alps is associated, significantly, with the vision of the mortuary and its long-frozen dead' (DN, p. 358) – which seems to me to constitute the real strength of the criticism, and to validate Leavis's claims for his approach. Unfortunately, the Leavisian-Lawrentian vocabulary in which Dickens's themes are discussed makes the thought as a whole seem less subtle than it often is. Asserted throughout is the status of the novel as criticism of life. *Little Dorrit* is described as 'an inquest into contemporary civilization' which 'might equally be called a study of the criteria implicit in an evaluative study of life' (DN, p. 286). The suggestion is that it is the novel form alone which makes this possible. In a familiar collocation, 'life', 'the real', 'the concrete', 'the individual' are equated:

> Dickens's capacity for effective thought about life is indistinguishable from his genius as a novelist . . . he doesn't need to be told that he must take a firm hold on the truth that life, for a mind truly intent on the real, is life in the concrete; that life is concretely 'there' only in individual lives; and that individual lives can't be aggregated, generalized or averaged. (DN, p. 286)

If by virtue of its form the novel is able to present individual lives concretely, to define them in their specific relations to one another, to constitute the real for us, so, in Leavis's acceptation, the constitution of the real is also its very subject matter. As he does with Lawrence, Leavis stresses Dickens's capacity for thought, his intelligence. His work is 'an enterprise of thought' which needs to be recognised as such. It is 'the thinking intelligence directed to a grasp of the real' (DN, p. 286). Leavis conceives society to be presented in *Little Dorrit* by the interplay of the various characters who are in some sense representative of more than themselves, their qualities defined by their interactions. They embody complexes of values. Thus little Dorrit 'stands in a relation of contrast to more than one of the *dramatis personae*' (DN, p. 311). As opposed to Mrs Clennam she represents 'reality, courage, disinterestedness, truth, spontaneity, creativeness – life' (DN, p. 311). Little Dorrit's creativity is not that of the artist, however, and here Doyce the inventor stands in a relation of contrast to the pseudo (and hence anti) artist, Gowan. It is Doyce who brings 'the becalmed and debilitated Clennam into touch with strong and intransigent creativity' (DN, p. 313). The vocabulary in which Leavis describes him is closely connected with that he has used of Little Dorrit: his 'disinterestedness' is a compound of 'commitment and resolution and undeflectable courage' (DN, p. 313). Perhaps rather strangely, Leavis sees Flora Casby as another artist-surrogate, pointing out the richness of her fantasies which are allied with, at times inseparable from, a firm grasp on the real.

In order to make clear the full contrast between Little Dorrit and Mrs Clennam, Leavis invokes his favourite Blakean distinction between identity and self-hood which brings into play the notion of the religiousness of truly creative art, so Dickens 'insists . . . that the individual is a centre of responsibility towards something that is not him-(or her-)self' (DN, p. 302). By contrast with Little Dorrit Mrs Clennam is locked in the paralysis of self-hood, she is life become mechanism. However, Mrs Clennam represents a social as well as a psychic formation for:

> What Dickens hated in the Calvinistic commercialism of the early and middle Victorian age – the repressiveness towards children, the hard righteousness, the fear of love, the armed rigour in the face of life – he sums up now in its hatred of art.   (DN, p. 285)

Leavis detects similar themes in *Dombey and Son*. Again, there is a stress on the importance of the child to creativity – 'To repress the spontaneity in children . . . is to thwart and discourage life' (DN, p. 45) – and again a social ethos is portrayed as deathly: 'The stress falls on the reinforced spirit of class, with its cold, brutal and extreme repudiation of what Lawrence calls 'blood-togetherness' (DN, p. 28). As with *Hard Times*, Leavis sees the essential subject of both novels as the struggle of authentic, creative, individual life against a utilitarian, mechanising, quantitative, deathly civilisation, and claims that in Dickens's masterpiece, *Little Dorrit*, by the 'intrinsically normative' 'creative nisus' we are brought to the recognition that 'the disinterested individual life, the creative identity, is of its nature a responsibility towards what can't be possessed' (DN, p. 351). But for Leavis to say this is, in his scheme of things, to place Dickens with Lawrence as having an essentially religious grasp of life, and, as on other occasions, he quotes Tom Brangwen's words, 'he knew that he did not belong to himself'. Lawrence and Blake, then, are potent presences in Leavis's chapters on Dickens, and Blake and Dickens together have come to represent for him the strength of the Romantic movement which 'enriched the human heritage in ways not as a rule given clear or full recognition' (DN, p. 359).

The distinction between form and subject matter has been overcome in a new way in Leavis's criticism of Dickens, for just as formally the novel creates its own reality, so it enforces the perception that reality is what *we* create, and that human life, in so far as it *is* human, is not to be set in any sharp opposition to art. Hence it is that in his late criticism we find Leavis treating characters, writers, contemporaries as all inhabiting the same world and having the same status. The stress on creativity and Leavis's association of it with a religious sense is, moreover, one of the points at which doctrine now enters his criticism. For Leavis, a religious sense, by definition, cannot involve the acceptance of an externally defined dogma, for he connects it with the nisus, the *ahnung* of creativity, the creativity of either the artist or the fully achieved human being. Such creativity demands responsibility, a responsibility to that which lies beyond the individual. It is exploratory, heuristic, and above all active, and being active is necessarily time-bound, the product of the whole being.

It is this definition of the religious that forms the intellectual component of Leavis's often distasteful attack on *Four Quartets* in *The Living Principle*. Just as his criticism of Lawrence has a biographical bias (hagiographical would perhaps be a better word) so these late essays on Eliot emphasise the poems as products of a personality, and an inadequate one at that. Phrases such as 'Eliot's desperate inner need' proliferate, and he is accused of 'a limitation of self-knowledge that he can't transcend' (LP, p. 189). On rather little evidence he is seen as identifying with the Coriolanus figure at the end of *The Waste Land* in a nightmare of 'self-enclosure'. Leavis's account of the poems is long and tortuous, simultaneously paying tribute to Eliot's sensitivity to language and denying that he has any. The essays give the impression of a settled determination to find fault, to punish Eliot for his sacrilege in not being entirely won over by Lawrence. However, when this kind of animus is discounted, the attack seems to focus upon Eliot's beliefs. This shows itself particularly clearly in Leavis's discussion of the description of the dancing peasants in 'East Coker' where he attributes to Eliot 'the American blankness' about language that he finds in Pound. Leavis's reading of the passage as exhibiting a kind of reductive snobbery seems perverse, for Eliot is insisting on the importance of the sacramental in human life rather than on the animality of the peasants. He is, precisely, using the language of the church, just as elsewhere in the poems he uses the language of negative mysticism to define and describe his experience, and to give value to human life. There is no 'American blankness' about this. His language, to adopt a Leavisian phrase, is 'time-honoured', reaching back beyond Shakespeare. It seems to be Leavis with his atavistic Protestantism and hatred of the sacramental and ritual who is blank at this point. How much Leavis's opposition is towards Eliot's *beliefs* emerges explicitly in his statement that 'his poem . . . affects the reader profoundly, and one's disagreement is profound' (LP, p. 228). For Leavis significance is to be found within the processes of time, and by definition, any movement toward transcendence is a denial of that creativity which is true spirituality. Blake and Lawrence are summoned once more to point the right path. With all his insistence that Eliot is a great poet the dominant note is one of dismissal.

In *Thought, Words and Creativity*, his final book on Lawrence, Leavis completes the incorporation of life into art, and the final melding of all his enterprises. The growing insistence in his later work on the necessary intelligence of the artist becomes an insistence here that the heuristic intelligence of the great writer is the proper and necessary human intelligence, to be set against the analytic, conscious, cerebral thought of philosophy, against an exclusively 'mental consciousness' that makes the mind 'the enemy of life' (TWC, p. 21). According to Leavis, 'It is with thought, lived and living thought . . . that Lawrence sets about rescuing life from this inner mechanization' (TWC, p. 26). This emphasis on a lived and bodied thought which is imbued with the power of saving us marks Lawrence's apotheosis, for whereas in *D. H. Lawrence: Novelist* Leavis's admiration was laced with criticism, the tone is now almost wholly adulatory. The change is notable, particularly in Leavis's treatment of *The Plumed Serpent*, a novel about which he had been dismissive in the past. Now it presents him with 'an exquisitely delicate problem' (TWC, p. 55). His language writhes in the attempt to exonerate Lawrence while maintaining some critical self-respect: 'He must inevitably lie under the suspicion of having yielded, at least a little, to temptation' (TWC, p. 35). Leavis's problem arises out of his insistence upon Lawrence's complete intelligence, on his greatness as a critic as well as a novelist, and it must be stressed that he does in fact engage with the problem rather than avoid discussing the book that Lawrence described as 'my most important thing so far' – a description which Leavis adopted as the title for his chapter on it. In Leavis's new account the failure of the novel is now seen to rest not so much on its themes as in Lawrence's fascination with Mexico and his attempt to identify this interest with his 'devoted concern for the life-theme' (TWC, p. 55). The importance of the book for Leavis now lies in its resistance to the Cartesian mind/ body dualism.

How much the novels are now treated as being completely normative shows in the detail of Leavis's style. Ursula and Birkin are referred to, not as fictional characters, but as people with an historical existence: 'Ursula . . . knew that she had for husband a man whose individual life was open to the deep source, to the unknown, and who had his part in the creativity that kept civilization rooted and changing – that is alive. But he couldn't have been that without her' (TWC, p. 91). It is this relationship that Leavis invites us to see as normative for all male/female relations. Again, we are invited to generalise out from specific incidents in the novels to acceptance or condemnation of real social phenomena, so that, for example, philanthropy, social benevolence are attacked, not just as they manifest themselves in the elder Crich, but absolutely.

It is here that Leavis's social and literary criticism become one, fashioned in a seamless web, for it is through the language he shares with his readers that the writer is able to evoke 'what his readers know already', if only unconsciously, 'a specificity of imagined experience out of which the apprehension flashes on the reader' (TWC, p. 27). But the language is, precisely, a language of values, values which are given weight and force by the imagined experiences with which they are connected. Imbued with that weight and force they then enter life invested with a mythic power.

Conclusion

In 1957 J. B. Priestley mounted a resentful, clumsily humorous attack on a lecture he had heard Leavis give at Nottingham, entitled 'Literature in my Time'.[1] Recalling Leavis's judgement that 'no time need be wasted on Priestley' the novelist conferred on the critic the title of 'Chief Controller of Literary Passports' and attacked him for his narrowness, intolerance and arrogance in dismissing those who, unlike him, were creative writers. However ironically intended, Priestley's title had some truth, for Leavis was the most important and influential critic in the middle decades of this century and his followers were prolific and committed. Most critics of stature, even when they have taken issue with him have engaged with his ideas seriously and paid tribute to his distinction. Among them Wellek, Steiner, Trilling and Raymond Williams perhaps stand out. Moreover, Leavis's fame was not confined to the academic world, but extended to the quality journals he so much despised. Following his attack on C. P. Snow, an article in *The Observer* (11 March 1962), 'The Hidden Network of the Leavisites', traced the most notable of those academics he had influenced, and the involvement of some of them in the periodical *The Use of English* and in the *Pelican Guide to English Literature*, edited by Boris Ford. Although the writer of the piece distances himself from the Leavis ethos, Leavis's importance is taken for granted and he is placed with perhaps a little irony in the category of 'Great men of ideas'. Leavis, then, was a fact to be reckoned with, and not only in this country, but in the United States and even more in Australia, in the universities of Sydney and Melbourne. An Indian admirer, C. D. Narasimhaiah, who was at Christ's College, Cambridge in 1947, saw Leavis ('this benevolent man') as one whom everybody of intelligence and integrity wanted to study under at that time; he suggests his impact on Indian universities in the late 1950s and early 1960s was enormous – ' "Leavis is all the rage here" ', he quotes one student as remarking – and praises the British Council for its efforts in supplying books, Leavisite teachers and even portraits of the great man.[2]

A distinguished and influential thinker, a stern moralist, a charismatic teacher, so much seems certain; and to say so much might seem in other cases to be enough. In Leavis's case it is not, for his adversarial stance to almost all features of modern culture makes any simple, detached recognition impossible to those who do not accept unquestioningly his diagnosis of society's ills, while his urgency and his own rigorous standards demand that he should be judged rigorously. Such judgement will entail, of course, the judge's recognition of his or her own position.

Throughout the preceding chapters I have identified contradictions and paradoxes in Leavis's thinking. They occur perhaps most notably in his ideas about rootedness; in his accounts of the standards and processes by which we evaluate a work of literature; in his descriptions of the kind of reality that literature conveys, and the means by which it does so.

Thus, he insisted that in earlier times popular culture was rooted in an agricultural way of life to the extent that the rhythms of physical work permeated the English language itself, and so flowed into and enriched a wider culture; but his definitions of this culture remained abstract, cerebral; and the continuity he believed in was asserted but not demonstrated. The rootedness he saw as so necessary to culture and creativity, and its physicality which he stressed so strongly, emerge on the whole as having little to do with any implication in a particular landscape, society or milieu, or even in some cases with the use of English as a native language, for many of the writers he praised as being rooted were cultural or linguistic exiles, while the rootedness of others was deemed to show itself in or be attributable to their grasp of the Classics or their affinity with a society other than their own.

Similar tensions may be felt in what Leavis has to say of evaluation, and of literary standards in general. First of all, there is at least a potential contradiction in the aims of Richards's practical criticism classes, aims to which Leavis subscribed wholeheartedly and made his own; a contradiction between teaching discrimination, which implies training in a rule-bound activity, and the aim of encouraging the student in charting a personal response to the poem under consideration. There is, I think, a further contradiction in Leavis's assumption that standards of judgement are immanent in literary works – that the works themselves create the criteria by which they are to be judged – and his declared belief that standards are the product of critical consensus. Although his later location of standards of judgement within a third realm that is constituted by language, and his perception of the human world as both creative and collaborative, offer to resolve both these tensions, the very offer of resolution on a conceptual plane seems to highlight the practical difficulties of such an attempt in the kind of pluralistic society he abhorred. However, the conflict is not only between the conceptual and the practical; it is in essence a conflict between different, incompatible concepts of language. Set against the notion of language as essentially creating human meaning and reality is that of language at its most highly charged gesturing toward reality, a meaning beyond itself, and effacing itself in the process. Put like this the two might seem to be one if Leavis's notion of the protensive pull of creativity is brought into play. Language, in the hands of the creative artist, brings a new reality into being. However, at times, even in his later work, Leavis speaks rather as if language at its most powerful effaces itself, not to create a new meaning, but to reveal a pre-existent, extra-linguistic reality. It becomes, that is, a gateway to a world beyond itself.

On the one hand there is a desire to ground all meaning in physical experience, so that language follows after and mimes sensation, and on the individual level, a form of tactile response is the highest validator of meaning and value. Language, then, is the means by which the reality of existence is *expressed*, but because physical reality and meaning are so closely related, meaning in an important sense pre-exists language. It is something to be discovered rather than made. On the other hand Leavis needs to make individual judgements compelling, to give them an authority in the world at large. Thus language becomes for him, not the means by which reality is expressed, but the very condition of its creation; meaning, a shared activity, brings reality into being. Leavis's ideas about rootedness, about judgement, about language, thus reveal themselves to be closely related, and the struggles and tensions within and between them a product of his attempt to transcend the Cartesian dichotomies of body/mind, physical/cerebral, individual/society, he so much hated. That despite his attempts, the old patterns reinsert themselves in his discourse is hardly to be wondered at, for those structures are embedded deeply in the language. This battle with meaning, however, does not seem to be one he lost, for, long before the the post-structuralists, he made visible the assumptions implicit in the structures of the language.

Another, less fertile, contradiction between Leavis's beliefs and practice is to be identified. Early in his career he put forward the notion of the canon as an entity which changed according to the needs and values of succeeding generations, and in these early years he taught and wrote about texts that were contemporary in the strongest sense of the word, texts that were so new as to be unsupported by any critical commentary. Part of his perception of the human condition was that we are temporal beings, implicated in the movements of history, but in his last books, although he still – perhaps even more insistently – proclaimed that life was growth and change, his conception of the canon seems to have hardened so that he no longer *in practice* saw literature as the result of a process of interaction between literary works and different generations of readers, but hypostatised it into a body of already received texts. The committed Leavisite would deny that this position is contradictory, and claim that because of the state of our civilisation nothing of significance has been written since those modern texts with which Leavis first concerned himself. However, arguments about the merits of individual mid and late twentieth-century works seem unnecessary in the face of Leavis's capacity to transform his own temporally grounded judgements into something timeless. If literature changes for every generation then one would expect changes of valuation in response to new needs and circumstances; if individual life is heuristic, if there is within it a protensive pull, then new insights, changes in valuation, seem inevitable.

What are we to make, then, of a critic who was committed in the abstract to such notions, but who resisted change so thoroughly in the concrete, publishing without alteration, as we have seen, material written decades previously?

The contradiction stems, I think, from Leavis's desire for an absolute which is yet contained within the shifting movements of time; from his sense of the necessity for a spiritual dimension to life that is combined with a resolute free-thinking which he himself associates with membership of a Protestant tradition. There is for him no court of appeal beyond the temporal, no transcendent signifier to arrest the wheeling of history, and yet for meaning to be possible there must be that upon which humans can rest, some offer of certainty persisting through change. One certainty for Leavis is that supplied by the physical; the visceral reaction that enables one to say '*I* know this'. It is the valuing of this certainty which leads to his adoption of Lawrence as prophet and which betrays also his residual Protestantism. Certainties are personal and must be felt in the bone, as it were. However, to be absolute in any real sense they must be demonstrable and shared, and it is here, as we have seen, that Leavis saw language as linking the feeling, judging individual with others and with the past. It was within language that he located the authority for the individual judgement, for judgements can be made only within language, and at bottom presuppose agreement in a form of life. Hence the urgency with which he fought rival constructions of reality, or even moderate argument, for it was only through agreement that the absolute he sought could be brought into being. It was this necessity to locate an absolute within the movement of time, to define as absolute his individual perceptions, that led, too, to his tendency to mythologise, for myth is an attempt to invest the temporal with universality, and to discover necessity within the apparently accidental. To believe oneself to be a constantly growing being, always moving toward the perception of new truths, and yet to regard one's perceptions and insights as in some sense absolute is not an easy position to maintain. It is perhaps because of this difficulty that in later years Leavis seems in certain aspects not unlike Ted Hughes's hawk:

> Nothing has changed since I began.
> My eye has permitted no change.
> I am going to keep things like this.   ('Hawk Roosting' 11. 22–4)

As I suggested earlier in this book, Leavis's search for the absolute is to be linked with his rejection of any form of philosophy, save that of Grene and Polanyi in his last years. The essence of philosophy is that it is dialogic, that it admits the possibility of other positions in its examination of the status of different kinds of argument. It always demands self-examination (even if not always of the most fruitful kind). Leavis's opposition seems to me to be a version of the quarrel between Rhetoric and Philosophy, between Gorgias and Socrates in Plato's *Gorgias*, with Leavis as a latter-day Gorgias constructing reality by means of a persuasiveness and urgency that purports to reveal the self-evident, pre-existent, the always already there. His stance is, at bottom, totalitarian and not the less so because of his moral urgency.

But to come to this conclusion about Leavis is to come to understand my own position with greater clarity; to recognise that my Catholicism is as much a matter of abiding temper as adopted belief, and as strong as Leavis's Protestantism. My scepticism about the absolute validity of personal judgements is absolute. At the same time, Leavis's idea of human life as process, as a creative movement towards truth, the notion of life as growth and change seems essential. Essential, too, is his belief that what we are and what we do *matters*. Writing this book, setting myself in opposition to one who has helped to shape my thinking and yet one to whom I have nearly always felt some antagonism, has enforced yet again in me the conviction that a certain kind of scepticism – scepticism about ourselves and our own motives and capacities – is absolutely vital to any properly human existence. It is only by fostering such scepticism in ourselves and – equally – demanding it of others that we might eventually attain something like our full humanity. We need to know our limitations as well as our strengths. Sadly, although Leavis did not lack the courage to try to change what could be changed, he had neither the serenity to accept what could not, nor, perhaps, the wisdom to know the difference.

Notes

Introduction

1. Fred Inglis has stressed Leavis's membership of an English tradition, placing him in a political context of 'stubborn idealism, and durably liberal and critical temper'. Interestingly, Inglis's tradition contains figures such as John Maynard Keynes, towards whom Leavis was consistently hostile. See F. Inglis, *Radical Earnestness: English Social Theory 1880–1980* (Martin Ro ertson, Oxford, 1982).
2. F. Engels, *The Condition of the Working Class in England* (Grafton Books, London, 1982), p. 39.
3. R. Williams, *The Country and the City* (Chatto & Windus, London, 1973).
4. *Nor Shall My Sword: Discourses on Pluralism, Compassion and Social Hope* (Chatto & Windus, London, 1972), p. 132.
5. M. Bell, *F. R. Leavis* (Routledge, London and New York, 1988), ch. 4.

Chapter 1

1. D. J. Palmer, *The Rise of English Studies* (Oxford University Press, Oxford, 1965).

2. *English Literature in our Time and the University: The Clark Lectures, 1967* (Chatto & Windus, London, 1969), p. 14.
3. I. A. Richards, *Principles of Literary Criticism* (Kegan Paul, Trench, Trubner, London, 1924). See also Richards's *Practical Criticism: A Study of Literary Judgement* (Kegan Paul, Trench, Trubner, London, 1929). In *Practical Criticism* Richards described the conduct of his practical criticism classes, and published some of the analyses produced for them by participants.
4. 'Beginnings and Transitions: I. A. Richards Interviewed by Reuben Brower', in *I. A. Richards: Essays in his Honour*, (eds) R. Brower, H. Vendler, and J. Hollander (Oxford University Press, New York, 1973), p. 24.
5. Palmer, *op. cit.*, p. 17.
6. *The Teaching of English in England* (HMSO, London, 1921), pp. 9, 14, 20.
7. Bell, *op. cit.*, p. 23.
8. I. A. Richards, *Science and Poetry* (Kegan Paul, Trench, Trubner, London, 1926), pp. 82–3.
9. *Principles of Literary Criticism*, *op. cit.*, p. 58.
10. *ibid.*, pp. 60–1.
11. P. McCallum, *Literature and Method: Towards a Critique of I. A. Richards, F. R. Leavis and T. S. Eliot* (Gill and McMillan, Dublin, 1983), p. 211.
12. Leavis, 'What's Wrong with Criticism', in *For Continuity* (Minority Press, Cambridge, 1933), pp. 68–9.
13. J. Bennett, ' "How it Strikes a Contemporary": The Impact of I. A. Richards' Literary Criticism in Cambridge, England', in *I. A. Richards: Essays in his Honour*, p. 45.
14. *Practical Criticism*, p. 3.
15. *The Living Principle: 'English' as a Discipline of Thought* (Chatto & Windus, London, 1975), p. 19.
16. *Education and the University: A Sketch for an 'English School'* (Chatto & Windus, London, 1943), pp. 76–83.
17. D. Thompson, *Reading and Discrimination* (Chatto & Windus, London, 1934; revised and reprinted, 1954), p. 157, revised edn.
18. *The Living Principle*, p. 23.
19. *The Cambridge Review*, 8 February 1929, pp. 254–6. Reprinted in *'Valuation in Criticism' and Other Essays*, (ed.) G. Singh (Cambridge University Press, Cambridge, 1986), pp. 11–16.
20. *Nor Shall My Sword*, pp. 30–1.
21. F. Mulhern, *The Moment of Scrutiny* (New Left Books, London, 1979).

22. C. K. Stead, *The New Poetic* (Hutchinson, London, 1964), p. 14. For Abrams's schema, see M. H. Abrams, *The Mirror and the Lamp: Romantic Theory and the Critical Tradition* (Oxford University Press, London, 1953), pp. 6–7.

23. *The Cambridge Review*, 8 November 1929, p. 100.

24. *The Living Principle*, p. 21.

25. Mulhern, *op. cit.*, p. 30. See also F. L. Lucas, 'English', *University Studies*, (ed.) P. Wright (Cambridge University Press, Cambridge, 1933), p. 259. Like Leavis's, Lucas's concern is with standards and intellectual rigour. He objected to the new emphasis on evaluative criticism which he described as 'airing opinions about authors' merits', and saw a danger of university English courses becoming 'organised orgies of opinion' (p. 275). Lucas saw rigour as synonymous with scholarship, and also wanted to add a compulsory paper in Latin, and unseens in Middle English (p. 289). E. M. W. Tillyard, one of the earliest members of Cambridge English demonstrates a different, less disinterested hostility in *The Muse Unchained* (Cambridge University Press, Cambridge, 1958). Significant is the almost complete elision of Leavis from the story. Only his intolerance is noticed: 'For Leavis, at that time, Richards was one of the small company of right people' (p. 102). Even in suggesting that *Scrutiny* pandered to students who needed to be told what to think, Tillyard avoids naming him.

26. Q. D. Leavis, *Fiction and the Reading Public* (Chatto & Windus, London, 1932).

27. *A Selection from Scrutiny*, compiled by F. R. Leavis in two volumes (Cambridge University Press, Cambridge, 1968), vol. 1, p. xi.

28. Mulhern, *op. cit.*, p. 302.

29. *ibid.*, p. 30.

30. *ibid.*, p. 108.

31. *ibid.*, p. 183.

32. *ibid.*, pp. 268–9.

33. L. Lerner, 'The Life and Death of *Scrutiny*', *London Magazine*, 2 (1955), p. 68.

34. 'Two Cultures? The Significance of C. P. Snow', *Spectator*, 9 March 1962, pp. 297–303. The lecture was subsequently published under the same title together with an essay by Michael Yudkin on Snow's lecture (Chatto & Windus, London, 1962). Leavis later incorporated it into *Nor Shall My Sword*.

35. C. P. Snow, *The Two Cultures and the Scientific Revolution* (Cambridge University Press, Cambridge, 1959).

36. *Cultures in Conflict: Perspectives on the Snow–Leavis Controversy*, (eds) D. K. Cornelius and E. St Vincent (Scott, Foresman and Co., Chicago, 1964).

Chapter 2

1. I. A. Richards, *Principles of Literary Criticism*, p. 61, in *For Continuity*, p. 14.
2. 'Mass Civilization and Minority Culture', in *For Continuity*, p. 15.
3. A. Megill, *Prophets of Extremity: Nietzsche, Heidegger, Foucault, Derrida* (University of California Press, Berkeley and London, 1985).
4. J. Klugman, *Culture and Crisis in Britain in the Thirties*, (eds) J. Clark, M. Heinmmann, D. Margolies, C. Snee (Lawrence and Wishart, London, 1979), pp. 13–36.
5. 'Restatements for Critics', in *For Continuity*, p. 184.
6. 'Mass Civilization and Minority Culture', in *For Continuity*, p. 15.
7. 'Under Which King, Bezonian?', in *For Continuity*, p. 163.
8. George Sturt originally published his work under the name of George Bourne. I have used the following editions: George Sturt, 'George Bourne', *The Wheelwright's Shop* (Cambridge University Press, Cambridge, 1963). George Bourne, *Change in the Village* (The Country Book Club, London, 1956).
9. I. A. Richards, *Principles of Literary Criticism*, p. 61. Quoted by Leavis in *For Continuity*, p. 14.
10. 'Mass Civilization and Minority Culture', in *For Continuity*, p. 15.
11. T. Carlyle, *Essays. Scottish and Other Miscellanies* (Dent, London, 1915), vol. I, pp. 227 and 228.
12. *Unto This Last*. Library edition of the works of John Ruskin, (eds) E.T. Cook and A. Wedderburn (London, 1903–12), vol. x, p. 192, quoted by P. Fuller, *Theoria: Art and the Absence of Grace* (Chatto & Windus, London, 1988), p. 108.
13. J. L. and B. Hammond, *The Village Labourer* (Longmans, Green and Co., London, 1911); and *The Town Labourer* (Longmans, Green and Co., 1917)
14. H. G. Wells, *Tono-Bungay*, (ed.) B. Bergonzi, (Houghton Miffin Co., Boston, 1966).
15. R. Williams, *The Country and the City*, pp. 9–12.
16. P. Lasslett, *The World We Have Lost* (Methuen, London, 1965), p. 201.
17. R. S. and H. M. Lynd, *Middletown* (Harcourt, Brace and World, 1929), p. 496 and pp. 33–4.

18. H. S. Hughes, *Consciousness and Society: The Re-Orientation of European Social Thought, 1890–1930* (McGibbon and Kee, London, 1967).

19. T. E. Hulme, *Speculations: Essays on Humanism and the Philosophy of Art*, (ed.) H. Reid (Routledge and Kegan Paul, London, 1924), pp. 173–7.

20. F. Kermode, *Romantic Image* (Routledge and Kegan Paul, London, 1957), p. 124.

21. T. S. Eliot, 'The Metaphysical Poets', *Selected Essays* (Faber and Faber, London, 1932), p. 287.

22. Leavis refers to Hulme dismissively in 'Romantic and Heretic', a review of Nehls's *Composite Biography*, *Spectator*, 6 February 1959; reprinted in *D. H. Lawrence: A Critical Anthology*, (ed.) H. Coombes (Penguin, Harmondsworth, 1973), pp. 393–7.

23. Bell, *op. cit.*, pp. 36–54.

24. *The Decline of the West* was published in two volumes. Vol. 1 appeared in 1918 (translated into English, 1926); Vol. 2 in 1922 (translated into English, 1928). Page references in the body of my text are to the abridged English edition: O. Spengler, *The Decline of the West*, (ed.) A. Helps (George Allen and Unwin, London, 1961).

25. 'D. H. Lawrence', *For Continuity*, p. 138.

26. J. Hone, *W. B. Yeats* (Penguin, Harmondsworth, 1971), p. 397.

27. J. Lacan, 'The mirror stage as formative of the function of the I as revealed in psychoanalytic experience', *Ecrits, A Selection*, translated by A. Sheridan (Tavistock Publications, London, 1977), pp. 1–7.

28. Henry Ford in collaboration with Samuel Crowther, *My Life and Work* (Doubleday, Page and Co., New York, 1926). In his apologia for his business practices Ford insists that 'There is a most intimate connection between decency and good business', protesting 'we do not want any hard, man-killing work about the place' (p. 100). The alternative is the assembly line: 'Some men do only one or two small operations, others do more. The man who places a part does not fasten it . . . The man who puts on the nut does not tighten it' (p. 83). The financial insecurity of Ford workers emerges in Ford's protestations about the importance of paying high wages: 'We closed down to get our bearings', he remarks casually (p. 135).

29. R. Hoggart, *The Uses of Literacy: Aspects of working-class life, with special reference to publications and entertainments* (Chatto & Windus, London, 1957).

30. *For Continuity*, pp. 164–5. 'Under Which King, Bezonian?' first appeared in *Scrutiny*, 1 (December 1932) pp. 205–14. It was republished in *For Continuity*, pp. 160–75, in the following year. It has

also been reprinted in '*Valuation in Criticism*' (ed.) G. Singh, Cambridge University Press, Cambridge, 1986.

31. Georg Lukács, in *The Historical Novel* (first published in Russian in 1937).

32. G. Lukács, *Studies in European Realism*, trans. E. Bone (The Merlin Press, London, 1972), p. 89.

33. *The Living Principle*, p. 10.

34. J. Wain, 'A Certain Judo Demonstration', *Hudson Review*, 1962, pp. 253–60.

35. *Higher Education: Report of the Committee appointed by the Prime Minister under the Chairmanship of Lord Robbins 1961–63* (HMSO, October 1963).

36. *The Living Principle*, p. 10.

37. *Lectures in America*, with Q. D. Leavis (Chatto & Windus, London, 1969), p. 5.

38. M. Grene, *The Knower and the Known* (Faber and Faber, London, 1966); M. Polanyi, *Knowing and Being. Essays*, (ed.) M. Grene (Routledge and Kegan Paul, London, 1958); M. Polanyi, *Personal Knowledge* (Routledge and Kegan Paul, London, 1958).

39. See note 18 above.

40. Ian Robinson has pointed out that Grene's treatment of the fact and value issue is over-simple. In a rejoinder to F. R. Leavis's ' "Believing in" the University', *The Human World* 15–16 (1974), p. 109, he describes her book as a 'well-meaning but rather tripey work'.

41. In a detailed examination of Leavis's modes of argument John Casey has pointed Lo the way in which he 'seeks to compel critical agreement' through 'the equation of concepts' so that there is an elision of any distinction between the descriptive and the evaluative. Of Leavis's claim that Lawrence is never cruel he comments wryly, ' . . . if one admits Lawrence's "genius" – as everyone does – it is, by this very admission, impossible to ascribe cruelty to him – although some people who *think* that they recognise his genius do so', *The Language of Criticism* (Methuen, London, 1966), p. 170.

Chapter 3

1. See *The Living Principle*, p. 19. He remarks on the lack of such a manual in *Education and the University*, p. 69.

2. *Education and the University*, p. 16.

3. Mulhern, *op. cit.*, p. 184.

4. *English Literature in Our Time*, pp. 3 and 58.

5. *ibid.*, p. 30.

6. Brookes Otis, 'Thoughts after Flexner', an essay 'which appeared in a short-lived periodical *The New Frontier*, run by young graduates of well-known Eastern Universities.' (*Education and the University*, p. 22); A. Meiklejohn, *The Experimental College* (Harper, New York and London, 1932); F. R. Leavis, 'An American Lead', *Scrutiny*, 1 (1932), pp. 297–300.

7. Central to the later definition is Leavis's articulation of a 'third realm' that is neither merely private nor purely objective. See *English Literature in Our Time*, p. 48.

8. The link between 'realisation' and 'enactment' in Leavis's use of the terms is discussed by V. Buckley, *Poetry and Morality: Studies in the Criticism of Matthew Arnold, T. S. Eliot and F. R. Leavis* (Chatto & Windus, London, 1959), pp. 163–4.

9. P. de Man, 'The Rhetoric of Temporality', in *Blindness and Insight: Essays in the Rhetoric of Contemporary Fiction*, 2nd edn (Methuen, London, 1983), p. 207.

10. Leavis himself rejected the term in an early essay: ' "sincere" is not a very useful term in criticism', 'This Poetical Renascence', *For Continuity*, p. 199.

11. See, for example, *D. H. Lawrence: Novelist* (Chatto & Windus, London, 1955), p. 18; *Dickens the Novelist*, with Q. D. Leavis (Chatto & Windus, London, 1970), p. 25; and 'The Americanness of American Literature', *'Anna Karenina' and Other Essays* (Chatto & Windus, London, 1967), p. 145.

12. In denying the relevance to English of Wittgenstein's work on language Leavis criticises Ian Robinson, his former pupil and editor of *The Human World*, claiming that Robinson had been unduly influenced by the 'inappropriate criteria . . . that go with a philosophical training'. This and similar criticisms in ' "Believing in" the University' seem to have been provoked by Robinson's criticisms of Grene. See Chapter 2, note 40, above.

13. Leavis's preoccupation with standards finds new expression around this time. 'Valuation in Criticism', *Orbis Litterarum*, 21 (1966) (reprinted in *'Valuation in Criticism' and other Essays*, p. 276) seems to have been a step towards his position in the Clark lectures.

14. Robinson queries the value of these terms in a very respectful discussion of Leavis in *The Survival of English: Essays in Criticism of Language* (Cambridge University Press, Cambridge, 1973), p. 239. Leavis's rejoinder is part of the debate referred to in note 12, above.

15. L. Wittgenstein, *Philosophical Investigations*, translated by G. E. M. Anscombe (Basil Blackwell, Oxford, 1978), p. 88. On standards see, for example, Wittgenstein's discussion of uses of 'good' and 'correct' in *Lectures and Conversations on Aesthetics, Psychology and Religious*

Belief, (ed.) C. Barrett (Basil Blackwell, Oxford, 1978), p. 5. Compare also Leavis on realisation with Wittgenstein on exactness, *Philosophical Investigations*, p. 41, section 88. Relevant to Wittgenstein's description of language as agreement 'in form of life' is Leavis's description of Eliot's apparent acceptance of individual isolation as 'ominous'. Leavis refers to Eliot's quotation, in his notes to *The Waste Land*, of the philosopher F. H. Bradley on the privacy of external sensations. See *Thought, Words and Creativity*, pp. 30–1.

16. 'Memories of Wittgenstein', *The Human World*, 10 (1973), p. 79.

Chapter 4

1. R. Wellek, 'Letter', *Scrutiny*, 5 (1936–7), pp. 375–83. See also F. R. Leavis, 'Literary Criticism and Philosophy', *Scrutiny*, 6 (1937–8), pp. 59–70.

2. de Man, *op. cit.*, p. 130. Bell, *op. cit.*, pp. 27–56.

3. 'Criticism and Literary History', *Scrutiny*, 4 (1935–6), pp. 96–100. The review initiated an exchange between Bateson and Leavis, printed in succeeding issues of *Scrutiny*. It and the ensuing correspondence are collected in *The Importance of 'Scrutiny'. Selections from 'Scrutiny': A Quarterly Review, 1932–1948*, (ed.) E. Bentley (New York University Press, New York, 1964), pp. 12–22.

4. T. S. Eliot, 'Tradition and the Individual Talent', *Selected Essays*, p. 15.

5. See W. B. Yeats, *Autobiographies* (Macmillan, London, 1961), pp. 354–5 and 'Edmund Spenser', in *The Cutting of an Agate*, reprinted in W. B. Yeats, *Essays and Introductions* (Macmillan, London, 1961), pp. 356–83.

6. J. Middleton Murry, *The Problem of Style* (Oxford University Press, London, 1922), pp. 98–9. See also T. S. Eliot, *Selected Essays*, pp. 288 and 305–16.

7. This seems to be an occasion on which Leavis sacrifices his beliefs to a *bon mot*, for elsewhere he remarks of Keats, 'That exquisitely sure touch . . . cannot . . . go with spiritual vulgarity'. *Revaluation: Tradition and Development in English Poetry* (Chatto & Windus, London, 1936), p. 265.

8. T. S. Eliot, 'Tradition and the Individual Talent', *Selected Essays*, p. 10.

9. E. Pound, *How to Read* (Desmond Harmsworth, London, 1931).

10. H. G. Gadamer, 'The Universality of the Hermeneutical Problem', in *Philosophical Hermeneutics*, translated and edited by D. E. Linge

(University of California Press, Berkeley, Los Angeles, London, 1977), pp. 3–17.

11. Leavis remarks of Shelley's verse that its success depends on 'inducing . . . a kind of attention that doesn't bring the critical intelligence into play', *Revaluation*, p. 207. Again, commenting harshly on Matthew Arnold's 'To Shakespeare', he says 'the sonnet imposes the kind of attention, or inattention, it needs', *Education and the University*, p. 74.

12. In fact, his judgement has been challenged at some length by Donald Davie who stresses the forcefulness of the verbs in the earlier passage, *Articulate Energy* (Routledge and Kegan Paul, London, 1955), pp. 110–15.

13. 'I can only regret that Shelley did not live to put his poetic gifts, which were certainly of the first order, at the service of more tenable beliefs – which need not have been . . . beliefs more acceptable to me', *The Use of Poetry and the Use of Criticism* (Faber and Faber, London, 1933), p. 97.

14. John Casey in *The Language of Criticism* (Methuen, London, 1966) has discussed the tension in Leavis's criticism between expressionism and the mimetic: see p. 157.

15. *Scrutiny*, 5, p. 375.

16. Leavis would have disputed this. He ends his discussion of 'By the Statue of King Charles at Charing Cross', 'We do not, of course, argue from the poem to Lionel Johnson's personal qualities', *The Living Principle*, p. 86. However, the need to make such a comment suggests the reality of the danger his mode of discourse poses.

17. *How Many Children Had Lady Macbeth?* (Gordon Fraser, The Minority Press, Cambridge, 1933) was later collected in L. C. Knights, *Explorations* (Chatto & Windus, London, 1946).

18. '*Hard Times*: An Analytic Note', *The Great Tradition* (Chatto & Windus, London, 1948), p. 227. Significantly, this piece first appeared as 'The Novel as Dramatic Poem (I): *Hard Times*', *Scrutiny*, 14 (1947), pp. 185–203.

19. Knights himself later acknowledged, '. . . today I should make far more allowance for the extraordinary variety of Shakespeare's tragedies', *Explorations*, preface, p. x.

20. G. Wilson Knight was highly praised in the columns of *Scrutiny*. His essay on *Othello* appears in *The Wheel of Fire* (Oxford University Press, Oxford, 1930).

21. G. Santayana, 'Tragic Philosophy', *Scrutiny*, 4 (1935–6), pp. 365–76.

22. 'Yeats, the Problem and the Challenge', in *Lectures in America* (1969); 'Justifying One's Valuation of Blake', *The Human World*, 7 (1972), pp. 42–64; 'Xenia' in E. Montale, *New Poems*, translated and

edited by G. Singh (Chatto & Windus, London, 1976). Essays on, and discussions of, Eliot appear in *D. H. Lawrence: Novelist* (1955), *English Literature in Our Time* (1969), *Lectures in America* (1969) and *The Living Principle* (1975). Leavis's notes on Wordsworth are published as an appendix to the collection, *'Valuation in Criticism' and Other Essays*.

23. The lecture was published in *On Poetry and Poets* (Faber and Faber, London, 1957), pp. 146–61. The intricacies of Leavis's relations with Eliot and Lawrence have been traced by B. Bergonzi, 'Leavis and Eliot: The long road to rejection', in *The Myth of Modernism and Twentieth Century Literature* (Harvester, Brighton, 1986), pp. 85–112. The subject is touched on by E. Greenwood, *F. R. Leavis* (Longman, London, 1978), p. 47.

24. P. J. M. Robertson, *The Leavises on Fiction* (Macmillan, London, 1981), p. 27.

25. Leavis proposed extracting and publishing under the title of *Gwendolen Harleth* those parts of *Daniel Deronda* of which he approved, and insisted on referring to the whole novel as *Gwendolen Harleth*. Collected in *The Critic as Anti-Philosopher: Essays and papers*, (ed.) G. Singh (Chatto & Windus, 1982) is a previously unpublished piece written as an introduction to an edition of *Gwendolen Harleth* proposed by Bodley Head. Leavis later admitted that 'the surgery of disjunction would be a less simple and satisfactory affair' than he had once thought, 'George Eliot's Zionist Novel', *Commentary*, October, 1960 (reprinted in *'Valuation in Criticism'*, p. 64).

26. This formulation was to have repercussions some ten years later when Leavis took John Wain to task for a similar use: ' . . . to anyone really contemplating the nature of Conrad's greatness it must be plain that "choice" in the sense imputed cannot have played any such part . . .', 'Joseph Conrad', *Sewanee Review*, 66 (1958), pp. 179–200 (later republished as 'The Shadow-Line' in *'Anna Karenina'*, p. 93). Wain retorted by quoting the relevant passage from *The Great Tradition* and Leavis in turn, admitting that he had not read through what he had written 'twenty years ago', insisted that Wain had distorted his sense by omitting vital sentences, and that anyway he had not used the word 'choose', as Wain had, with the implication that Conrad had calculated which language his books would sell best in, 'Correspondence', *Sewanee Review*, 66 (1958), pp. 689 and 690. (Leavis's rejoinder, 'Conrad's "Choice" of English', is reprinted in *Letters in Criticism*, (ed.) J. Tasker (Chatto & Windus, London, 1974), p. 69. The exchange, in addition to illustrating Leavis's refusal to concede gracefully, and his tenacity in argument, also testifies to his sense that a

language cannot in any simple sense be seen as separable from user and use.

27. *D. H. Lawrence* (Gordon Fraser, Cambridge, 1930) reprinted in *For Continuity*, pp. 111–48.

28. T. S. Eliot, *After Strange Gods. A Primer of Modern Heresy*. The Page-Barbour Lectures at the University of Virginia, 1933 (Faber and Faber, London, 1934).

29. Leavis comments on the trial in an essay which first appeared in *The Spectator*, February, 1961 (reprinted as 'The Orthodoxy of Enlightenment' in *'Anna Karenina'*, pp. 235–41).

30. See J. Middleton Murry, *Son of Woman: The Story of D. H. Law-rence* (Cape, London, 1931). Murry's main emphasis is, perhaps, on making some sense of his painful relationship with Lawrence. Although Murry's picture of Lawrence the man, whom he knew intimately, is very different from the one Leavis constructs it is not to be described as simply as Leavis suggests. Murry pays tribute both to Lawrence's psychic disabilities *and* his greatness. In an otherwise admiring piece R. J. Kaufmann comments that there is a side of Lawrence, 'petulant, domineering, immature' that Leavis 'simply denies', 'F. R. Leavis, The Morality of Mind', *Critical Quarterly*, 1 (1959), p. 251.

31. 'Anna Karenina', *'Anna Karenina'*, p. 22.

32. F. Kermode, *The Sense of an Ending: Studies in the Theory of Fiction* (Oxford University Press, New York, 1966), p. 39.

33. See 'The Americanness of American Literature: A British Demurrer to Van Wyck Brooks', *Commentary*, November, 1952, pp. 466–74; M. Bewley, *The Complex Fate* (Chatto & Windus, London, 1952), pp. vii–xv; *Pudd'nhead Wilson: A Tale by Mark Twain* (The Zodiac Press, London and The Grove Press, New York, 1955); and 'Pound in his Letters', *Scrutiny*, 18 (1951), pp. 74–7. Page references in the body of my text are to *'Anna Karenina'* where all these essays are reprinted.

Conclusion

1. J. B. Priestley, 'Literature in my Time', in *Thoughts in the Wilderness* (Heinemann, London, 1957).

2. C. D. Narasimhaiah, *Better Literary History and Better Literary Criticism: The Work of F. R. Leavis and How it Strikes an Indian* (Mysore: Rao and Raghavan, 1963).

Select Bibilography

1. Critical Works by Leavis

Mass Civilization and Minority Culture (Gordon Fraser, Cambridge, 1930).

D. H. Lawrence (Gordon Fraser, Cambridge, 1930).

New Bearings in English Poetry: A study of the contemporary situation (Chatto & Windus, London, 1932).

How To Teach Reading: A primer for Ezra Pound (Gordon Fraser, Cambridge, 1932).

For Continuity (Minority Press, Cambridge, 1933).

Culture and Environment: The training of critical awareness, with Denys Thompson (Chatto & Windus, London; Oxford University Press, Toronto, 1933).

Towards Standards of Criticism: Selections from *The Calendar of Modern Letters* edited and introduced, (Wishart, London, 1933).

Determinations: Critical Essays, ed. (Chatto & Windus, London, 1934).

Revaluation: Tradition and development in English Poetry (Chatto & Windus, London; Macmillan, Toronto, 1936).

Education and the University: A sketch for an 'English School' (Chatto & Windus, London; Macmillan, Toronto, 1943).

The Great Tradition: George Eliot, Henry James, Joseph Conrad (Chatto & Windus, London; Clarke, Irwin, Toronto, 1948).

188

Mill on Bentham and Coleridge, edited and introduced (Chatto & Windus, London; Clarke, Irwin, Toronto, 1950).

The Common Pursuit (Chatto & Windus, London; Clarke, Irwin, Toronto, 1952).

D. H. Lawrence: Novelist (Chatto & Windus, London; Clarke, Irwin, Toronto, 1955).

Two Cultures? The Significance of C. P. Snow with an essay by Michael Yudkin on Snow's Rede Lecture of 1959 (Chatto & Windus, London; Clarke, Irwin, Toronto, 1962).

'Anna Karenina' and Other Essays (Chatto & Windus, London; Clarke, Irwin, Toronto, 1967).

A Selection from Scrutiny, 2 vols, edited (Cambridge University Press, Cambridge, 1968).

Lectures in America, with Q. D. Leavis (Chatto & Windus, London; Clarke, Irwin, Toronto, 1969).

English Literature in Our Time and the University: The Clark Lectures, 1967 (Chatto & Windus, London: Clarke, Irwin, Toronto, 1969).

Dickens the Novelist, with Q. D. Leavis (Chatto & Windus, London; Clarke, Irwin, Toronto, 1970).

Nor Shall My Sword: Discourses on pluralism, compassion and social hope (Chatto & Windus, London; Clarke, Irwin, Toronto, 1972).

Letters in Criticism, edited by J. Tasker (Chatto & Windus, London; Clarke, Irwin, Toronto, 1974).

The Living Principle: 'English' as a discipline of thought (Chatto & Windus, London; Clarke, Irwin, Toronto, 1975).

Thought, Words and Creativity: Art and thought in Lawrence (Chatto & Windus, London; Clarke, Irwin, Toronto, 1976).

The Critic as Anti-Philosopher: Essays and papers, edited by G. Singh (Chatto & Windus, London; Clarke, Irwin, Toronto, 1982).

'Valuation in Criticism' and Other Essays, edited by G. Singh (Cambridge University Press, Cambridge, 1986).

Note

Among the most important early essays and pamphlets reproduced in later collections, *D. H. Lawrence* (1930) appears only in *For Continuity*; *Mass Civilization and Minority Culture* appears in *For Continuity* and in *Education and the University*, 2nd edn; *How to Teach Reading* appears in *Education and the University*. Many of the essays in *For Continuity* appear elsewhere.

2. Critics on Leavis

Anderson, P., 'Components of the National Culture', *New Left Review*, 50 (May/June 1968), pp. 3–57. A Marxist discussion of Leavis as a cultural critic.

Bell, M., *F. R. Leavis* (Routledge, London and New York, 1988). Describes Leavis's stance as 'principled' rather than theoretical. Traces parallels with some Continental philosophers.

Bergonzi, B., 'Leavis and Eliot: the long road to rejection', in *The Myth of Modernism and Twentieth Century Literature* (Harvester, Brighton, 1986). Traces Leavis's changing attitude toward Eliot.

Bergonzi, B., 'Leavis, Lewis, and Other Oppositions', in *Exploding English: Criticism, theory, culture* (Oxford University Press, Oxford, New York, 1990). Takes Leavis and C. S. Lewis as representative figures of contrasting approaches to literary studies.

Bilan, R. P., *The Literary Criticism of F. R. Leavis* (Cambridge University Press, Cambridge, 1979). Comprehensive but rather uncritical survey.

Boyers, R., *F. R. Leavis: Judgement and the discipline of thought* (University of Missouri Press, Columbia, Mo., 1978). Addresses fundamental issues of value in an attempt to arrive at 'some plausible and legitimizing account of the critical vocation'.

Bradbury, M., 'A Matter for Serious Scrutiny: F. R. Leavis in the 1950s', in *No, Not Bloomsbury* (André Deutsch, London, 1987). A semi-autobiographical account of the impact of Leavis in the 1950s, emphasising his appeal to students in the red-brick universities.

Buckley, V., *Poetry and Morality: Studies in the criticism of Matthew Arnold, T. S. Eliot and F. R. Leavis* (Chatto & Windus, London, 1959). Places Leavis within a familiar configuration.

Casey, J., *The Language of Criticism* (Methuen, London, 1966). A rigorous examination of the modes of argument of Leavis and other critics.

Cornelius, D. K., & E. St Vincent, *Cultures in Conflict: Perspectives on the Snow–Leavis controversy* (Scott, Foresman, Chicago, 1964). An anthology of comment on and material apposite to the controversy. Contains extracts from both Leavis and Snow.

Critical Quarterly, 1 (1959) contains a symposium on F. R. Leavis.

Eagleton, T., 'The Rise Of English' in *Literary Theory: An introduction* (Basil Blackwell, Oxford, 1983). Despite its stress on Leavis's importance in the constitution of English studies, a rather tendentious and belittling account of his work.

Greenwood, E., *F. R. Leavis* (Longman, London, 1978). A short but cogent introduction.

Hayman, R., *Leavis* (Heinemann, London; Rowan & Littlefield, Totowa, N. J., 1976). A rather superficial account of the life and work.

Inglis, F., *Radical Earnestness: English social theory 1880–1980* (Martin Robertson, Oxford, 1982). Places Leavis within a specifically English liberal tradition of protest and dissent.

Kinch, M. B., W. Baker and J. Kimber, *F. R. Leavis and Q. D. Leavis: An annotated bibliography* (Garland, London, New York, 1989). An invaluable aid to any extended study.

McCallum, P., *Literature and Method: Towards a critique of I. A. Richards, T. S. Eliot and F. R. Leavis* (Gill and McMillan, Dublin, 1983). Rebarbative style, but cogent criticism of the contradictions in liberal essentialism.

Mulhern, F., *The Moment of 'Scrutiny'* (New Left Books, London, 1979). An invaluable account of the history of *Scrutiny* and of Leavis's milieu.

New Universities Quarterly, 30 (December 1975). Symposium in honour of Leavis on his eightieth birthday.

Robertson, P. J. M., *The Leavises on Fiction: An historic partnership* (Macmillan, London, 1981). Takes the criticism of fiction to be of central importance.

Steiner, G., 'F. R. Leavis', in *Language and Silence: Essays 1958–1966* (Faber & Faber, London, 1967), pp. 249–66. A sympathetic recollection of Leavis at Cambridge combined with a critique of his limitations.

Strickland, G., *Structuralism or Criticism? Thoughts on how we read* (Cambridge University Press, Cambridge, 1981). Contrasts English and Continental attitudes to literary studies.

Thompson, D., (ed.), *The Leavises: Recollections and impressions* (Cambridge University Press, Cambridge, 1984). A fascinating collection of memoirs and critical assessments.

Trilling, L., *A Gathering of Fugitives* (Beacon Press, Boston, 1956), pp. 101–6. An American assessment, stressing the importance of class.

Walsh, W., *F. R. Leavis* (Chatto & Windus, London, 1980). An account of the work that verges on the hagiographical.

Walsh, W., 'A Sharp, Unaccomodating Voice', in *A Human Idiom: Literature and humanity* (Chatto & Windus, London, 1964). A claim for the value of Leavis's approach in education.

Watson, G., *The Leavises, the 'Social' and the Left* (Brynmill Publishing Co., Swansea, 1977). A partisan and rather too detailed account of the Leavises' dealings with the literary establishment.

Wellek, R., 'F. R. Leavis and the *Scrutiny* Group', in *A History of Modern Criticism, 1750–1950*, Vol. 5 (Yale University Press, New Haven and London, 1986), pp. 239–64. An overview of Leavis's career and writings.

Williams, R., 'Two Literary Critics', in *Culture and Society* (Chatto & Windus, London, 1958), pp. 244–64. Examines the preconceptions of I. A. Richards and F. R. Leavis.

Index